INTERCULTURAL EDUCATION: THEORIES, POLICIES AND PRACTICE

Intercultural Education:
Theories, Policies and Practice

Edited by
DEREK WOODROW
GAJENDRA K. VERMA
MARIA BEATRIZ ROCHA-TRINDADE
GIOVANNA CAMPANI
CHRISTOPHER BAGLEY

Ashgate

Aldershot • Brookfield USA • Singapore • Sydney

Published by
Ashgate Publishing Ltd
Gower House
Croft Road
Aldershot
Hants GU11 3HR
England

Ashgate Publishing Company
Old Post Road
Brookfield
Vermont 05036
USA

British Library Cataloguing in Publication Data

Intercultural education : theories, policies and practice
   1. Multicultural education - Europe
   I. Woodrow, Derek
   370.1'17'094

Library of Congress Catalog Card Number: 97-74443

ISBN 1 84014 118 2

Typeset by
AME Wordprocessing
161 Lower Brownhill Road
Southampton, SO16 9LD

Printed and bound by Athenaeum Press, Ltd.,
Gateshead, Tyne & Wear.

Contents

vi

Acknowledgements

The assistance and support given by these people in the production of this book is gratefully acknowledged:

Janet Grimshaw
Tony Neasham
Colin Lees
Angie Evans

1 Introduction and overview

Derek Woodrow and Gajendra K. Verma

This book is the result of a number of European Union and Council of Europe initiatives. The major stimulus came from an intensive course held in Lisbon in 1994 as part of two Erasmus networks exploring the nature of intercultural studies on a European-wide basis. The participants, lecturers and postgraduate students, came from Italy, Spain, Portugal, France, England and Scotland under the title of the network 'Intercultural Relations and Education: Theories, Policies and Practices'. It has two clear focuses of concern, one is the development of the issues relating to mutual understanding between nations, societies and cultural groups in order to lessen tensions and promote and enable meaningful communication between the citizens of Europe and the World. The second is derived from the inner problems of States and communities in ensuring equal opportunities and individual rights within multicultural societies and tackling the problems of discrimination.

The importance of this initiative within Europe is immense and can be seen from the range of initiatives which have been sponsored. These are described by Rocha-Trindade and Mendes who review the development of growth of these policies, and contributions within this volume derive not just from the sponsoring Erasmus project but also from a Tempus project (designed to provide support for Eastern Europe in its moves towards democracy by sharing academic knowledge and programmes), another Erasmus project concerned with the development of a European Certificate in Comparative and International Educational Studies and from an international conference organised by the Adam Institute for Democracy entitled Education for Democracy. The issues discussed in this book are clearly significant in the development of modern societies as they seek to come to terms with the revolution in intercultural relations brought about by mass communications and

1

global transport. The world is rapidly having to come to terms with cultural and social differences which can no longer be kept separate in their protective groups in the manner discussed by Vinsonneau. Indeed the very nature of cultures now has a dynamic and volatility which is beginning to concern cultural leaders, and has led to the protestive resurgence of fundamentalism which challenges world order and harmonious society.

The book broadly follows the dichotomy indicated earlier, with the first half essentially looking at the theoretical underpinnings of intercultural studies, leading to considerations of multiple interpretations of both interculturalism and of comparative conceptualisations in different cultures. Campani looks at the dynamic reconstruction of intercultural education, as it develops into a theoretical rationale for the policies of multiculturalism and pluralism which have been central to the social policies of Member States. Combatting racism and xenophobia has been a central tenet of European development ever since the Second World War. Vinsonneau discusses the way in which these 'protective' boundaries are created by groups and those in power situations. The preservation of power and authority are central to the rise of discrimination by introspective looking sectarian movements. Yet the more communication and interchange increase, the more interdependent peoples become and these motivations become outdated yet still remain as central social drives. In this context, notions of 'self' and of 'identity', whether of individuals or groups, are severely challenged. Their meaning in a world with changing and flexible boundaries is clearly in need of reassertion and redefinition as they respond to the wider context of globalisation, and this is taken up by Oriol as a basis for understanding the role and reaction of groups to the threat to their identity. This increasingly dynamic nature of cultures and of their conceptualisation is discussed by Garcia-Castano and Pulido-Moyano. They argue against the traditional fixed view of culture as a static and meaningful categorisation of what are in fact groups of varied and fluid individuals, each dependent upon their own reality rather than being cloned images of some idealised cultural image.

The central section of the book is concerned more with comparative data, contrasting different societies and their different historical philosophies. Within one text, only a limited number of comparative issues can be developed in any depth but equally the total agenda for greater knowledge of intercultural assumptions and mores needs to be kept in perspective if coherent development is to take place. The implications of these social parameters on Educational beliefs and purposes are then taken up. Woodrow looks at the significant differences between different cultures in theoretical beliefs about how learning

2

takes place. Even theory, it is maintained, is culturally created and leads to different conceptualisation in different societies. These differences are again turned into discriminating consequences by the social power brokers. The next two papers look at aspects of teacher training. Besalu considers the nature of teacher training in the context of interculturalism, looking at the nature of preparing teachers for a world view and for the development and delivery of a curriculum for equity, a curriculum for all. Ribero uses teacher training courses to examine the difficulties in transferring educational curricula and systems from one context to another, again challenging the notion that any society has absolute solutions to educational problems. This view of two societies and their educational needs is in the context of developing and developed countries, the north-south division to which answers must be found which respect rights and needs if the global world into which we are being drawn is not to be one of conflict and critical antagonism. The comparison of contexts is taken up in the remaining two papers in this section, both looking at inter-national comparisons. Johnson presents a different picture of intercultural knowledge in his research designed to illuminate the differing social ambiances which form the micro-societies of particular classrooms in different nations. By looking at such concepts as 'friction' and 'cohesion' within the primary classroom he illustrates the wealth of comparative data which is needed for meaningful inter-cultural discussion about schools and education. Bagley then looks at the nature of social reaction to mixed marriages and the children of mixed marriages in The Netherlands and Britain. He presents questions about differences in the two societies, both with traditional imperialist histories, and also raises issues about discrimination and racism, with which the final section of the book is concerned.

This volume brings together a number of papers which challenge the social assumptions and basis of democracy within modern societies. It returns to the fundamental rights of citizenship which form the critical raison d'être of both the United Nations and the European Community. In looking at the social and political conditions of discrimination and participation they touch upon the very heart of democracy and human development. Verma reviews the political and educational development and meaning of terms such as 'multiculturalism', 'cultural pluralism' and 'interculturalism'. He defines three goals and processes to which it must adhere. Gundara looks at representation and the meaning of citizenship in the complexity of a pluri-cultural Europe in a review of the political use of nationalism to exclude 'migrants' from rights and belonging, attacking Eurocentrism as a major problem in Europe. He also looks at the rise of xenophobic violence as a feature of insecure nationalism and the role of education as a counter-influence. Garratt and Robinson then look at the way in which issues such as citizenship could be employed positively to form the core and driving force for school curricula, helping to forward an agenda for harmony and understanding across Europe and the world. Using the English National Curriculum as a vehicle for analysis they review the varying and divisive underlying forces which drive social, and even economic, issues out of the agenda of education in schools. Heathcote then looks at the politicisation of health education and promotion, commenting on the way in which such terms as empowerment, born in a context of equality and enfranchisement, nevertheless lead almost inevitably to implicit discrimination and the empowerment only of those already with power. Grant and Monasto look at particular national creations of interculturalism, critically reviewing developments in their own countries and at the way in which boundaries are maintained and supported. Grant reviews the recent history of intercultural relations within the United Kingdom, both of the complex internal nationalistic compromises, contrasts, cultural subordination and conflicts and also of the xenophobic antagonisms created towards groups of immigrants from outside the U.K. Monasta in a polemic article about Italy, sums up many of the frustrations and anxieties about unfeeling and unresponsive societies which seem to work to maintain divisiveness and privilege.

This book seeks to capture the complexity and breadth of intercultural studies in the modern world. It presents views of this debate from many quarters of Europe. There may be different conceptualisations, different priorities and concerns, but there is a common view of the critical importance in our newly globalized, open and mobile world society that discrimination, xenophobia and dismissive disparagement of others cannot be sustained without conflict and turmoil. Recent wars, financial catastrophes and environmental catastrophes have emphasised the interdependence of modern societies. Regressive nationalism cannot in the end be sustained, despite the fervour of some proponents. Education, as a major socialising agent, must assume responsibility for forwarding a world curriculum, an education for all, a quality education for all. This requires knowledge, understanding and an acceptance of varying perceptions and identities, all valid and 'right' in their context. Contrasts and varying conceptualisations are natural and sustainable, even individuals are now only temporarily and momentarily defined, individual cultures are constantly in flux and development in a world of continuous transformation and movement. Like the arrow in Zeno's paradox of motion, the definition of identity (of self or culture) once made describes its own inapplicability. It is the debate of the twentieth century, but its determination becomes ever more pressing as the century reaches its closure.

Part I

Educational policy and theories of identity

2 Intercultural education: policies within Europe

Maria Beatriz Rocha-Trindade and Maria Luisa Sobral Mendes

The plurality of human groups is translated at the material level by the diversity of their geographic settlements and by differences of ancestral ethnic origin. At the cultural level this plurality is explained by linguistic and religious diversity and historical collective memory: a conceptual set of features known as cultural identity. Throughout the centuries, the settlement of different groups in well-defined territories where they became majorities gave rise to the creation of nations. These nations presented a certain degree of homogeneity as far as the above-mentioned material and conceptual characteristics were concerned. Whenever their stability and safety involved the establishment of sovereign regions, externally recognised as such and exercised within their respective territories, these nations became States (see note 1).

The reciprocal relations between State and Nation were not always established nor did they always prevail. Invasions, wars and treaties, as well as massive population movements, put an end to them and led to the co-existence of several nations within the same State. Colonial occupations also produced similar consequences. Many of these situations are now stable and it is common for a country to have several regions, differentiated by major nationalities and cultures. These nationalities and cultures have diverse characteristics in regard to language, religion, or ethnic origin. The creation of semi-autonomous regions with a certain degree of self-government is a sound solution to potential conflicts among the several socio-political forces operating within the same State. In other cases such conflicts may develop into major confrontations or even civil wars leading to fragmentation of the State.

So far a type of conceptual situation has been described that is clear cut, where each culture may be considered fairly homogeneous in a clearly defined territory. However, there are exceptions, including situations such as frequent

7

international migrations where the permanence of the movement leads to the settlement of foreign minority communities in the host countries. There are also post-decolonisation situations that leave a remnant of residents from the previous colonial power in the new independent countries, thus originating other types of minorities. It should also be noted that post-colonial situations usually produce migratory movements from the new States towards the previous imperial powers. This does not constitute a return migratory flow but in a way conveys a closing of the circle of bilateral mobilities.

Moving from these generalised historical frameworks, it is important to analyse the present and to project the current tendencies into the future. In many countries in Europe it is evident that there are communities of migratory origin, sometimes in significant numbers and whose differences become noteworthy. Within the European Community there have recently been several waves of individuals who have joined immigration movements for economic reasons. There are political or war refugees from African, Asian, Middle Eastern, Central and Eastern European countries presently experiencing volatile situations. These mass movements will often increase drastically when a generalised famine situation occurs in one of these countries (see note 2).

In spite of efforts to limit the entry of newcomers, the already settled minorities represent a very significant presence which needs to be taken into consideration in any political project. This is valid at the European Community level as well as at that of each State (the subsidiarity principle) aiming at the well-being of and social justice for all elements of the resident population.

Any political project designed to deal with this situation cannot be based upon goals of integration/assimilation of the minority groups in the majority societies. During the last three decades the American 'melting pot' dream has lost its credibility. The 'multicultural' approaches, which may be defined as a diversified set of different communities, whose interaction and social mobility are not necessarily taking place, also provide incomplete solutions (see note 3). Intercultural perspectives may well have more beneficial consequences. The term aims to convey a dynamic state of permanent interaction among present cultures. In order to achieve the good communications on which it depends it is necessary always to keep in mind two realities - universality and diversity. Quoting Lévi-Strauss - "La découverte de l'altérité est celle d'un rapport, non d'une barrière".

If one attempts to express the differences among the three previously mentioned approaches in another manner, one would delineate:

- an ethno-centric character to be the idealised concept of the 'melting pot' as it promotes the rule of generic culture as a result of the fusion of all present cultures;

- an ethno-plural character to the multicultural perspective based on a verified judgment of plurality;

- an ethno-interactive character to the multicultural vision brought about by a logic of contact, interpenetration and mutual influence of cultures.

Intercultural education is the action medium, the tool which results from this concept. The expression includes in the term 'education', all the components of formal and non-formal teaching, of family or community education and of all the other processes of organised social interaction aiming at the education of the individual. It also, therefore, includes the State's pedagogical role in the production of rules and laws and the role played by the media in the shaping of public opinion.

With the economic development that took place following World War II, specifically from the 1960s onwards, the industrialised European countries welcomed the arrival of foreign workers from diversified cultural and linguistic backgrounds searching for better working and living conditions. Since then, the educational systems of the host-countries have been continuously receiving a large number of students from immigrant families. These families of diversified origins were faced with great adaptation difficulties of a social, cultural and linguistic nature. Consequently, those difficulties were also reflected in their children's academic success.

The educational studies previously attempted in this field in other countries were not very conclusive. In the United States the studies of Bilingual Programmes were limited to language teaching and in practice they assumed a remedial methodology. In Canada the Heritage Language Programmes were conceived in response to local social circumstances. The cultures present were individualised but the programmes did not contemplate social interaction. In practice these educational policies proved inadequate to the needs of European countries due to the diversity of situations present in the heterogeneous character of the target populations.

Notwithstanding a previous practice of pedagogy which included several cultures involved in the educational process (as referred to in the Work Group Final Report Project 7) it became necessary to develop and to implement educational projects and experiences that comprised:

9

- actions developed by the educational authorities of the country of origin and the host-country;

- permanent information to all teaching agents concerned with the social, cultural and educational realities involved in the education of migrant populations;

- a commitment on the part of the institutions in charge of the education and training of teachers, either in the host-countries or in the countries of origin;

- the organisation of studies applying the knowledge acquired in the area of Human and Social Sciences to the teaching of migrant populations.

Moreover, the pioneering role played by the Council of Europe throughout the 1970s should be stressed.

As early as 1970 (Resolution 70/35 of the Council of Europe Committee of Ministers) and following the concerns felt by the institutions which implemented the education of migrants' descendants, the Member States were alerted to the situation in migrant communities and to the need to eliminate the difficulties of social and academic adaptation experienced by students of migrant origin; they were also alerted to the advantage of maintaining cultural and linguistic ties with the country of origin as well as to prepare their reintegration should those students ever decide to go back.

In 1975 (IX Permanent Conference of European Ministers of Education) all concerned Governments were invited to take measures aiming at promoting equal educational opportunities for migrant children as well as providing them with the possibility of learning the language and culture of the host country and of their country of origin. It was at about this time that the initiatives of the European Community concerning education in a multicultural context started to be observed. In 1977 the Council of Ministers of the European Community in accordance with Directive 77/486/EEC of July 25, adopted the following guidelines:

- to provide equal opportunities for basic education to the children of migrants;

- to provide courses on the language of the host-country using methodologies adequate to the students;

10

- to organise courses on the language and culture of the country of origin with the collaboration of all countries involved whenever possible;

- to implement educational programmes from an intercultural perspective.

Once the need to act was recognised and using the guidelines established by the Council of Ministers of the Community and by the Council of Europe, this latter organisation assembled a working group (1977-1983) coordinated by a Swiss researcher, Micheline Rey, to study the said guidelines and the issue of teacher training. Teacher training was designed to:

- make teachers aware of the practice of education in multicultural societies;

- introduce teachers both from the host-countries and from the countries of origin to the cultures involved as well as to their respective teaching systems;

- incorporate in basic training and in continuous training the intercultural perspective;

- implement the organisation of seminars and courses on intercultural pedagogy, addressed to teachers and other teaching agents;

- create training courses, documentation and continuous in-service teacher training, as for example the CEFISEM did in France.

The Ministers of the Member States participating in the Council of Europe approved Recommendation R (84)18 concerning teachers' training for the education and full comprehension of interculturalism, namely in migratory contexts which reinforced previous initiatives. Following the already mentioned Project, a new one was launched - The Education and Cultural Development of Migrants Project 7 (1983-1986). The main guidelines contained in the original document (CDCC's Project Group No. 7 doc. CDCCC (84)10), which provided a basis for all actions subsequently developed in Europe at an international level, state:

'1. by now most of our societies are multicultural and will become increasingly so;

11

2.   each culture has its own specific features, to be respected as such;

3.   multiculturalism is a potential asset;

4.   to make multiculturalism an asset in reality, we must achieve communication and interaction between all the cultures without obliterating the specific identity of any, and we must mobilise the multicultural situation to make it truly intercultural, with all the dynamism which this implies (in terms of communication and interaction especially).'

It is perhaps interesting to compare the characteristics of the positions assumed by the Council of Europe and by the European Community (presently the European Union) regarding intercultural issues. In the writers' opinion, based on numerous documents on the politics of both organisations, it is evident that the Council of Europe is quite explicit concerning the concept, the description of the contexts and the launching of Projects and initiatives aimed at the development of Intercultural Education. The European Union has broader objectives revealing implicitly a concern with European construction and integration processes. Thus, the European Union promotes Intercultural Education in an implicit manner through its broad range of Programmes.

Programmes such as LINGUA, ERASMUS, DELTA and TEMPUS (to name but a few) have produced results throughout the years. They aim to introduce cultural communication into the education and training of European populations, acknowledging their respective diversities and attempting to make them interact to promote a better mutual understanding. More recently, the 4th Framework Programme, to be approved during the current year, reassigns previous Programmes. This task is to be performed in accordance with another organisational scheme which takes into consideration social, training and administrative aspects. The intercultural dimension is not necessarily explicit in this new scheme, but it is implicit in almost all the other Programmes.

This legislative 'prudence' is understandable if we consider that the Community Programmes call for astronomical financing from the Member States, especially within a continuing controversy between the well-being and social progress of the indigenous populations versus the cost of the absorption of immigrant or refugee populations. The outcome is usually expressed by feelings of rejection or xenophobia.

In 1989 the Council of Ministers of Education of the EEC discussed issues relating to co-operation and community policies for 1993 in the area of education (89/C27/04). The result was the establishment of five main objectives considered by the Member States as capable of promoting their closeness in the subjects of education and training.

- A pluricultural Europe.

- A Europe of mobility.

- A Europe of training for all.

- A Europe of skills.

- A Europe open to the World.

Subsequently the Treaty of the European Union, known as the Treaty of Maastricht (February 1992), dedicated three articles (Articles 126, 127 and 128) to Education, Vocational Training and Youth. Hence, an integrated policy is clearly defined, aimed at deriving better knowledge of the educational systems and encouraging the exchange of teachers and students. This knowledge is not limited to the European Union's political borders, but is extended to other countries and international organisations.

The acknowledgement of different historical paths, of rich national cultural heritages and of the plurality of artistic expressions in European society introduced courses of action in pedagogy directed by reciprocal knowledge and opening routes to pedagogical innovation. For instance, distance teaching is mentioned as a feasible innovative route to the achievement of all these goals. The interest in different aspects of Interculturalism expressed by international organisations such as UNESCO and OECD should also be stressed. Diverse cultural initiatives (seminars, conferences, publications) are dedicated particularly to the Intercultural Education of young people and adults. Proof that this issue is of great importance in today's Europe is that it is within its geographical area that these initiatives are taking place, attracting experts from all over the world (see note 4). Intercultural Education is nowadays acknowledged as an adequate methodological strategy concerning the plurality of cultures that co-exist in the European social context. Its educational and training potential with the intent to manage the tensions among the several resident groups and communities is accomplished through the reinforcement of communication among cultures aimed at attaining a constructive interaction and a mutual knowledge and respect for their differences and specificities.

European Community Programmes on Education and Training

Programmes	Description	Years
COMETT	Co-operation Programme between University and Enterprises for Technologies Training.	1986-94
ERASMUS	Community Programme on Students Mobility	1987
PETRA	Programme for Youth Professional Training and for Youth Professional Life	1988-94
Youth for Europe	Programme to promote student exchange within the Community	1988-94
IRIS	European Network Programmes for Women's Occupational Training	1983-93
EUROTECNET	Programme to promote innovation in professional training resulting from technological change in the European Community	1990-94
LINGUA	Programme to promote the knowledge of foreign languages in the European Community	1990-94
TEMPUS	Trans European Mobility Programme for Higher Education	1990-94
FORCE	Community Programme for the Development of Continuing Professional Training	1991-94

Source: Rapport de la Commission au Conseil, Au Parlement Européen et au Comité Economique et Social, Bruxelles, 1993, p.4.

References

Balibar, E. and Valerstein, I. (1990) *Race, nation, classe. Les identités ambigues* (Paris, La Découverte).

Challiand, A. et al. (1985) Les minorités à l'âge de l'État-nation (Paris, Fayard).

Commision de la Communauté Européenne (1993) *Livre vert sur la dimension Européenne de l'éducation* Bruxelles.

Conseil de L'Europe (1986) Final report of the project group Strasbourg, C.E.

Costa-Lascoux, J. and Weil, P. (dir. de) (1989) *Les minorités et leurs droits depuis 1789* (Paris, L'Harmattan).

European Journal of Intercultural Studies, Vol. 4, (2), 1993.

European Journal of Intercultural Studies, Vol. 4, (3), 1994.

Hammar, T. (1990) *Democracy and the Nation State. Aliens, denizens and citizens in a world of international migration* (Aldershot, Avebury).

Ministério da Eduçao (1991) *Guia de Portugal* Lisboa.

Ministério dos Negocios Esrrangeiros (1992) Tratado da Uniao Europeia (Lisboa, M.N.E.).

OCDE (1987) - L'éducation multiculturelle (Paris, OCDE).

Perotti, A. (1989) L'éducation interculturelle: en jeux et stratégies in *Migrants-Formation* vol.77 pp13-16.

Perotti, A. (1990) L'éducation dans les sociétés pluriculturelles en Europe in *Migrations-Sociétés*, vol. 2 no.8 pp.29-54.

Perotti, A. and Toulat, P. (1990) Immigration et médias in *Migrations-Sociétés*, vol. 2 no.12, pp.9-45.

Porcher, L. (1981) *The education of the children of migrant workers in Europe. Interculturalism and teacher training* (Strasbourg, Council of Europe).

Quast, M. and Ingenhoff, A. (1990) Les migrations des peuples de l'est in *Migrations-Sociétés*, vol. 2 no.8 pp.55-68.

Rey, M. (1986) - *Former les enseignants à éducation interculturelle. Les travaux du Conseil de la coopération culturelle (1977-1983)* (Strasbourg, Conseil de L'Europe).

Rocha-Trindade, M- B. (1990) Migrants et espaces de migrations: cadres conceptuels de référence culturelle in *Sociétés*, vol.29 pp.37-44.

UNESCO (1983) *Introduction to intercultural studies: Outline of a project for elucidating and promoting communication between cultures 1976-1980.* (Paris, UNESCO).

Notes

1. The extensive bibliography published from the mid 1980s on the concepts of State and Nation, their features and approaches, illustrates the interest these issues generated at the time. The evolution of the current political situation denotes the concern of the authors who in general have academic backgrounds in the areas of International Law, History and Cultural Anthropology. See for instance the set of articles that the Groupement pour les Droits des Minorités published in the book "Les minorités à l'âge de l'État-nation" (Challiand, 1985) and also Thomas Hammar (1990); Balibaret Wallerstein (1990); Costa-Lascoux (1992).

2. Mikael Quast and Amina Ingenhoff (1990) analyse the reactions of the German press to the migrations from the Eastern countries. The factual chronology and the dramatic situations implicit in that long process help in an understanding of the shaping of public opinion concerning such

situations. The reason for quoting this article was to present an example which would demonstrate the evolution and the effects of certain migratory movements.

3. See M.B. Rocha-Trindade (1990) who analyses how each country's historical origins and political route determine their pedagogical direction regarding educational issues.

4. The Conferences and Projects of OECD organized by the Centre for Teaching Research and Innovation have analysed the consequences to educational systems of the cultural and linguistic changes published during the second half of the last decade. In 1983, UNESCO issued "Introduction to Intercultural Studies" in which it outlines a project meant to illustrate and promote communication among cultures for the period between 1976 and 1980. The thematic issues of specialized international scientific reviews are also a good indicator of the actuality and interest of the subjects in question. "Migrations Société" edited by CIEMI, under the co-ordination of A. Perotti, are good examples. Also the recent issues of European Journal of Intercultural Studies (Vol.4, 2 and 3, 1994) which had as Guest Editors Giovana Campani and Jagdish Gundara, outline the profile of Intercultural Education in 11 European countries (France, Belgium, Denmark, Luxembourg, The Netherlands, Portugal, Spain, United Kingdom, Germany, Greece and Italy).

Council of Europe (CDCC) Intercultural Education Projects

1983-86 The Education and Cultural Development of Migrants
- Experts' Meetings (4)
- Colloquies (4)
- Seminars (9)
- Study Visits (4)
- Case Studies (16)
- Studies and Reports (5)

1977-83 Working Group on Teacher Training for Intercultural Education
- Socio-Cultural Information (15)
- Socio-Cultural Situation of Migrants (8)
- Seminars (4)
- Meetings

1972 Experimental Classes

ICP-93-UK-2040/05 and ICP-93-I-1050

These were the two programmes under which the Lisbon Intensive Course was planned, and which formed the basis for the major part of this book.

The ICP-93-2040/05 is a three-year programme begun in 1993. It succeeded a series of one-year EEC grants, that suffered from the usual problem of lack of continuity and the impossibility of long-term planning; consequently, although an earlier programme was able to set things in motion, the introduction of a three-year ICP was welcome, ensuring an element of stability. The earlier ICP-90-UK-0314/05 (1990/91) was coordinated by the University of Glasgow, and included the Kobenhavns Universitet and the Universitat Autonoma de Barcelona. This ended in 1991 after the first meetings to establish the European Certificate in Comparative and International Educational Studies.

The next ICP-92-UK-2040/05 was applied for in 1991 and began in 1992. Coordinated by Glasgow, it included in the first instance Kobenhavns Universitet, l'Università degli studi di Firenze, l'Universitat de Illes Balears, and l'Universidade Aberta de Lisboa. A planning meeting was held in Palma de Mallorca in March 1993, and an intensive seminar was put on at l'Universita degli studi di Firenze in May 1993, organized by Professor Attilio Monasta; the theme was 'Teacher education in Europe'. Staff and students from the participating universities presented papers, and there were many discussion seminars. The 1994 seminar - the present one - is being organized by Professor Doctor Maria Beatriz Rocha-Trindade of the Universidade Aberta de Lisboa, to which our thanks are all due, and to whose Rector we are appreciative for his welcome.

There has been some expansion of the consortium since its first year. In 1993, l'Universitat de Barcelona was admitted, and in Autumn of 1994 Trinity College, University of Dublin, also joined our ranks. The three-year period will see the group with some members for northern and southern Europe: Glasgow, Copenhagen and Dublin from the north and Lisbon, Barcelona, the Balearic Islands and Florence from the south. We are all extremely grateful to the Universities that have given so generously of their time to organize the intensive seminars.

The programme gained funding not only for the intensive programme, but also for student mobility and curriculum development. Student mobility supports students to go to one of the other universities for three to six months, both under this ICP and others, and most of us have already or will shortly have students from elsewhere working with us. There may, according to circumstances, also be involvement in curriculum development as well as taking part in the regular courses available.

The main activity under this head is the European Certificate in Comparative and International Educational Studies, planned to be fully compatible with the European Diploma in Education and Training, ICP-93-I-1050, conducted by the University of Florence. Both are post-graduate programmes, usually taken by students currently or having recently taken post-graduate degrees in their own Universities. For the Certificate, four courses are required (four modules of about 20-30 hours) in the field of Comparative and International Education. Two of these can be taken at the home University (they can already be part of the home-based degree), and two have to be taken in another EU country. A full intensive seminar (like this one) counts as one course, and a three-month period of study counts as two. (The same rules operate for the European Diploma, five plus three in this case.) Students will also be expected to prepare a paper or make a presentation upon the educational value of their experience, and a group of staff from the consortium recommends the award.

Procedures for certification differ. The European Diploma is awarded in two versions by the University of Florence, one in English and one in the student's own language. The Certificate is awarded by Glasgow in one version, namely Latin; even with our present membership, it would otherwise have to be

18

in Danish, Portuguese, Italian, Spanish, Catalan, Scots, Gaidhlig and Gaelge (Scottish and Irish Gaelic) - and, of course, English. It would have to be as long as a piece of wallpaper, Latin sounded simpler.

The ICP-93-I-1050 programme also includes annual intensive course and post-graduate student and staff mobilities. It is organised from the University of Florence and incorporates Universities in Florence, Girona, Granada, Nice, Paris, Perugia, Lisbon, Viseu, London and Manchester, and more recently Umea and Reykjavic.

3 The epistemological status of the theories of identity

Michel Oriol

The claims of the theories of collective identity are nothing less than obvious. There is no clearly defined set of phenomena (characteristics of identity) to which theories bring more and more suitable interpretations, in the way in which theories of perception progressively lead to a better realisation of the perceptive processes. Therefore, the first question to be raised is whether such theories are essentially descriptive or primarily explanatory, or in some manner a combined function. (Lapierre, 1984)

However, we are forced to recognise that using a theoretical justification for the concept of identity is all the more difficult when, on the one hand, it involves a polysemic signifier (being able to denote logical, mathematical, metaphysical, personal and political signifiers), whilst, on the other hand, it is increasingly commonly employed in primarily ideological usage. It is certainly not the only term, defined in the context of psychological theory, that later finds itself absorbed in a generally uncontrolled manner within the natural language use (one only has to think of the semantic derivative of concepts such as 'complex' or 'motivation'). However, in the case of the term 'identity', the problem is even more difficult to resolve because its ideological function is typically performative: to invoke collective identity in the language of protest, is to identify a need to establish, defend or redefine it.

The social psychologist is not at liberty to extract the common meaning from its confused usages by mere virtue of its epistemological and methodological exactness. Therefore, we have to put forward what is meant by 'membership identity' (a term deliberately chosen because it is unusable in natural language), the theoretical signifiers which serve to describe and/or interpret the dynamics concerning extended groups and their members. (Oriol, 1985)

21

Without at this point considering the genesis of the concept in its psycho-social use (this remains an epistemological task to be undertaken), we can schematically distinguish three stages in its definition and usage:

- a usage inspired by culturists, originated by Erik H. Erikson (1964), who described identity as an ensemble of properties situated at the nexus of the individual and society. This term would then appear to belong to a tradition of 'clinical' interpretation. (Clapier-Valladon, 1976)

- a usage more clearly inspired by experimental tradition in social psychology that attempts to construct from a certain number of fundamental notions, such as categorisation, an axiomatic set of conditions and consequences of belonging . It derives from the central and significant works of Henri Tajfel. (Codol, 1975)

- a usage we could consider as 'dialectical'. That is to say, one which presents identity as a group of properties linked to situations and the strategies which are developed to cope with them. Rather than being concerned with the construction of a general theory, it aims to provide a better understanding of actual situations in their psychological, sociological and historical contexts.

In the search for articulations which encompass the individual psyche and the social dimensions of the relations between subjects, we remain deeply indebted to the way in which culturists have contributed to highlighting the relativism of the fundamental concepts of psychology. (Erikson, 1964) Asserting that cognitions and affects depend profoundly upon primary processes of socialisation not only sets down a theoretical assumption, but also the definition of an area where there still remains much to tackle.

However, at the same time, it is reasonable to ask oneself what the theoretical significance is of the emphasis put on the variation of psychological traits attributable to separate human groups. Referring to the term 'basic personality', as it is called, Kardiner and his followers attempt to make more intelligible the connections between clearly different practices of cultural groups; the way children are socialised, the functioning of institutions, the ideological and mythical outcomes. 'It is not a question ... of a descriptive or classificatory concept, but of a highly abstract and interpretive explanation that embraces a whole of psycho-sociological theory and rests upon a system of correlative ideas'. (Kardiner, 1961)

22

However, emphasising the fact that common traits (produced by shared socialisation) explain the cohesion, and thus in a sense the very structure, of cultural groups, leads to uncertainty as to whether culturalism truly manages to improve upon a simple common sense theory. Everything happens as if the proverb 'birds of a feather flock together' was the fundamental axiom necessary for realising the belongingness of cultural groups: socialisation functions as a product of similarities, similarities function as a factor (and norm) in the cohesion of groups and cultures.

The arguments put forward by culturalists are, of course, more sophisticated than the application of 'implicit theory' where recurrent expressions are easy to pinpoint in even the most varied politically-ideological discourses. However, to be expressed with more detail and precision does not necessarily make it more efficient than common sense in constructing a truly critical theory of social relationships. The axiomatic culturalist takes group/cultural unity to be a product of homogeneity of personal attributes, themselves being derived 'naturally' from common education. This results in neglecting three levels of objection that psycho-social theories and socio-historic comparisons (in the genetic study of the creation of relationships) can easily help establish:

- Similarity/difference systems are not given, inherent constituents of the natural and social environment. Studies on categorisation and social comparison show in the same way that they depend upon the structures and strategies, both perceptive and conceptual, of the cognising subjects.

- Belonging should therefore not be conceived as a kind of natural outcome from given causes. It is a prime regulator of the way in which subjects assume, ignore or deny for themselves one or other attribute with which they compare themselves with those who are commonly considered as bearers. As a subject states his belonging as being something 'natural', he often fails to make a simple acknowledgement: he sets as a desirable norm whatever is the collective attribute he owns. (This is the same reason for there only being a 'Galilean' theory of identity distinct from the 'Aristotelian' confusion of fact and theory: social psychology does not aim to rectify common sense theories, but to consider them as a part of the events that must be interpreted. (Lewin, 1956))

- One of the performative roles of explicit claims of belonging is precisely to affirm the unity of the group in spite of its diversity (and not because of its homogeneity). This is what anthropologists have in turn recognised by considering cultures as entities of difference (between men and women, young and old, superiors and inferiors, fiancées and divorcées, etc...) and not as rigid systems of uniform representations and practices.

While remaining in the conceptual field of culturalism, Erikson has clearly envisaged this theoretical difficulty which represented for him the tangible diversity of members of a 'cultural group'. However, he endeavoured to account for this by creating an effective synthesis of both the identity of the individual and that of the group. 'Ego-synthesis' combines, in his eyes, the fundamental traits of personal identity (unity and stability) interwoven with consideration of collective ideals, without summing up the totality of identifications formed in the course of primary and secondary socialisation.

Erikson's approach maintains in a sense a true reality, since personological research remains concerned with the necessity to combine the idiosyncrasies of individual backgrounds and the cultural norms from which it cannot be disaggregated. However, in his interpretation of membership, he simply failed to take fully into account the relational nature of the issues he was considering. Erikson irreversibly marked, from a lexical view point, the field of social psychology by being the first to use the term identity in his application to groups. He has left us with an invaluable source of psycho-anthropological descriptions. We had to wait, however, for the critical contributions of H. Tajfel (1981) for problems aimed at creating an epistemologically rigorous definition.

Tajfel's first distinction, in this respect, is to ascertain the existence or rejection of collective identities as processes dependent upon more fundamental psycho-social determinations (i.e. categorisation, social comparison and the elimination of dissonance). In other words, even if he himself did not formulate it as schematically as our account has done, Tajfel proves through experimentation (occasionally socio-historic comparison) the fact that belonging is assumed or rejected according to principles which best correspond to those that Bruner (1956) and his school of thought had clearly established in relation to social cognition (even if this expression had not as then been applied) and those that Festinger had raised regarding the inevitable recourse to social comparison in the evaluation of self esteem (Festinger, 1957).

We can therefore acknowledge Tajfel's worth for having produced in a particularly precise fashion what is known as, according to the term advanced by Merton (1957), a 'middle theory'. The way in which subjects perceive and judge social groups is no different in its results from the most general of perception theories (accentuation of intra-group similarities and inter-group differences and the attribution by inference of valued or devalued characteristics). The evaluation of self-esteem by disowning (cognitive isolation) or over-valuing the appertaining group and its attributed common traits, originates precisely from Festinger's fundamental hypotheses, (Festinger, 1957). (The great works of Codol on the dissymmetry of comparisons between the subject and others only confirm these theoretical opinions by rectifying and refining them. (Codol, 1975)

However, once established, social identity effectively brings about clearly established community behaviour (and hence discrimination). Tajfel, indeed, has ingeniously shown that the establishment of social identity could arise purely from social categorisation factors, with apparently, very little influence from economic and social motives.

Defined in this way identity designates an area of investigation with greater clarity than Erikson's 'ego-synthesis'. It relates to what, in the creation and representations of a person, are determinants which arise from his assumed membership. We can, on that note, return to conceptualisations through which sociologists endeavour to construct what they refer to as a 'specific rationale of social groups'. (At the end of his life, Tajfel was very conscious of the need to contribute to the production of synthesis by relating more closely psychological and sociological analyses. His untimely death in 1981 did not allow him to carry out such a project (personal interviews).)

This necessity to articulate, in the study of group identities, personal specificities and collective attributes is found in the most of the recent work carried out in France, notably by those who were led or inspired by Carmel Camilleri (1990). His contribution to this study was to make clear the relevance of two concepts: that of combination (or alternation) and that of strategy. (Oriol, 1985)

He highlighted the diversity of observable behaviours in the midst of groups which were liable to be categorised according to their roots (such as second generation immigrants). He stated the diversity of assumed or denied characteristics, but he moreover constructed typologies which primarily relate to the way in which subjects more or less deliberately select their roots by focusing at different stages on the closure or openness of the group, the ideologisation of their status and the more private or public nature character of their chosen signifiers. This led to the recognition of the notion of identity strategies. The notion of pattern, precious to culturists, is then only relevant when it refers to traits taken into account through 'intracultural' or 'intercultural' interactions.

Taboada-Leonetti (in Camilleri, 1990) contains precise arguments relating to the process of recognition: "the notion of strategy suggests that, from the moment that we apply this to social or psychological events, we have to assume a certain freedom of action by the actor on possible social or existential determinants. This happens whether the notion of strategy be understood as 'a group of temperaments taken by actors in order to attain a given goal' (Larousse), or, with reference to the theory of games in maths, as 'a group of decisions based upon hypothesis formed on the behaviour of players' (a definition which has the advantage of introducing the idea of interaction). As for the notion of identity strategies, this indisputably presumes that actors are capable of acting on their own definition of themselves. This concept is a logical consequence of the definition of identity as the result of an interaction and not as a nominalist definition". (Taboada-Leonetti in Camilleri, 1990)

Are we still at the same stage in the epistemological register as the work of Tajfel? In one sense, we can consider that these works confirm that collective identity clearly falls within middle theories, introducing intelligibility to issues which the more general psychological interpretations or the more global sociological analyses do not on their own help us to understand, or even indeed to predict concrete outcomes of assumed or denied membership. However, in another sense, the notion of strategy widens the field of relations within which it is convenient to situate expressions of identity; no longer only containing the individual and the groups of potential belonging or reference, but also the sets of resources (practical and symbolic) which can be used to recognise or modify the statutes of collective order. Therefore, let us imagine that the suitable epistemological model (to which it is necessary to refer the theories of collective identity) is that of dialectical rationality. On one hand the subject's characteristics can only have meaningful identity if they find themselves objectivised by established codes, recognised behaviour and accepted practices. On the other hand, this set of resources (real or potential) only makes sense through the theories of internalisation/rejection without which they are nothing more than purely formal attributes. We are therefore sent from one extreme to the other i.e. from the make-up of the group by objective means (institutional aggregation) to its concrete recognition by individuals in their representational system and their practical strategies (existentialist aggregation), (Oriol, 1984).

Dialectically constructed in this way, it seems that the array of theories of collective identity is more a question of food for thought than a fait accompli. It is probably where social psychology and the disciplines with which it is inevitably associated (sociology, history, semiology) prove the least certain in the prediction of events and the prevention of crises. All the more reason for further work.

References

Bruner, J., Goodnow, J.J., Austin, G.A. (1956) *A study of thinking*, (New York, London; J.Wiley and Sons).

Camilleri, C. (avec Kartersztein, J., Lipiansky, E.M., Malewska-Peyre, M., Taboada-Leonetti, I., Vasquez, A.) (1990) *Stratégies identitaires*, (Paris, PUF).

Clapier-Valladon, S. (1976) *Panorama du culturalisme*, (Paris, Epi).

Codol, J.P. (1975) On the so-called 'superior conformity of the self behaviour': twenty experimental investigations, *European Journal of Social Psychology*, vol. 5.

Erikson, E.H. (1964) *Enfance et société*, (Genève, Delachaux et Niestlé).

Festinger, L. (1957) *A theory of cognitive dissonance*, (Stanford, Stanford Univ. Press).

Kardiner, A. (1961) *L'individu dans sa société*, (Paris, Gallimard).

Lapierre, J.W. (1984) L'Identité collective, objet paradoxal ; d'où nous vient-il? in *Recherches Sociologiques* vol.XV no.2/3, (special edition on 'L'identité ethnique et culturelle', ed. M.Oriol).

Lewin, K. (1956) *Psychologie dynamique*, (Paris, PUF).

Maisonneuve, J. (1973) *Introduction à la psychosociologie*, (Paris, PUF).

Merton, R.K. *Social theory and social structure* (Glencoe, The Free Press).

Oriol, M. (1984) (ed.) *Les variations de l'identité, vol.1* (Nice, IDERIC).

Oriol, M. (1985) Appartenance linguistique, destin collectif, décision indivduelle, *Cahiers Internationaux de Sociologie*, vol.LXXIX.

Tajfel, H. (1981) *Human Groups and Social Categories, Studies in Social Psychology*, (London, New York; Cambridge University Press).

4 Social construction of theoretical beliefs

Derek Woodrow

Introduction

Much of the initiative leading to the current universal concern for intercultural studies (and related multicultural and pluralist policies) derives from a concern for inequalities and discrimination. There is little issue with the conclusion that all individuals differ, yet they do form groups based upon shared concepts, attributes, values. Elsewhere in this volume the ways in which differences are converted into discrimination and denial of rights and access to power are considered. In this chapter differences in conceptualisation of ways of learning are discussed, and this raises the rarely discussed phenomena of 'academic discrimination'. Where schools are viewed as exclusively concerned with the intellectual development of the pupil, and where there is no concern for the social consequences or encouraging the growth of spiritual, moral and social values then academic differences and the creation of intellectual hierarchies amongst pupils are not seen as discriminatory, yet the effects on 'self-image' and life-confidence are clearly significant. This intellectual discrimination is most rife in western Europe, where a strong sense of 'belonging where you are born', of belonging to a Nation State, serves to provide a strong enough sense of identity able to withstand such discrimination. This widespread discrimination in western societies is evident in the way in which particular academic attainments (such as success in mathematics or Latin) are used to select and choose people for many jobs, when the abilities used in such discriminatory choices do not relate in any way to the actual skills needed. Societies make many implicit assumptions about the worth of members of their communities based upon academic attainment. In the United States, where in the first half of the century most people were immigrants, this intellectual challenge was notably diminished and the 'American Dream' was of making good, not of being clever. Where pupils learn in different styles, especially if styles differ from those assumed by the teacher, then difficulties and classroom discrimination are obvious and unrelated to the pupil's real intellectual ability and make the judgments doubly false. These are the issues which this chapter begins to explore by looking at the cultural and societal influences on theories of cognition.

There is little doubt that different cultural traditions result in significant variations in artistic output. Whilst they may vary over time they also contain some lasting resonances. English folk song and choir techniques differ from the German choral, Italian 'bel canto' and the French 'impressionist' traditions. The Russian novel has traditions as distinctive as those within which Kafka and Zola reside, and film-making has its own distinctive nation-related qualities such as the French cinéma vérité and the lush romanticism of Indian film-making. Of course, for the western world there is some doubt as to how long this will survive the influence and pressure of television, with its ability to present the same images to everyone. Yet even in this international medium the travelling viewer cannot but be struck by the variations in style and content. I find British television unchallengeably the best - naturally since I am British! I am intrigued by what I perceive as the animated discourse on French television and flamboyant shows of German T.V. I find American T.V. bitty and sparse in content, but these observations are not necessarily true - it is merely that I am conditioned to such expectations. They can be changed, and my tastes in time-wasting have certainly been adapted and redeveloped as I have grown older, but they remain largely a reflection of the social milieu in which I move. I belong now to a subculture of serious viewers, opera goers and 'intellectuals' who analyse and discuss theatre. That is not my original cultural setting of soap operas, quiz shows and tabloid newspapers.

The obvious existence of varying culture and national identity has had just as clear an impact on formal education. Reviews of different societies show the variation in informal child-rearing and adult-initiation practices. Formal education is itself socially created and only becomes universal with the rise of the urban industrial dwelling. Different societies have different perceptions of authority and respect for elders, different perceptions of freedom (especially for children) and different assumptions about gender roles and gender relationships. In Western Europe the Marxist educationalists of the 1960s and 70s clearly established that education is a vehicle for socialisation, for confirming and continuing the social order and for conditioning the populace to their varied roles. In more recent times it has been viewed, with fewer overt political overtones, as a vehicle for enculturation. It is this notion of enculturation which has underwritten much multicultural and plural education in that it presupposes that there is the possibility of affecting future generations into a conformity of acceptance rather than the enculturation of the pupils by their own social racist setting. This view of education as controlled and managed enculturation has bred a sense of historical inevitability since any society will enculture its own values and is therefore impotent in making significant changes in society. This results in the replacement of the mediaeval entrapment of serfdom with the modern impressment of being a servant to the state. Thus in England, Bernstein talked of 'codes' and 'mental structures' and in France, Bourdieu described the 'habitus' in which learning takes place - both concerned with socially constructed and imposed frameworks within which learning is created and facilitated, and which mediates personal consciousness and society at large. Such frameworks relate not just to social behaviours and interests, but to ways of learning and the meaning of 'learning', and it is this notion of the social determination of acceptable theory which I wish to consider.

Cognitive functioning and rational argument are constructs within the culture within which a person resides. On a macro level the dialectic between culture and learning presents problems in that different societies (often unwittingly) misunderstand each other, and on the micro level it can create a mismatch between local subculture and that of the wider society within which that subculture exists, leading individual learners to a sense of dissonance.

By culture I will take as a definition the continuation into the present existence of an individual of all the traditional mental images with which he/she has been imbued by virtue of the society within which the individual is immersed. Good (1973) defined a culture pattern as 'an interrelated, interwoven and virtually inseparable group or cluster of cultural traits that taken together produce an established and typical result such as a way of thinking, living or acting'. Such a concept is not, of course, a static structure, but a continuing dynamic between 'traditional' values and virtues imbued by upbringing and family and the more recent social milieu within which a person functions. Culture, too, is often difficult to disentangle from ethnicity, and, like the debate on nature and nurture as causal factors in psychology, may ultimately be unresolvable. For many educators whether a particular factor in learning derives from nature or nurture is not important, what is required is that its existence is recognised and there is a response to its consequences. At a more fundamental level, however, is the sense that a nature-related (or ethnically derived) feature is essentially less amenable to change than those derived from nurture (or culture). Whilst recent developments in genetic engineering suggest that this

31

may also in due course become a question of societal choice rather than preordination as in the past, the problems such issues raise illustrate the deep-seated society beliefs on which it touches.

Antagonism to geneticism

The influence of 'ethos' and 'culture' and 'time' on thinking can be seen in the debates stimulated by particular groups of psychologists. For example there was intense concern and heated debate in the late 1960s when cultural/ethnic differences were allied to the notions of general ability (see, for example, Jensen, 1969). This derived from debate within the U.S.A. where the then dominant belief in IQ tests as predictors (rather than mirrors) of intelligence and developmental potential led to the proposition that intellectual ability is an innate and inborn characteristic of a person, a notion which stretches back to the work of Thorndike and Burt. The tests were at that time viewed as largely independent of culture and representing mental responses unsullied by the mediation of language and other socially dependent factors, and hence 'true'.

It was a time too of the overwhelming realisation of the power of newly discovered genetic encoding, and it was not surprising that such a remarkably powerful discovery led to the assumption that intelligence was also a part of that encoding. It is a debate which has recently returned as more detail and awareness of genetic power has emerged. Nature not nurture was the inevitably the dominant issue, Jensen (1969) assessed that about 80% of intelligence was attributable to genetic factors, and Herrnstein and Murray (1994) estimated 60%. A number of psychologists (Cronbach, 1970; Jensen, 1972) simultaneously pressed the hereditary position. The implications of such genetic determinism was the clear implication that underachieving minorities such as the American black population (and even power-starved majorities such as women) were deemed to be in such a position for ever since their intelligence was written in their genes. This rightly caused a furore since it enshrined, 'on the average', white male dominance as an inevitable and immutable law of nature. This proposition of racial stereotypes in IQ also arose (and was also rejected) in England in the work of Hans Eysenck (1971). Typical anti-Jensenian commentary can be found in Gartner et al. (1974) which represents both the academic and polemic versions of disapproval (see also Jacoby and Glauberman, 1995). Its recent reemergence in the work of Herrnstein and Murray (1994) has, despite a careful apologia, caused yet another flurry of outraged rejection. The Sunday Times (23rd October 1994) reported how when the journal 'The New Republic' published an article by Murray and Herrnstein in 1994 they felt compelled to include simultaneously a large number of critical responses. Many critics whilst pointing to the inevitability of interaction between nature and nurture and their basic indivisibility in the development of intelligence then stress the social, societal and interactional factors as if they were both predominant and in some way adaptable.

The power of genetic encoding and its current valuation in scientific thought brings with it a serious issue of identity from the implications both of external control and manipulation of individual characteristics and the frustration of individual impotence to effect changes. Recent reports in *Science* (Cardon et al., 1994) suggest a link between Dyslexia and chromosome 6 and there are assertions that aggressive behaviour has a biological cause through the brain chemical serotonin. It remains clear that rejection of such 'theories' in relation to the emotive issue of IQ is often not driven by falsehood or truth as by the worth to society and the value judgments placed upon them by those who propound such views. Many genetic traits lead to diversity and different contributions to a rich society and as such are acceptable. When, as in the presentation of IQ, they contribute to a single measure of value then they represent an unacceptable valuation of individuals. It is the attached value judgments which occur when IQ is seen as the critical determinant in human functioning and social success which make genetic determinism so unacceptable, and that is a commentary on the kind of society which enables such value judgments to emerge. The dismissal of these ideas then becomes as much to do with social or cultural acceptability as with logical exactitudes and there is a need to give a good deal of thought to ways of conducting such a debate in acceptable value terms. Despite the general and universal dismissal of genetic inheritance as a significant factor as compared to social factors, many still believe that mathematicians (or even more especially, musicians) are born rather than made!

The problem derives in part from the attempt to mirror in human cognition and thinking the realities of human physical development. This linking of mind and body remains a crucial feature in describing the insensible and intangible in terms of metaphors drawn from the observable and evident. The vehicle by which we explore the world (namely our senses) determines the meaning and realities we impose on the world. As in scientific investigation the choice of measuring instrument almost inevitably contains within it a presumption of what it will discover and disclose. The 'ghost in the machine' may be invisible to that machine but it is still a decisive factor. The choice of the language in which to describe learning and knowing carries implicit with it the structure by which it will be analysed. The subtleties found in a language mirror the implicit values and concerns of the society in which it was created and help to maintain those values. The omnipresence of genetic predictability leads to biological determinism (a product of contemporary thinking) contrasting the historical determinism identified by earlier European educationalists. Such determinism is not restricted to European psychology. R.K.Narayan comments "College teachers!...I revere college teachers, our Gurus. Meritorious deeds in previous births make them gurus in this life". Education is seemingly caught between the Scylla of predetermined physical limitation of a person's intelligence and ability to learn knowledge and the Charybdis of being a socially constructed vehicle to confirm and reinforce a predestined role for a person.

A similar hypothesis to IQ and its supposed genetic derivations appears in other modern 'biological determinisms' such as in the notion of right and left hemispheres of the brain and the assumed dominance of one or the other for different people, and more especially different groups of people, of these spheres of mental control. Dunn (1988) reports that these hemispheric differences appear to lead (or relate) to such preferences as for group based learning as opposed to individually managed styles and to preferences for traditional or for less conventional learning situations. The attribution of such 'naturally occurring' (and hence by affiliation 'pure') cognitive factors is also present in the growth of 'artificial intelligence' descriptions of cognitive functioning, related to the powerful language of computing which describes the brain in terms of synapses and neural networks. These biological determinants of achievements raise far fewer outcries and resistance than occurs with IQ. This is in part because the overall relationship to knowing and learning is not yet apparent and predictive and the 'machine' related context is felt to be really about small details rather than grand design and over-all functioning. It is also because they allow for different values to be attached to alternative strengths and weaknesses. Potentially, however, this approach to cognition provides for an equally predictive assessment of learning capability. Such determinism becomes acceptable or unacceptable depending upon one's view of the 'rightness' of existing relationships between the groups concerned (e.g. gender roles) or the extent to which the power determinants and the values they imply are viewed as changeable and compensatable.

Changing definitions

These debates derive from a notion that for each individual there exists 'general intelligence'. It is this notion that suggests that people's innate ability to learn can be measured by a single measure, whether it be by I.Q. test or by counting synapses. An alternative development avoids the problems implicit in the notion of general intelligence by looking at a profile of specific cognitive elements. The breakdown of general intelligence (Thurstone and Thurstone, 1941) into domains such as spatial ability, verbal ability, number, etc. leaves open the option of alternative kinds of knowledge and ability and makes it more difficult to categorise and compare individuals. The most recent presentation is that by Gardner (1983, 1992) who defined a minimum of seven intelligences in his theory of 'multiple intelligences'; linguistic, logico/scientific, spatial, musical, kinesthetic, interpersonal and intrapersonal. It is interesting that Gardner also provides indirect support for the importance of innate intelligences, claiming that by three years of age children already exhibit their dominant qualities. His work in education through Project Zero seeks to provide a curriculum which acknowledges individual attributes. This is clearly valuable in supporting the self-identity and self confidence of pupils and in motivating them to succeed through this self confidence. Whilst providing respect and support for each person's strengths is regularly supported as an ideal of democratic educational systems, it is clear that western societies still discriminate heavily towards linguistic and logico/scientific qualities in career and selection procedures. Gardner himself maintains some significance for IQ tests in his claim that they relate to these first two qualities in his list. In England an attempt to widen the criteria for selecting and approving students through the provision of a 'Record of Achievement' disappeared with the National Curriculum which returned all valuations to academic criteria - basically linguistic and logico/scientific intelligences and essentially the old IQ criteria. Power outcomes often devalue many altruistic educational developments.

The attachment of these 'factors' to specific skills and knowledge makes them very attractive, but the correlation between these tests and actual abilities in various disciplines of knowledge is a little tenuous. Mathematicians, for example, fall into a variety of categories, some displaying spatial awareness and others algebraic or manipulative abilities. In societies where children more often than not follow in father's footsteps there is likely to be a greater belief in innate/hereditary abilities and a stronger sense that identifying these characteristics might be helpful in guiding people into appropriate roles. More mobile societies are likely to pay less attention to such predetermining characteristics and to lay more stress on the consequences of experience and application in developing role specific skills.

More recently Western psychologists and academic-curriculum creators have provided new 'process-driven' categories of cognitive style which mirror the move of the school curriculum from content and facts towards strategy and process. Much of the methodology related to these mental processes is reminiscent of attempts during the 1960s and early 1970s to identify 'creativity' as a specific domain (see e.g. Guilford, 1967). This involved tests of 'divergent' and 'convergent' thinkers and later to axes such as whether a person adopted a 'scanning' approach to a problem or a 'focussed' approach, whether people are reflective or impulsive, holistic or serialists. In a return to the search for more general descriptors (c.f. Jungian psychology) these were condensed by Witkin in biblio (1967) into a single 'field dependent' or 'field independent' description. There has been quite a significant amount of research in the U.S.A. to identify how various disadvantaged groups (such as native Americans or black Americans) might be collectively associated with such differences as an attempt to provide non-social explanations of their disadvantage (e.g. Jones, 1986; Jacobs, 1987; Dunn et al., 1990). It is interesting to find Berry (in Modgil et al., 1986) describing social factors such as hunting communities v. agricultural societies, nomadic v. sedentary settlements, nuclear v. extended families as creating different field dependent or field independent cognitive styles. Similarly Dawson (1981) attributes different cognitive styles (field dependent or field independent) of two major groups of Hong Kong Chinese to their different ambient life styles, fishing and agrarian. Thus different ethnic/cultural groups are assessed as exhibiting differing cognitive profiles attributed to social and hereditary factors. Once again the academic framework however attractive needs also to be placed within the context of societal values, and research is needed into ways in which employers and others can utilise and support distinctive characteristics if discrimination is to be removed. This is one of the critical issues focussed upon within the feminist movement, do you compensate for apparent weakness or do you find ways of revaluing discarded criteria? The recent concern with the learning of process skills and strategies also has some interesting societal based origins. The reasons are clearly very complex, perhaps to do with the modern availability of factual knowledge which makes emphasising its use a more effective discriminator of people than knowledge on its own. In higher education the growth of computer based strategies has reformed the nature of some areas of study leading to redefinitions of its purpose and underlying premises. The move to a process curriculum is also in part a response to the explosion in knowledge in that not only is it difficult now to 'know everything' but that knowledge is continually being outdated. As far back as 1951 Kellaway reckoned that the 'shelf-life' of an engineering education was little more than ten years, and yet the pace of innovation has increased significantly since that time. It perhaps is also to do with maintaining the academic authority of the teacher. Students now have easy access to high powered techniques and at school level children now have access through television to much vicarious experience to which the teacher is no longer party. The teacher is therefore no longer the major owner of information and can only be authoritative in the more expert use of facts and knowledge. Indeed as a child all the knowledge I knew was provided by parents or teachers, and was thus bounded by my culture and society. My teachers knew what I knew. Today information, facts and even experiences are abundantly available to pupils and students and teachers are no longer in control of that function of learning. Thus the ability to use and manipulate facts becomes the focus and purpose of education. The new intellectuals are not those who know but those who can. Such factors have no doubt been influential in the increased interest in 'problem-solving skills' and 'investigation', not just from the expressed concern for cognitive abilities but perhaps as much as for a concern about the teachers' own self-image - not from a self interested or self promoting position but more altruistically in the need to confirm and authorise such a role within every particular society. As societies change, so too do these critical authority relationships.

Cross-cultural comparisons

Before looking further at issues relating to individual cognitive/learning styles it is informative to consider the macro/national variations in what is meant by knowledge and its acquisition. As a particular context we shall consider the world wide reforms of mathematics teaching which occurred during the 1960s and early 1970s. The 'new mathematics' swept the world. Having initially arisen in America, Continental Europe, and Britain it was then carried by the power of evangelism to many other countries, in particular British and American texts appeared throughout Africa. Yet the nature and content of the developments in the originating western countries were significantly different, with a general categorisation being represented by an American drive towards knowing things, a British drive towards doing things and a French drive towards understanding things. (A comprehensive analysis of these differences will be found in Howson et al., 1981.) This reflects the different educational principles and beliefs which underpin the systems. The American priorities throughout this century have been directed towards creating a national identity, and it is for this reason that a cumulative, modular and essentially non-intellectual (even at times anti-intellectual) philosophy was fundamental to the creation of a sense of belonging and furthering the American dream. In contrast to this Western Europe had no crisis of belonging, simply being born somewhere confirmed national membership, so that the educational philosophies were concerned with division and stratification, finding and nurturing the intellectual elite. Within this European context the 'nation of shopkeepers', England, holds a matching pragmatic quasi-practical approach, whereas in mainland Europe there has been a greater concern for grand ideas. As Grace (1994) stated recently 'English education has never been as hospitable to education theory as other European systems'. As Howson (1981) states 'The emphasis on logic, orderliness of mind, and clear thinking associated with the French - ce qui n'est pas clair n'est pas français - characterises their 'modern maths' texts in the same way in which a pragmatic approach does that of their English counterparts.' The various school texts produced by the three different systems of mathematical curriculum proved almost totally unexchangeable during the major reform periods, for example contrast the English 'Schools Mathematics Project', the Belgian course produced by Georges Papy entitled 'Mathématique Moderne' and the American 'School Mathematics Study Group'.

"... These stereotypical variations are also represented in the dominant field psychologies to which the three educational systems have generally adhered.

- British education has been dominated by Piagetian developmental psychology, in which children are presumed to grow into knowledge if placed in the right supportive experiential environment. Thus Hungarian colleagues commented that in England "Not to hurt the 'self image' of the children is more important than to force them to achieve better results, there is more emphasis on creativity than knowledge" (Hatch, 1993). In Britain the teacher has (until recently) been entirely responsible for the curriculum since it resides in the classroom environment. Teachers have been the creators of projects for curriculum change and practitioner/action research is normal. In one sense Piagetian psychology removes any guilt for the English teacher who alone was responsible for ensuring that all pupils did their best all the

38

time - in such an impossibly demanding position it was a relief that the teacher did his/her best and the pupil did his/her best it was just that the pupil was not ready that caused any failure.

- American education is dominated by behaviourist psychological notions in which learning is broken down into small manageable elements and incrementally learned, thus the curriculum responsibility is vested in the 'programmed' teaching materials and the tests by which this progress is measured rather than the teacher. Curriculum change is vested in projects created by University educationalists and taught to 'master teachers'. As Howson (1983) says "In the U.S.A. the teacher is seen as a consumer of curriculum materials..." In such a system again people are never really at fault - it is the material which does not quite work.

- European education is more underwritten by gestaltian traditions in which grand ideas are the object and end points rather than particular skills. National syllabi created by mathematicians are the fulcrum of curriculum development and mathematical structures lie at the heart. The pupil usually bears, and accepts, the responsibility for any failure in learning, and the Baccalauréate is the major endpoint for testing."
(Woodrow, 1995)

Clearly there is much dangerous stereo-typing in such statements, but like all stereo-types they arise from momentary if partial truths and become dangerous only when over-perpetuated.

As intimated above it is in these Western countries that the nature of education has moved from being founded on knowledge and facts to a concern for the process skills and problem solving application of fundamental mental abilities. There is a search for generalisable abilities which can be applied to an ever changing world. Mention has already been made to the impact of television as more than just entertainment and time-absorbing, it provides information and knowledge through which understandings of the world and its functioning emerge implicitly for viewers. This attention to generalised process skills as the central feature of education is not true of learners in some other countries, where knowledge is still rooted in facts, and where the investment possible in education makes very large classes inevitable, and teacher knowledge precarious. Where factual knowledge and algorithmic skills are precarious they maintain their central importance. Learning in this situation is inevitably 'book bound' and rote-learned skills are not just valued but found useful. Students and teachers believe that success comes from being told what to learn and this can then be memorised for success. Sham (1995) has identified 'behavioural rules' which affect (determine) Chinese attitudes to learning:

- 'respect for superiors' and 'loyalty and filial piety' - leading to conformity and suppression of deviant responses and hence low creativity and originality. (Liu and Hsu, 1974)

- 'learning is memorising by practising' - partly consequential on how the written language is learned and is perhaps why Chinese tend to excel at subjects which can be learnt by memorising (science) and practice (mathematics).

Kember and Gow (1990) also found that the Chinese favour learning which is based on a step-by-step processing of information, an extensive training based upon memorisation rather than argumentation. It is perhaps this inclination which leads to stronger preferences by Chinese students towards Science and Mathematics, usually seen as subjects for which facts and rules predominate as curriculum elements.

I recall a friend returning to India with her daughter and relating how she was taught to read from a standard English primer. There in the middle of the Bihar plain where it had not rained for two years was a little Indian girl reading about fair skinned, fair haired Anglo-Saxon children playing in the snow. It is not conducive to learning with understanding and would tend to impose rote, memorising learning as the natural learning paradigm. Thus a Hong Kong educated student investigating different teaching and learning styles between England and Hong Kong commented on the problems that arise from the English habit of asking open ended questions and setting projects rather than examinations. The notion too that a teacher might gather the views of the pupils as a vehicle for discussion was also problematic in transferring from an authority-based culture to one which prizes autonomy. Again in those educational systems in which discussion is rare (e.g. the Chinese and African systems) then 'target language' methods in foreign language teaching would become frustrated by the pupils' non-response, it is interesting that the Chinese word for 'disobedience' is translated as 'mouth-back'.

Constructivism and authority

Many of these concerns lie with the notions of authority and correctness. Cultures which have strong respect for ancestors and elders will tend to have a view of knowledge which is heavily based on the notion of a 'body of knowledge' rather than knowledge as a creative and individual voyage of discovery. The search in mathematics and science for truth rather than goodness or quality will relate to some cultural mores rather than others. Fasheh (1982) points to this issue of authority as also relating to political needs and sees the moves towards investigatory and exploratory methods as removing or undermining that authoritarian culture which some societies feel they require. Individual identity as contrasted with belonging to a societal group be it family, ethnic or cultural, will bear fundamentally on such issues. The growth of 'constructivist' theories in both mathematics and science education relates to the rejection of 'bodies of knowledge' and extrinsically created truth and authority which challenge individuality and self determinism. It is an interesting apparent paradox that the development of the current psychological focus on 'constructivist theory' should have taken place in the two subjects perceived as least related to individual construction as opposed to external truth and objectivity. In radical constructivist theory it is held that there is no knowledge other than that which is owned by the individual. The role of the teacher is therefore to create situations for experiences which present the learner with new ideas to rationalise. It is a 'teaching for meaning' psychology in which metaphor and language exploration are the vehicles for development. This places enormous emphasis on the images and constructs which the pupil owns, and many of these will be focussed within, and derived from, the pupil's own culture rather than that of the teacher or society at large.

It is also perhaps no accident that the 'constructivist' theory should have arisen largely within USA and English education as a response to the commitment of the culture and society to capitalistic and self-reliance philosophies. It is related too to the role and responsibility accorded to the teacher and pupil. It assumes the possibility of a negotiated position between teacher and pupils in which pupils have autonomy and rights. One of the basic outcomes of the right wing 'Thatcher/Reagan-ite' policies is that the 'state' ('there is no such thing as society' said Mrs Thatcher) is no longer responsible for individuals. Their current position as employed or unemployed, rich or poor, is their responsibility - all they need to do is to exert their entrepreneurial talents. Guilt is passed on to the individual rather than the responsibility of collective society. So in radical constructivism were there is no knowledge except that known by the pupil and it is individual self exploration which is central. It becomes more problematic as a theory when family rather than self is the identity unit and social responsibility rather than self aggrandisement is the motivating force. Constructivism is also a difficult theoretical position when the role given to the teacher by the learner is founded in a culture which values authority and leadership. Where authority rather than autonomy is valued then it is likely that the traditional teaching of mathematics and science will cause fewer stylistic conflicts and constructivist theories will not find favour. "Radical constructivism can therefore be seen as a theory created to be in concert with the societies in which it is assumed, societies for which individual autonomy rather than social responsibility is preferred" (Woodrow, 1995). Just as when modern right-wing philosophies are troubled by the lack of recognition in their approaches of a concern for 'mutual support and care' they revert to a notion of 'family' (even though this concept is now very limited) so the constructivists when equally troubled by the exclusion of social views of mathematics/science have created the notion of the micro-culture of the classroom. There is, however, an irony in that many of those who espouse constructivism (identified by the above as a right-wing tendency) are castigated by the right-wing as 'soft lefties' because their beliefs in individualism lead them to abandon traditional didactic teaching for more activity based teaching. It is such contradictions which demand a new clarification educational philosophy, just as in most European societies the notions of democracy and of right/left, capitalist/communist/socialist divisions are undergoing some redefinition. Even such recent terms as 'empowerment' which gained currency as a means towards more equitable societies are now seen to maintain discrimination (see Heathcote in this volume).

The substantive issue raised in mathematics and science education by many of the proponents of constructivism is the same as that of many other adherents to learning (or indeed to many social) theories; they tend to believe that their own theory is the only one which can be valid. It is the problem of holding such theories as faiths rather than beliefs, it is possible to hold multiple beliefs but not multiple faiths (Woodrow, 1995). Indeed in reality most people are quite capable of holding two mutually contradictory beliefs and then applying whichever one suits their purposes in a particular situation! As suggested by Cobb (1994), there is no 'true' theory of learning - merely one which is viable at the time of use. It is undoubtedly true that, whatever the classroom assumptions of the teacher or researcher, learners 'construct' knowledge and that without the cooperation (witted or unwitted) of the learner's mind the teacher teaches to no effect. There is knowledge, however, which exists to the teacher and in the context of which the pupil learns. There is 'social' knowledge and environmental knowledge in which the learner is embedded and to which the mental structures resonate and adapt, provided that the learner can find the right connection. Learning right and wrong, learning what is acceptable and learning what is dangerous are all transmitted from a context of social mores and common knowledge, and it is important that the teacher maintains a sufficiently broad learning ambiance in which all the pupils can find something to which they can respond. The teacher and the way in which the presentation of subject knowledge is structured affect the learning and it is therefore vital that the teacher has a sense of the nature and role of the knowledge being transmitted and of the view-point of the pupil.

It will be seen therefore that for students who have to change the cultural contexts of their studies there may well be issues and problems which arise from the different assumptions and principles which underlie the very meaning of what it is to learn. Although there has been some debate as to the connection between particular theories such as constructivism and the actual pedagogy of the classroom (see e.g. Driver, 1994) the way in which classroom interaction is described and valued in the current debates contains an implicit recognition of learner autonomy as opposed to teacher authority, they are in the context of learning rather than instruction. The debates take place within clear cultural/social assumptions which remain implicit, but of course these assumptions are not universal. Both Driver et al. (1994) and Cobb (1994), in interesting linked papers exploring the dichotomy of constructivism and sociocultural perspectives, seek to defuse the conflict through the notion of multiple beliefs held simultaneously and utilised in a pragmatic manner. The claim is that for individuals truth is replaced by viability. So too for social groups and social beliefs, they will be based upon viability leading to local (but not universal) truth. This, of course, is one of the reasons for the notion of 'culture' as a varying and unstable entity. This attempt to mediate between theories does not deal with the problems which emerge when contemporaneous theories held by an individual are in conflict rather than peaceful coexistence. The problem is compounded when these theories are simultaneously held by the teacher/curriculum but not the pupil. There are national and/or dominant attitudes to learning within all societies and there will inevitably be subcultures which may or may not respond sympathetically to these encultured systems.

Individual/societal cognitive conflicts

In order to look at the way in which societal assumptions and cultural pressures might influence individual learning, the concerns about learning the mathematics will be used as a context. This subject forms a good case study in that it has been reported as being a very selective attractor to students. Not only does it seem to appeal strongly to only a minority of students it is also reputed to create 'fear' and 'anxiety' in many others. It is often seen as an 'innate' ability, people are either born able to do it or not as the case may be, practice and hard work not always being rewarded. There are also wide differences in its adoption as a subject of study by different ethnic groups and between the two genders. Mathematics is essentially a very discriminatory subject of study, creating a highly structured measure offering fine differentiation in academic ability between people. Many societies may dislike discrimination in terms of gender, religion, race, size or age but most will accept intellectual discrimination, preferring these attainments rather than Gardner's kinesthetic or even artistic intelligences to give people status and power. There is ample evidence of mathematics discriminating not just between individuals but between different ethnic/cultural groups (Taylor, 1993: Modood, 1993).

In an influential proposition, D'Ambrosio (1985) coined the term ethno-mathematics to identify some of the issues he found in teaching mathematics. His study of Brazilian street-children led to the thesis that young learners have two types of knowledge and skills, one that they learn 'on the streets', which might be termed native wit, and another which formal education attempts to inculcate (see Nunes, 1992). There is a well known syndrome in mathematics that students who function very well in working out the odds in gambling, or in calculating change and money in the market place, frequently do not transfer these skills into the classroom where formal structures are taught by teachers. The conflict between learning the formal relationships of number as defined by the teacher and the intuitive notions of the everyday world which the student finds to work in practice make the student hesitant and confused. The more formal methods may be known to be more effective and powerful in the long term but they can appear complicated in the short term, and for the student who does not go on to fully complete the learning process there may be a net loss. It might be sometimes better to remain with less efficient but locally effective strategies.

Various aspects of 'multicultural'' and anti-racist' implications within the curriculum of mathematics were discussed during the 1980s (Woodrow, 1987). The actual understanding and meaning of concepts can be culturally determined.

Bishop (1989) discusses mathematics education as an enculturing activity and looks at differences in such basic activities as counting, locating, measuring, playing, designing and explaining. Similar issues have also been raised by Lancy (1983). Emblem (1986) in describing her response as an English teacher looking at the mathematical learning environment in Pakistan commented on the arithmetic rich context of life in Pakistan. 'Shopping' there is a daily process and involves a high number of transactions for different goods and foods. Children are surrounded by barter and exchange and everyday monetary transactions. In modern English society children are rarely present on many shopping occasions, most of which are supermarket placed with little arithmetic involvement and a single monetary transaction. This paucity of experience must reduce the prioritisation of arithmetic skills in the child's mind and produces a different attitude to arithmetic to which teaching approaches need to respond. It is not difficult to imagine the way in which Pakistani parents will disparage English schooling as failing to teach arithmetic well, when in practice it is the pupil's context which has changed. The regular calls for teaching methods which are effective in Japan or Taiwan to be transported into English school fail to recognise not only the contextual ambiance within which teaching takes place but the effects of this on the way in which pupils organise their learning. Stevenson et al. (1992) identified essential differences in the learning assumptions of Japanese and Taiwanese parents (and hence pupils) who believed that success related to effort, whereas American parents believed success was due to ability. The effects of the immediate environment on motivation for learning is seen in the parallel assumption that a 'book-rich' environment leads pupils to easier learning of reading, and conversely a paucity of reading material in the home to a lower rate of reading development. The way in which television provides information and story in a much more accessible way than do books, and this again may reduce the priority to read for some pupils, makes the teachers task in achieving reading standards more difficult. In just the same way a lack of regular immersion in number activities can diminish the child's preoccupation with number and slow down the learning of number relationships. This immersion and quantity of number involvements can be seen too in the impact of calculators in the classroom. Despite some popular belief that calculators may reduce achievement in number skills, they do give access to a far wider range and variety of number involvements, and this richness can be an advantageous motivation to counter changed societal experiences.

A number of studies have been conducted into the under-achievement of particular social and ethnic groups in mathematics. Some conjectures on reasons include such factors as:

- Mathematics is a failing subject - by which is meant that progress is measured by the point at which students fail. Until a student gets something wrong it is difficult for the teacher to help. Successful progression through mathematics therefore demands an ability to survive being wrong. It is suggested, for example, students who are very 'teacher dependent' may have more problems with mathematics than with other subjects. American research (e.g. Dunn et al., 1990.) has shown that some groups of students (e.g. girls, some black students) are measured as being more teacher dependent and these subgroups have also noticeably not traditionally been mathematically motivated.

- Early mathematics is focussed on arithmetic, in which detail and accuracy are the essential ingredients. Later on mathematics moves into algebra and geometry in which structure and wider views are required. Thus, groups of students who have both focussing and serialist cognitive styles will do well in early mathematics, but later success comes from more of a scanning and holistic style of learning. In English society traditional play styles of boys and girls appear to encourage more holistic and structure related activity in boys (e.g. ball games and wide ranging outdoor activities) and rather more introspective and focussed tendencies in girls (e.g. dolls, and skipping and hopscotch as outdoor activities).

- Mathematics has a traditional dependence on subject authority, where rightness and wrongness are externally validated. Mathematicians are therefore generally drawn from those for whom external and authoritarian structures form their natural style. This would in turn be reinforced by mathematics teachers tending to teach in an authoritarian and externally motivated style which will perpetuate this discriminant attraction of the subject. Different attitudes to authority are clearly features of the different cultures and would lead to differential affinity to mathematics as a subject.

Dunn et al. (1990) considered a group of 21 elements in a 'Learning Styles Inventory' (LSI) which revealed some interesting differences between Mexican-American, Chinese-American, African-American and Greek-American fourth, fifth and sixth-grade pupils. The LSI included personal construct items (such as responsibility/conformity, authority, self-motivation, parent and teacher motivation) together with methodological issues (such as learning alone, preferring a variety of approaches, tactile and kinesthetic approaches) and contextual issues (such as morning/afternoon working, noise and temperature preferences). The African-American and Chinese-American profiles proved to be consistently opposites, almost perfect mirror-images. Aloneness was a strikingly strong positive for Chinese and an equally strong negative for the African, indeed 15 of the 21 items were statistically significantly different. All the profiles contained some significant differences, the two nearest being Greek- and Mexican-Americans with only six significantly different attributes. Chinese-Americans seem to require a variety of instructional approaches, whereas African-Americans prefer established patterns and routines to their learning. Best time of day for learning was also variable, but most mathematics in primary schools takes place in the morning and many teachers seem to anticipate morning learning being more productive. The cognitive style approach is complex but it does highlight important issues about individual learning styles. In the context of this argument it would appear that it may be significant that such stylistic differences are based within subgroups of the society. The factors which create these differences would therefore appear to be culturally or socially (or even ethnically) based and will lead to the prioritisation by different groups of different descriptions of the learning act as better descriptors of how learning takes place.

The marked preferences for varied or standardised approached to learning which emerge from the cognitive style research makes the recommendations of the Cockcroft Report (1982) that 'mathematics teaching at all levels should include ...exposition, discussion, practical work, consolidation of skills, problem solving and investigational work' a much more complex statement than it appears. It contains within it assumptions of broad meanings of knowledge, of learning as an active rather than passive activity, which would be denied by other cognitive frameworks. Some of these differences are seen in the debates about approaches to assessment. The experiments with 'course-work assessment' in recent school exams in England presuppose a belief in learning as experiential and concerned with process skills. Recent moves to pull back the extent of course-work marks the pressure from those with more traditional beliefs who see learning as knowledge and the ability to perform skills. One of the strong arguments with which this retrenchment has been countered is the evidence of improved confidence and achievement in mathematics from girls as a result of incorporating a course-work element in the assessment.

Discrimination by assessment may be acceptable for a society in which finding and creating an educated élite is its educational objective, but for a mass education provision predicated on achieving the best for all its peoples, it is difficult to justify. Real beliefs may not be the same as expressed principles.

Consequences on careers

The results of cultural effects upon learning would not ultimately be of significance provided that they did not affect future career and life patterns in an adverse manner. The fact that I am not fitted or motivated to excel at basketball is ultimately not a significant factor in my life. The real discrimination lies in the outcomes of schooling on future life choices. The fact that twice as many boys than girls continue studying mathematics beyond compulsory schooling would not matter if mathematics were not a significant vehicle for future control of one's destiny. The influence of societal expectations runs strongly throughout research findings on career choices. Tanna (1990) reported that a number of Asian higher education students had chosen to study 'A'-level science subjects because of their future 'career' value rather than from academic strength in those subjects, even though this led to a need for longer periods of study to compensate for lower initial ability in the chosen subjects. Where Asian girls proceed to higher education, medicine and science are major attractions (Vellins, 1982; Taylor, 1993). For Chinese students there is a strong tendency to study mathematics, engineering and some aspects of finance and accountancy (Modood, 1993; Taylor, 1993).

Career choices are often made around the ages of fourteen and sixteen and determine much of the future study pattern. The dominance of either future career prospects as opposed to current enjoyment and perceived attainment is likely to be different in different cultures (Siann and Knox, 1992). Another feature in this choice preference may relate to the greater influence of parental and family advice in some Asian families. Parental influence has been explored by Ghuman (1990), Siann et al.(1990), Siann and Knox (1992), and Brah (1993), and there are clear indications of family decision making in a number of Asian contexts. Adult choices will tend to favour longer term advantages of career related decisions compared to the more individualistic and immediately attractive choices made by students within white U.K. society in which personal 'enjoyment' and/or perceived ability may play a more significant element. Comment has been made earlier on the tendency of Asian pupils to obtain A-level results through resits, and this has been associated with their choice of 'good career' subjects rather than subjects in which they have high achievement. It is also related to their belief that success comes from application, study and practice rather than through specific abilities (Stevenson et al., 1992). By comparison, the issue of vocational education continues to be problematic in English education, which has never quite determined its attitude to vocational as contrasted to academic commitment. The ambivalence towards 'technical schools' was evident in the variable response to the 1944 Butler Act and the promises of the ROSLA ('raising of the school leaving age') debate in the early 1960s quickly evaporated into a uniform, academically based provision. Current attempts to introduce National Vocational Qualifications have yet to be seen to resolve the basically anti-vocational philosophy of English schooling. This is clearly a culturally embedded issue and different cultures have different attitudes towards the vocational purposes of education.

There is in England a general trend in the unattractiveness of teaching to students from ethnic minority groups, with the black students in particular spurning the vocation. This has been evident from a number of the access courses run nationally, whose outcomes support the assumption that black students will be attracted to social studies and youth and community work but not to teaching. It could be, of course, that the institutionalised discrimination (by way of curriculum and teaching methods and educational assumptions) is too strong an experience to be ignored, but there might also be other reasons connected with the perceived opportunity through a high degree of personal action and autonomy to support their particular community.

Many societies are concerned at the differential response of girls to mathematics and science. The reasons may be economic rather than ones of values in that to increase the supply of a technologically aware workforce, the most effective response may not be to increase even further the proportion of males but to look towards increasing the much smaller contribution of females. Evidence is available from France, Finland, Kenya, America as well as England that there is real concern on this issue. The solution, however, probably resides in issues concerned with values in education and in the ways in which this affects cognitive assumptions. There is evidence that groups with a matched attainment profile exhibit significantly different confidence profiles, and confidence eventually affects learning. Social assumptions have been shown to have a strongly influence on self perceived ability and hence choices of study (e.g. Okebukola, 1992; Devine, 1993; Duane and Duane, 1992; Head, 1985). Figures for recruitment to Higher Education in England show that about 4% of white students apply for medicine and dentistry whereas about 18 % of all the Asian groups apply for medicine, about 17% of white students apply for social sciences compared to 33% for black students, 20% of white students apply for Maths and Engineering compared to 35% of Chinese students. There are clearly different career intentions allied to different ethnic groups and different social factors would appear to lead to different cognitive preferences.

Much of this evidence on career choices derives from students who have succeeded in the educational system. Of those young people belonging ethnic minority groups, it would be expected that these students represented those who had been most assimilated, yet culturally distinct choices still clearly prevail. The notions of cultural plurality and a multicultural society are dependent upon a society freer from value judgments and implicit discrimination if they are to succeed. Respectful coexistence and tolerance, esteem, mutual care and concern are fundamentally required to preserve harmony in society.

References

Berry J. (1986) Comparative Studies of Cognitive Styles and Their Implications, in: S.Modgil, G.Verma., K.Mallick, C.Modgil *Multicultural Education: The Interminable Debate* (London, Falmer Press).

Bishop A. (1989) *Mathematics as a Social Enculturation* (Dordrecht, Kluwer Press).

Brah, Avtar (1993) 'Race and Culture in the gendering of the labour markets: South Asian young Muslim women and the labour market'. *New Community* 19(3): pp441-458.

Cardon Lon R. et al. (1994) Quantitative Trait Locus for Reading Disability on Chromosome 6, *Science*, vol.266, pp 276-279.

Cobb P. (1994) Where is the Mind ? Constructivist and Sociocultural Perspectives on Mathematical Development, *Educational Researcher*, vol.23, no.7 pp 13-20.

Cockcroft W.H. (1982) *Mathematics Counts - Report of the committee of enquiry into the teaching of mathematics* (London, H.M.S.O.).

Cronbach L.J. (1970) *Essentials of Psychological Testing* (3rd Ed.) (New York, Harper & Row).

D'Ambrosio U. (1985) Mathematics education in a cultural setting, *Journal of Mathematics Education, Science and Technology*, vol.16, no. 4, pp 469-477.

Duane, R. and Daune, A.M. (1992) 'Women in Male Careers: The case of the higher technicians in France', *Training and Employment: Newsletter* 6: pp 1-4.

Dawson M (1981) The Bio-Social Adaption of the Boatpeople (Tanka) and the Hakka Agriculturalists of Hong Kong on Cognitive Style, Illusion, Susceptibility and Modernisation. *Unpublished manuscript*, University of Hong Kong.

Deutsch M., Katz I., Jensen A.R. (eds) (1968) *Social Class, Race, and Psychological Development* (New York, Holt Rinehart Winston).

Devine F. (1993) Gender segregation and labour supply: on 'choosing' gender-atypical jobs, *British Journal of Education and Work*, vol.6, no. 3, pp 61-74.

Driver R.,Asoko H., Leach J., Mortimer E.,Scott P. (1994) Constructing Scientific Knowledge in the Classroom, *Educational Researcher*, vol.23, no.7, pp 5-12.

Dunn R (1988) Introduction to learning styles and brain behaviour: suggestions for practitioners, *International Education*, pp 6-8.

Dunn R. et al. (1990) Cross-Cultural Differences in Learning Styles, *Journal of Counseling and Development*, Vol.18, pp 68-93.

Emblem V. (1986) Asian children in schools, *Mathematics in School*, vol.15, no 5/vol.16, no.1.

Eysenck H. (1971) *Race, Intelligence and Education* (London, Maurice Temple Smith).

Gardner H. (1983) *Frames of Mind: The Theory of Multiple Intelligences* (New York, Basic Books).

Gardner H. (1992) *Multiple Intelligences : The Theory in Practice* (Glasgow, Harper Collins).

Gartner A., Greer C. and Riessman (1974) *The new assault on Equality* (New York, Harper and Row) .

Ghuman, PAS. (1980) 'Punjabi Parents and English Education', *Educational Research* 20(12): pp 121-130.

Good L. (1973) *Looking in Classrooms* (New York, Harper and Row).

Grace G. (1994) Education as Scholarship *SCSE Conference* (London, 4th Nov. 1994).

Guilford J.P. (1967) *The Nature of Intelligence* (New York, McGraw Hill) .

Hatch Gillian (1994) Coming up to Russian Expectations, *Mathematics Teaching*, 146.

Head J (1985) *The Personal Response to Science* (Cambridge, Cambridge University Press).

Herrnstein R and Murray C,. (1994) *The Bell Curve: Intelligence and class structure in American life* (New York, Free Press).

Howson G., Keitel C., Kilpatrick J., (1981) *Curriculum developments in mathematics* (Cambridge, Cambridge University Press) .

Howson G. (1983) *Review of Research in Mathematics Education*, Volume B (Windsor, Nelson-NFER).

Jacobs RL. (1987) 'An investigation of the learning style differences among Afro-American and Euro-American high, average and low achievers'. Ph.D. thesis, Louisiana: Peabody University reported in Dunn et al. (1990) op. cit.

Jacoby R. and Glauberman N. (1995) *The Bell Curve Debate: History, Documents and Opinions* (New York and Toronto, Times Books/Random House).

Jensen A.R. (1969) How much can we boost IQ and scholastic achievement? *Harvard Educational Review*, 39 reprinted in Jensen A.R.(1972).

Jensen A.R. (1972) *Genetics and Education* (London, Methuen) .

Kellaway (1951) *Mathematical Gazette.*

Kember D. and Gow L. (1990) Cultural specifity of approaches to learning, *British Journal of Educational Psychology*, vol.60, pp 356-363.

Lancy J. (1983) *Cross-cultural Studies in Cognition and mathematics*, New York: Academic Press.

Liu M. and Hsu M., (1974) Measuring Creative Thinking in Taiwan by the Torrance Test, *Testing and Guidance*, 2, pp 108-9.

Modood T. (1993) 'The number of ethnic minority students in higher education: some grounds for optimism'. *Oxford Review of Education* 19(2): pp 167-182.

Nunes T. (1992) Ethnomathematics and everyday cognition, in D.A.Grouws (ed.) *Handbook of research on mathematics teaching and learning* (pp 557-574) (New York, Macmillan).

Okebukola, P.(1992) Differences in Socio-Cultural Environment Perceptions Associated with Gender in Science Classrooms, *Journal of Research in Science Teaching*, vol.29, no.8, pp 791-820.

Sham S. (1995) *Cultural differences in Teaching and Learning - A case study of Chinese Adolescents* paper given at European Conference on Educational Research; September; Bath, England.

Siann, G. et al. (1990) 'Parents, Careers and Culture: the view of ethnic minority and ethnic majority girls' *British Journal of Guidance and Counselling* 18(2): pp 156-169.

Siann, G. and Knox, A. (1992) 'Influences of career choice: the responses of ethnic minority and ethnic majority girls', *British Journal of Guidance and Counselling* 20(2): pp 193-204.

Stevenson H. & Stigler J. (1992) *The Learning Gap - Why our schools are failing and what we can learn from Japanese and Chinese education* (NewYork, Summit Books).

Taylor P. (1993) Minority ethnic groups and gender in access to higher education, *New Community*, vol.19, no.3, pp 425-440.

The Open University (1977) *The Curriculum and Cultural Reproduction Revision II* (Milton Keynes, O.U.Press).

Thurstone L.L. & Thurstone T.G. (1941) *Factorial Studies of Intelligence* (Chicago, Univ. of Chicago Press).

Vellins, S. (1982) 'South Asian students in British universities: a statistical note'. *New Community* 10(2): pp 206-212.

Witkin A. (1967) A Cognitive-style Approach to Cross-Cultural Research, *International Journal of Psychology*. vol.2, pp 237-38.

Woodrow D, (1987) Multicultural and Antiracist Mathematics; in *Perspectives*, (Exeter University) reprinted in *Mathematics Teaching: The State of the Art;* Ernest P. (ed.) (London, Falmer Press).

Woodrow D. (1995) The quest for multiple beliefs in learning theories and its frustration by single faiths, in *Chreods* vol. 9 pp 11-14.

5 Inequality and intercultural education
Gajendra K. Verma

The issue of inequality in education is not a new one. There is aconsiderable body of literature both in Europe and other parts of the world that bears testimony to this. Much of the writings reflects concern that sections of the population or society either get no access to any schooling at all or only access to one in which inequality of various kinds operates against their chances of success. Viewed from the macro-level, many of the factors involved transcend the boundaries of the education system itself and relate to socio-economic structure of particular societies.

This chapter attempts to focus a narrower frame of reference and highlights aspects of some of the issues associated with inequality within the educational process. It argues that intercultural education as a strategy is likely to reduce the present inequality which exists within the education system. This focus was based on the premise that education is an invaluable commodity which is important not only to individuals but also to the society in which they live.

Context

The post-war reconstruction of shattered cities and economies and the scarcity of men to do the work in all the European countries necessitated a wider search for suitable labour. Consequently, throughout the 1950s various European countries actively encouraged the recruitment of labour from their colonies or from countries newly given their independence. The result of this is the presence within nation states of a number of cultural, ethnic or racial groups. Since the process of migration and the history of different nations vary considerably, the cultural profiles of the settlers in different countries also vary.

However, the fact remains that most western European societies are now demographically diverse, characterised by two or more distinct groups. The groups are differentiated in terms of language, ethnicity, religion and cultural characteristics. In spite of such diversity, most countries have failed to recognise and support the heterogeneous nature of their societies. This failure extends to many areas of state provision including the education services. In many countries, debates and discussions are still continuing as to how educational institutions and their curriculum can be modified to meet the challenges of cultural plurality in society. There is no consensus in any democratic society as to how best to educate *all* children and young people in a culturally diverse environment. Social/educational reformers have been asking over decades what contribution education should be making towards creating a society in which life chances of *all* are better distributed. Can this be achieved without detriment or prejudice to the individual, or to his or her sense of identity or to that of other individuals?

A major obstacle to progress along these lines in education is the fact that educationists and education services function within the social and historical contexts of the states they serve. Most Western European states claim, and probably believe, that they espouse equality and that it is a central pillar of their law and administration. Unfortunately, however, arguments can readily be adduced to show that this is not so. The charge laid by reformers is that states by their laws and administrative processes are concerned to ensure the perpetuation of *in*equality so that those who have, retain their privileges and those who have not, continue to be deprived of them. Such an arrangement serves the social stability of the state well. Attempts to change matters by reformers run into the problem that the redistribution of privileges means that there are losers as well as winners.

Alongside this is the ambiguity inherent in the word 'equality' itself. This was considered by Saunders (1989) who teased out three meanings. These he identified as 'formal equality', 'equality of opportunity' and 'equality of outcome'. Formal equality he defined as equality under the rule of law; equality of opportunity meant that all individuals had an equal opportunity to achieve by developing their particular talents; a society based on the notion of equality of outcome he compared to a handicap race so perfectly calculated that all the runners arrived at the finishing tape together. The conclusion he arrived at was that 'formal' equality was incompatible with the other two meanings. That is to say, it was impossible to have equality of opportunity without compromising on the principle that everyone is equal and entitled to equal treatment.

Inequality and education

The term 'inequality' has an important part to play in any discussion on fairness and effectiveness in the educational process. It serves as an umbrella concept to enhance a variety of dimensions, in which certain sections of the population suffer from multiple disadvantages. Their ethnicity, language and culture differs from that of the host nation and there is sufficient evidence to suggest that they are not being given a fair chance in the field of education, employment and other aspects of life (Verma, 1986). Issues of inequality are currently examined within the 'equal opportunities' debate in Western countries, but seem to focus on the issue of gender.

Research, EEC reports, government inquiries, large and small-scale studies conducted over the last thirty years in many countries of Europe have clearly demonstrated that ethnic and cultural minorities remain the object of conscious or unconscious discrimination, and that this inhibits their life chances. It also deprives them of their right in democratic society to enjoy the economic and social mobility which are taken for granted by the dominant ethnic group. A turning point came in the 1970s when ethnic minorities throughout the world started asserting their rights. They became conscious of the fact that their identities were being eroded because of assimilationist educational and social policies. This awareness caused them to challenge the disparity between the declared values and principles of democratic societies and the realities of such policies as they experienced them.

Over the last three decades or so, the idea of a nation state as territory inhabited by a culturally homogeneous society has been challenged by the march of events. On the one hand there has been a powerful move towards European integration - politically, socially and economically - which many would say has now acquired a momentum which makes further progress in that direction inevitable. It has already affected and is likely further to affect the lives of citizens within the European Union. On the other hand, cultural, religious and linguistic differences between groups have come under scrutiny and have caused concern to many, who - at best - distrust their diversity.

There is sufficient evidence in the literature to suggest that European countries have deeply monocultural and assimilationist educational systems. This can been seen in the kind of curriculum they teach, the assessment techniques they use and the way teachers are expected to present other societies in the classroom. Of particular interest in this respect is Britain.

For most of the twentieth century education in Britain was something of a cottage industry. Schools were free within the law to teach pretty much what they wanted constrained only by the demands of the public examination system. The teaching profession itself was perceived as a rich mine of British eccentrics in a nation given to eccentricity. Such an arrangement for the education of children undoubtedly had its weaknesses but one of its strengths was that it allowed - indeed, positively encouraged - schools and teachers to address the needs of the children for whom they were responsible. Thus, the content, methods and objectives of teaching adopted by a teacher in an inner-city school, three-quarters of whose class was of South Asian origin, were markedly different from those of a colleague in another school teaching children of White British, middle class parents.

The advent of the 1988 Education Reform Act changed all that. The national curriculum became part of a legal entity and an elaborate system of testing was brought into being to ensure that its educational objectives were being realised. For the first time, government had determined what should be taught and did so, not as a result of discussion with educators but of its mere will. Schools and teachers were deluged with highly detailed instructions about what they were to teach and the length of time they were to expend on each element. Without going into fine detail, it is instructive to look at two areas of the curriculum as examples: History and Religion.

"History in the National Curriculum (England)" (DES 1991) is prefaced by a note which, although lengthy, is quoted in full because it gives the flavour of the new relationship between government and the schools and teachers. Note: The following attainment targets and programmes of study constitute the National Curriculum for History. The attainment targets and their constituent statements of attainment, specify the knowledge, skills and understanding which pupils of different abilities and maturities are expected to have by the end of each key stage. The programmes of study specify the matters, skills and processes which are required to be taught to pupils. The two types of requirement are complementary, and pupils will not be able to satisfy the statement of attainment without demonstrating a knowledge and understanding of the historical content of the appropriate programmes of study.

The examples printed in italics serve to illustrate the attainment targets and programmes of study and are non-statutory.

That extract is now followed by another under the heading of 'The Purposes of School History'.

1.   History can mean two things: the past and the study of the past. The past influences all aspects of our lives. It shapes the customs and beliefs of the communities to which we belong. Learning about the past and the

58

methods used to study it helps pupils make sense of the world in which they live.

2.   There are two main aims of school history:

- to help pupils develop a sense of identity through learning about the development of Britain, Europe and the world;

- to introduce pupils to what is involved in understanding and interpreting the past.

There follows a final extract from the document - the titles of the core study units for key stage 3, that is to say, for children between the ages of 12-14. They are:

1.   The Roman Empire
2.   Medieval realms: Britain 1066 to 1500
3.   The making of the United Kingdom: Crowns, Parliament and peoples 1500-1750
4.   Expansion, trade and industry: Britain 1750 to 1900
5.   The era of the Second World War.

The impact of these directions is best perceived when considered together. First, the History that is taught must be the history that is prescribed. Failure to do so on the part of the school and the teacher will result in the failure of the pupils and, since the prescription is backed by the 1988 Education Act, it must be supposed that legal action could be taken against the teacher or the school. Second, the study of History is clearly and overtly justified by its power to develop a sense of identity in the students. This is not the place to explore the sense in which the word 'identity' is being or might be used in this context. However, the core study units cited and the clear general direction of the rest of the document makes any conclusion other than that students were expected to form identities which drew heavily on England's development as a parliamentary democracy, its rise to head a glorious Empire and its relations with Europe very hard to sustain.

Had all this been intended for a homogeneous White British audience, some doubts might be expressed about the suitability of the curriculum in terms of the world picture it would present to the children. What seems not to have occurred to those who framed it is the fact that the perspectives of many of the children who were, by law, obliged to follow it, were very different from those of their White British peers. For them, it was the story of the subjugation of their ancestors and their countries by the triumphant British. For some, it was the story of their forefathers' enslavement. The History they were obliged to learn was a statement of their historical inferiority.

Let us now turn to consider the place of religion. The Education Reform Act requires all maintained schools to provide a daily act of worship and demands that, taken over time, these acts of worship should be mainly of a Christian nature. However, a conscience clause going back to the 1944 Education Act was retained which allowed parents to withdraw their children from school worship and the legislation included the possibility for parents arranging for their children to receive alternative opportunities for worship off the school premises.

Nevertheless, the general effect of the 1988 Act was to strengthen the requirements of the 1944 Act and appeared to take little account of the changes that had come about in the intervening years to the nature of British society. The requirements shocked and surprised many headteachers and members of religious minority communities (Skinner, 1995). One Muslim organisation warned parents of the need to withdraw their children from school worship otherwise they would pray to Jesus as the 'son of God' learn about the Trinity and thus commit the awesome sin of *Shirk*, associating others with Allah. This is the worst thing a Muslim can do (Sarwar, 1989).

In Britain, therefore, the introduction of the National Curriculum and its associated testing system in 1988 (DES, 1988), far from countering the inequalities which exist within the educational system in particular and in society in general, actually reinforced prejudice and inequality and backed it by the full force of the law. Concern has been expressed about the issue of freedom of religion. A powerful group is pressing for the removal of religious inequalities within the education framework of the 1988 Education Act for religious education and collective worship. Only time will tell if they are successful.

There is evidence from research to suggest that many of the conflicts that arise between the school and ethnic minority communities, and many of the cultural disparities that pupils experience, are caused by conflicting values, beliefs and behaviour (Pumfrey and Verma, 1990). Some ethnic and religious groups are socialised in homes and communities in which the sacred is valued more than the secular, and in which traditional cultural beliefs and religious values are strongly held. The attachments that people in this process contribute to the formation of cultural in-groups. The attitudes of in-group towards the outgroups are formed on the basis of this socialisation process. As Parekh (1989) wrote:

> All of us in our traditional settings, take lots of things about ourselves for granted. We are constantly growing and changing without being aware of it. The immigrant's position is different, especially for someone easily distinguishable by their colour or culture. Partly because of the conscious or unconscious pressure of an inhospitable society, partly because of their own sense of unease, they feel forced to define themselves, to say to others and even themselves, who they are, and what constitutes their identity or claim to distinction.

Unfortunately this strategy, whilst it is very easy to understand why it is adopted, deepens the gulf between the minority and majority groups. The school can play a mediating role by including intercultural education as part of the curriculum (Verma, 1993).

If we take the word 'culture' to denote the meanings and understandings which are learned, shared and evolve in groups, then intercultural education should be constructed in such a way as to create an environment in which it is possible, even desirable, to accept each other's cultures, ethnicities and communities. The culture of an educational institution should be a reflection of the best of the culture of the society of which it is part. Since most societies are multicultural, this ought to be reflected in the culture of the educational institution. In this analysis, culture encompasses almost every aspect of human experience - it represents a more or less consistent pattern of thoughts, feelings and actions, and it is structured.

Inequality and intercultural education

At the risk of accusations of pessimism, I begin with the following quotation:

> Individuals may act morally towards each other by reason and by principle and may show an altruism which cannot be explained in terms of self-interest. Groups, however, show an extraordinary, powerful and persistent egoism. It has been observed by Neibhur that relations between groups 'will be determined by the proportion of power which each group possesses at least as much by any rational or moral appraisal of the comparative needs and claims of each group.' (McIntosh, 1979)

In most western societies, academics have developed various models in the last thirty years or so and have used them to deal with the issues of inequality within the educational context. The most popular approaches employed to advocate and provide equality of opportunity have been multicultural and anti-racist education. These have had some effect on the perceptions and practices of some teachers - mainly, however, restricted to those who work in schools with substantial minority populations. It has to be said that teachers in schools where White British pupils are the norm have failed to see the significance of these approaches to them. The consequence has been that they have failed to change the ideological perceptions of society at large. There has been widespread failure to recognise the inequality within the education system and racial prejudice and discrimination in society at large remains at a high level.

More recently, the concept of intercultural education has evolved, particularly in Europe. This has featured increasingly widely in research reports and in the media, and thence in writings of those interested in social and educational policies. A framework of appreciation of diversity, with recognition of the potential for enhancement of opportunities for all, is essential to the development of intercultural education. The curriculum should be taught in ways that are as little biased as possible. Teachers should adopt a critical approach to cultural bias, racism and stereotyping in their teaching schemes. They should be equipped for their work by learning to recognise cultural diversity as a source of social and curriculum involvement. Schools have a duty to prepare children and adolescents to make their contribution to a multicultural society. Unfortunately, reality falls far short of theory. Unfair discrimination and racism remain potent everyday realities to members of minority ethnic, cultural, religious and linguistic groups for reasons that have been touched on earlier. The rise of the National Front in France, various neo-Nazi groups in Germany and the British National Party in the UK, all of them with the extirpation of ethnic minority groups from their countries as their prime purpose testify to this.

Viewed at the global level, inequality has both social and political implications. We live in an interdependent world where we have to work and interact with nations of different races, cultures, ethnicities beyond our borders and with people of varying cultural, linguistic, religious and ethnic groups within our borders, the one affecting the other. In such a world of increasing interdependence - economically, socially and politically - intercultural education can play an important role in challenging stereotypes, prejudices and ethnocentric perspectives of both the individuals and the groups. The Swann Report stated that:

We consider that a multiracial society such as ours would function more effectively and harmoniously on the basis of pluralism which enables, expects and encourages members to participate fully in shaping the society as a whole within the framework of commonly accepted values, practices and procedures whilst also allowing and, where necessary, assisting the ethnic minority communities in maintaining their distinct ethnic identities within their common framework. (DES, 1985)

Expressed like that, it seems an ambition both desirable and possible. Unfortunately, events across Europe since 1985 have shown how difficult it is to realise. They have also shown how important it is to continue to work towards it. The issue of intercultural education is becoming increasingly meaningful in today's world which is divided by conflict and tension between ethnic groups. Therefore there is all the more need for people at all levels of society to learn to understand each other and, through that understanding to develop tolerance and respect for each other.

It is clear that at the core of any discussion about intercultural education is the concept of culture. Culture is learned and is shared by society. It is concerned with ideas, values, attitudes and behaviours. It is also accepted that culture changes as shared ideas, values, attitudes and behaviours change/modify as a result of interaction among members of a defined cultural group and between members of different cultural groups. Thus, culture as a dynamic process changes because of its own internal dynamics and in relation to other cultures.

The main problem in intercultural education is how to make cultural groups accept and understand views, values and behaviours differing from their own. Such cross-cultural encounters often create friction, tension and conflict. It may even reveal ethnocentrism, xenophobia and pressure from the dominant group for assimilation. Proponents of intercultural education argue that it brings up people who are capable of assessing alternative values and views of life critically. In order to reduce ethnocentrism we need to know how people view the world around them which consists of individuals belonging to various cultural groups.

The goal of intercultural education should not simply be to recognise and appreciate cultural diversity in society, for this can amount to mere tokenism. People must understand the significance of a culture's history and tradition as part of the dynamic and multifaceted culture of any contemporary society. The education system therefore ought to develop curricula and pedagogies that integrate an understanding of cultural process and cultural continuity and changes within a framework of national identity.

It is easy to argue that education should not be held responsible for inequality of various forms in society, since this is beyond its direct control, particularly the socio-economic structure of society. Nonetheless, it is unalterably true that education can play an important role in leading the battle against inequality (Verma, 1993).

References

Department of Education and Science (1985) *Education for All: Report of the Committee of Inquiry into the Education of Children from Ethnic Minority Groups*, (The Swann Report) Cmnd 9453, London, HMSO.

Department of Education and Science (1988) *The Education Reform Act 1988*, London, HMSO.

Department of Education and Science (1991) *History in the National Curriculum. (England)* London, HMSO.

McIntosh, P. (1979) *Fair Play: Ethics in Sport and Education*, London, Heinemann.

Parekh, B. (1989) *Identities on Parade* in *Marxism Today*, June, 1989.

Pumfrey, P.D. & Verma, G.K. (1990) (eds.) *Race Relations and Urban Education: Contexts and Promising Practices*, London: The Falmer Press.

Sarwar, G. (1988) *Education Reform Act 1988 - What Can Muslims Do?*, London: Muslim Educational Trust.

Saunders, P. (1989) '*The Question of Equality*' *Social Studies Review, 5 (2)*.

Skinner, G.D. (1995) *Primary Schools With All Pupils from South Asian Backgrounds* Research Report to the Leverhulme Trust, Centre for Ethnic Studies in Education, University of Manchester.

Verma, G.K. (1986) *Ethnicity and Educational Achievement*, London: Macmillan.

Verma, G.K. (ed.) (1993) *Inequality and Teacher Education: An International Perspective*, London: The Falmer Press.

6 Issues and problems of representation in a comparative European context
Jagdish Gundara

Introduction

This exploratory paper will argue that three political and discursive realities are of central importance in understanding and acting upon the present growth in Europe of violence, xenophobia and nationalism. The three 'realities' are:

a)   governmental management of social diversity and migration in Europe;
b)   the mediation of issues concerning immigrant communities and academic concepts of 'otherness';
c)   the crucial role which formal and non-formal education have to play in demonstrating alternatives to chauvinism, xenophobia and violence.

There is no necessary connection between the three. What is being argued here is that there is much to be learned from bringing them together in order to highlight the ways in which the ideological and the governmental dimensions of European life together help to sustain or provide fertile ground upon which violence, particularly racist violence, can germinate and receive sustenance. It is also the contention of this paper that academic and popular discourses about issues of 'race', multiculturalism and exclusivity may be learned by, or legitimated for, most of the populace through the educational system. There is seldom recognition, by those who theorise about the ways in which racism and xenophobia are able to spread, that for many in Europe its origins lie in the educational system which provides the 'intellectual basis' for otherness and sustains a fear of the outsider. The central importance of both formal and informal education is as a means by which to combat the growth of xenophobia and violence. There are few grounds for arguing that education can provide any short-term panacea for the ills which beset European societies. However, if short term solutions are not provided then education will then be seen as too slow a process. Constructive and long-term action is needed, and it must not depend for its implementation on the maintenance of a sense of crisis.

Social diversity and the European state

The two European organisations which have had an impact on those educational developments which relate to social diversity in European society are the Council of Europe and the European Community. Their impact on national educational policies has, however, been limited because the European states have not allowed these organisations to interfere in the educational domain, which is seen only as being part of the national jurisdiction. The two bodies have focused on issues revolving around social diversity, through their concerns about the education of 'migrants'. The particular migrations which informed these policies started in the late 1950s when the de-colonisation process began to gather momentum. The Council of Europe began to survey the position of 'migrant' children's education in 1966. During each subsequent year resolutions were adopted by the Council on different aspects of the education of 'migrant' families. This process culminated in the launch of a five year 'Project No. 7' in 1980. The European Community developed a programme in the 1970s, and it also initiated discussions about the education of 'migrant' workers, and issued a Directive to this effect in 1977. The Council of Europe has increasingly focused on an intercultural approach to education, the underlying assumption appears to be that the European nation states are cohesive and coherent. What has so far developed in relation to educational policies, such as they are, is a response at the wider European level which does not take into account the underlying diverse natures of European societies. It instead concentrates on the immigrant dimension and ignores how, for instance, educational policies for immigrants ought to be formulated in the context of general educational policies which include provision for indigenous European minorities and policies concerning their education. There is also a lack of consideration of the educative role which the education systems can or should play. The concerns, however, ought to be broader than the immigrant communities.

There is particularly a problem at the present time because governance of nations, especially in Europe, has become an extremely problematic issue. The rise of violence and instability is made worse by the ways in which economic decline in many areas of Europe is leading to an increase in tensions and a disintegration of communities. Where these communities are diverse the tensions are greater. The development of narrow nationalisms east of the Elbe has had dangerous consequences in the western European context by providing strength to presumed purer 'ethnic' identities which have constructed an imagined past designed to exclude diversities. Social scientists in the so-called developed countries have been concerned for a long time with the integration of the new nations in the developing countries. What has been forgotten is that national integration is a permanent issue for all nations whether old or new, 'developing' or 'developed'. The tendencies towards disintegration may be linked to different factors in different contexts, but the need to reexamine the basis on which nations are governed requires continual appraisal.

At another level, systems of education have a major role to play in ensuring that the educational and informational process does take on the substantive issues of the 'belongingness' of all groups to the polity. The representation of 'the other' and the knowledge which constructs the immigrant as an alien do not help. The problems of housing and employment, or difficulties in education, are shared by many or all members of the community. These difficulties do not have to be given an ethnic or racial gloss. They are shared problems. The only justification for separating out issues which have to do with different communities would be to illustrate how shared problems are sometimes worse for minority groups. What tends to be projected and emphasised is difference.

The national project which set out to make 'one out of the many' has faltered. There is also a lack of solidarity because people have become surplus to the requirement of the state. The General Strike in Spain on 27th January 1994 is one example of the growing frustration of the workforce with the diminution of their significance and prospects. At the other end of the scale, IBM has recently become profitable once again - at the expense of 15% of its existing (international) workforce! This solidarity of all groups within Europe has to be an inclusive proposition so that the national minorities, immigrant communities and the under-class are all seen to belong to it. The notion of a nation state which is caring and nurturing of all the citizens has received a serious setback. In western Europe the malaise of racism has assisted in disintegrating communities, which may yet aid and abet the process of disintegrating nations, as it has in the case of the now fragmented Yugoslavian state and parts of eastern Europe (Denitch, 1990). There is a present danger that the rise of the violent notions of 'ethnic cleansing' might attain a form of legitimacy in Europe, only fifty years after they were defeated. The overflow of these abominable notions into other parts of Europe would have catastrophic consequences. It should also be noted that the phrase 'ethnic cleansing' has become acceptable for unproblematic use in many contexts in describing complex issues.

If citizens within the state feel that they are treated fairly, that they belong and are accorded their full rights, they would then fulfil their obligations. Therefore, the accordance of full citizenship rights would lead to the loyalties which are necessary for nation states to function. In the recent phase of frenzy about the market economy, social rights of groups have also been negated with a consequent withdrawal by groups from their social responsibilities. In the absence of greater equalities siege communities are being established which hark back to narrow nationalism and fundamentalisms (Gundara, 1992). Analysis of the aspirations of these communities is disregarded in the media. Instead the discourses of the new democracies are those of rabid monetarism disguised as radical reform. In such a climate racisms fester and grow.

The secular nation state has received setbacks at various levels. The lack of a commitment by politicians to secular ideals and a corruption of the polity has led to an increase of what Galbraith famously described as a private wealth and public squalor, and this has lost the state the loyalty of many people. In Britain references to the monarchy raise issues of whether it is worth keeping for financial reasons. Yet, at the underlying level, a Poujadist government has unleashed this argument. The irony is that they have undermined the legitimacy of the Crown by denying that there is any notion of society at the underlying level. This market-orientated approach applied to every aspect of British life, propelled by new conservativism, has led to the thinning of the glue that has held the imagined British national community together. The marginalisation of large groups of people from different localities, regions and nationalities in European countries undermines the fabric of European nation states. If at times of hardship and economic crises, immigrant groups are seen as being the only element of diversity in societies, they can be constructed as being the visible signifier of 'our' ills. In certain European contexts they are being blamed for causing many of the social problems, thus activating the syndrome of blaming the victim.

The European nation states have indigenous diversities on the basis of religion, language, and social class through regional or national minorities. Now, in the post world war period, many of these countries have acquired new groups of settlers. These groups have different patterns of settlement, social class affiliations, legal statuses, as well as levels of family reunification. The earlier distinction between the countries into which people migrated in northern

68

Europe and the southern European countries from which emigration took place has changed. Even the emigration countries in southern Europe have now become immigration countries. Schools in both northern and southern Europe all have extremely diverse student populations. With the signing of the Maastricht Treaty and the establishment of an open market in the European Union, a newer pattern of intra-European Union migration is also taking place. The position of the earlier postwar immigrants from outside Europe, who had to fight for their and their children's educational training rights, is markedly different from the European Union immigrants who now, as a matter of right, demand high levels of social policy and educational provision for their children.

As the larger processes of integration take place and there is a greater need for specialisation and social differentiation within societies, each nation state will have to ensure that economic, political and cultural policies are developed to enable greater co-operation. Such measures will also have to take account of the local and national peculiarities. Above all, such policies will have to be mediated - represented to the peoples through the media. There is no longer space (or time) for the reconstruction of comfortable ideological positions which mistake the recognition of culinary diversity for intercultural understanding, nor for communities based around spurious notions of blood and soil or other metaphorical abominations. In the 'new order' there will be a need for the polity to recognise diversity, tension and contradiction and to work through them to the establishment of communities in productive flux. Such communities do not need racism in order to thrive, nor do they need their 'nationalism' preformed and prepackaged.

Few European governments have afforded the newly settled communities a sense of confidence with their place in European societies.

Redefining nationalities

As the immigrants have become more settled in Europe there has been a concern about defining their legal and political position within European societies. In Germany the situation is compounded by the 'ethnic' Germans arriving from Eastern Europe and Russia and acquiring citizenship rights soon after arrival. This is in sharp contrast to the Auslanders who have been resident in Germany for a long time, and cannot acquire such rights. The new settlers to Europe have come from nation states and most of these states have diverse populations. These settlers are therefore either nationals of the country of origin or of the country of settlement. Their position in legal and political terms is continually being undermined through legislation. This legislation is racist in its intent and is not directed against the 'ethnicity' of the new settlers. The use of 'ethnicity' by social anthropologists has certainly not helped in clarifying this complex issue. It is necessary for those involved with such issues to undertake a more systematic analysis of the basis of European nation states in historical and contemporary terms so that a clear definition may emerge. For instance, what are the differences between the national minorities and 'ethnic' minorities? Do the national minorities (in Jura, Scotland, Brittany, Wales) accept the states as defined by the dominant nationalities? There is, furthermore, a need to define the nature of European societies and their relationship to the structures of the nation state.

The national minorities in Europe generally have a territorial basis (Scotland, Wales) which is constitutionally recognised by the state. The newly settled communities, however, also occupy urban spaces which may not be constitutionally recognised but which nevertheless, represent the birth of these new communities. The black communities in Brixton, Southall and Harmondsworth live as part of the working class. Similarly, the Turks in Kreuzberg in West Berlin live in a 'sanctuary' against racism which, nevertheless, they still experience. Schools in these neighbourhoods reflect the communities in which children live. But it has to be noted that such communities are often misrepresented as 'other' cultures which are planted in the 'host' communities. Apart from the somewhat spurious notion that before the arrival of others there have always been 'communities' living in idyllic harmony, the fact is that many of these so-called other communities are very much alive, growing and importantly changing. The black community in Britain has, through its music, been able to develop what has been described a sense of 'lived blackness', but it has also been influential on the 'cultural' identities of many other young people. Paul Gilroy has also pointed out that some of Britain's Asian community have

'borrowed the sound system [....] as part of their invention of a new mode of cultural production with an identity to match.' (Gilroy, 1993)

The point is that the new communities are something of which we are all a part. Attempts to halt change will not work. The ghetto-isation of otherness is one discursive means of dealing with communities which have to be constantly redefined as alien. So much of the violence and xenophobia which is mediated is premised upon a past sense of identity rather than one for the future.

Eurocentrism and education

At the basic level, the issue which is being raised is how does Europe construct itself as an entity and how are notions of inclusion and exclusion articulated, at least in the educational and knowledge domain? Knowledge systems confront dual challenges as European integration take shape. On the one hand Europe confronts a Eurocentric tradition in many domains of knowledge. These hegemonic understandings are informed by the imperialism of Europe. As Edward Said writes:

> 'Without significant exception the universalising discourses of modern Europe and the United States assume the silence, willing or otherwise, of the non-European world. There is incorporation; there is inclusion; there is direct rule; there is coercion. But there is only infrequently an acknowledgement that the colonised people should be heard from, their ideas known.' (Said, 1993)

As a result of the imperial enterprise, not only is Europe in the world but the world is in Europe. Ostensibly this has profound implications for the transfer of knowledge. Yet, discourses from the colonised peripheries are still treated as being marginal in contemporary Europe. Martin Bernal indicated how in the 18th century and 19th century Europeans developed a historiography which denied the earlier understanding that the Greeks in the Classical and Hellenistic periods had learned as a result of colonisation and interaction among Egyptians, Phoenicians and Greeks (Bernal, 1987). Part of the reason for this new historiography has been that with the rise of racism and anti-semitism in Europe, the European Romantics and racists wanted to distance Greece from the Egyptians and Phoenicians and construct it as the pure childhood of Europe. It was unacceptable from their perspective that the Europeans would have developed any learning and understanding from the Africans or the Semites.

The notion of a European culture separated from the world south of the Mediterranean is a mythical construction. The contributions to knowledge in the ancient period from this immediate region include Mesopotamian astronomy, the Egyptian calendar and Greek mathematics, enriched by the Arabs. As Samir Amin states:

> 'The opposition Greece = the West / Egypt, Mesopotamia, Persia = the East is a later artificial construct of Eurocentrism. For the boundary in the region separates the backward North African and European West from

the advanced East; and the geographic unities constituting Europe, Africa and Asia have no importance on the level of the history of civilisation, even if Eurocentrism in its reading of the past is projected onto the past the modern North-South line of demarcation passing through the Mediterranean.' (Amin, 1989)

The debate about how and where 'civilisation' arose is an interesting one for educationalists and students, but it is only a part of a wider concern with the intellectual straightjacket that Eurocentric education can become. In this sense it is always necessary to consider ways in which the curriculum, both formal and informal, can be modified or changed. As long as history is studied from the perspective of one or another nationalist claim to truth, rather than from one or another paradigm of historiography, education will remain trapped in the tramlines of nationalist tautology. And within this context questions of racism, xenophobia and violence will rattle around meaninglessly. Educationalists would do well to consider several alternative definitions of history before planning their lessons or mediations.

The dominant-marginal perspective in educational and media discourses needs to be constantly challenged and often redrawn. The issues being presented here are historically significant and of the gravest importance for the future of education as well as for the political and social structures of Europe. It requires a combination of pedagogical patience and persistence. There has to be a constant and fundamental reappraisal of the histories and national identities into which we have all been inducted with such care. The answer does not lie in trying to establish either a liberal or 'back-to-basics' curriculum founded in that Eurocentric, nationalist and empire-based intellectual milieu which has done so much to contribute to our present predicament.

For European education systems, the challenge is to engage in a wide ranging establishment of connections with other cultures and civilisations which are part of the fabric of contemporary European society, and also to develop an understanding of its past which includes Greece, Egypt and the Near Eastern connections. It is also a question of disentangling, of decoding, of identifying the operation and structures of those discourses which help to sustain the present relations of power and subordination in our societies. This of particular significance in relation to discourses which construct difference as suspect, culture as fixed (and 'ours'), and otherness as the root causes of violence, xenophobia and nationalism. It is not otherness which is the key educational issue, but sameness. The issue of Eurocentrism is not simply an issue of prejudices and errors which heighten xenophobia and chauvinism. Eurocentrism, according to Amin:

> 'has replaced rational explanations of history with partial pseudo-theories, patched together and even self contradictory at times ... The Eurocentric distortion that makes the dominant capitalist culture negates the universalist ambition on which that culture claims to be founded.' (Amin, 1989)

The Enlightenment came not as a universal phenomenon, despite attempts to learn from other cultures, but as a narrowly defined European response to the obscurantism of Christianity. There are obvious contributions that the academic and educational systems can make in the context of democratic egalitarianism which are also a feature of European societies. Such theoretical issues should have implications for what constitutes the common curricula and shared knowledge in European schools and communities. Without such a curriculum and educational changes, individual groups are likely to demand separate political structures, schools and media systems for their own religious or ethnic groups. The rise of ethnic, culturalist and fundamentalist nationalisms in Europe at the present has had dire consequences for nation states as currently constructed.

The political realities and the ideological underpinnings of developments in Europe need to become part of the discourses of those who consider themselves to be the 'normal' citizens of Europe.

References

Amin, S. (1989) *Eurocentrism* (London, Zed Books).
Bernal, Martin (1987) *Black Athena: The Afro-Asiatic Roots of Classical Civilisation, Vol.1* (New Brunswick, Rutgers University Press).
Denitch B.(1990) *The End of the Cold War: European Unity, Socialism and Shift in Global Power* (London, Verso).
Gilroy, Paul (1993) *The Black Atlantic: Modernity and Double Consciousness* pp.72-110 (London, Verso).

Gundara, Jagdish (1992) The Dominant Nation: Subordinated Nations and Racial Inequalities in J. Lynch, C. Mogdil, S. Mogdil (Eds.) *Equity of Excellence? Education and Cultural Reproduction,* Vol.III (London, Falmer Press).

Said, Edward (1993) *Culture and Imperialism* (London, Chatto and Windus).

Part II

Interculturalism and language issues

7 Theory, language and socio-political perspectives

Giovanna Campani

The intercultural curriculum: a perspective for the future

The need to develop an intercultural curriculum - in northern as much as in southern Europe - was born of essential reality. The need to accept immigrant children into schools, in both educational and cultural terms, is part of this reality. However, the issues which demand the creation of an intercultural pedagogy go beyond this particular situation and are very complex. The challenge of interculturalism, which begins in meeting others outside your door (be it a stranger or neighbour), in both its psychological and sociological perspectives, touches the central issues of our times:

- the social and political concerns of modern times, post-modernism, globalisation;
- the crisis of nationality and the new social relationships, new modes of integration and immigration;
- the relationship between state, communities and individuals;
- individual and social identities, in the context of multiple ties and the place of values in these multiple relationships.

Intercultural education draws on all the disciplines of the social sciences in order to create the necessary epistemological basis, which was precisely the theme of the Lisbon conference. This intercultural approach raises major social and political questions, related to problems of integration and thus the very patterns of society (including such concerns as the issue on the one hand of the wearing of Islamic scarves in French schools, and on the other, the demands of regional separatists in Europe). Thus it touches on many ideological domains.

Little by little, new hypotheses requiring the reform of educational institutions are created as a consequence of the debate about intercultural issues such as establishing a theoretical framework (which has resulted in intercultural concerns entering fully into the academic teaching of most European countries), researching its epistemological credentials; the varied practices, responding to various educational traditions, the social and political, in every European country, and the redefinition of patterns of social integration. In this sense, the connection between intercultural education and the academic preparation of the migrant children is comparatively trivial compared with the vast theoretical issues raised and the revelation of the contradictions in which education is entangled. It could well be that intercultural education could be the catalyst for the renewal of educational structures and the construction of new curricular patterns.

A number of authors have begun to support this notion, for example :

'The intercultural pedagogy awaits the return of Rousseau, but some ideas (developed in several places, through a variety of experiences, at various institutional, national and supranational levels) are definite and constitute the common heritage of all those who give their energies to providing multicultural societies with some educational hypotheses to meet the needs of educating children, who already encounter intercultural experiences.

We are constantly increasingly convinced by all the experiences of those who confront issues at a European level, by consulting the literature, by the recommendations of the international organisations and by the results of our researches, that of the educational hypotheses which appear to be the basis of future realities, the intercultural approach to education will be an important part of the educational action of tomorrow.' (Di Carlo, 1994, p.69)

Terminology and language

The expressions 'cultural plurality', 'multi-cultural', 'intercultural' are sometimes used as synonyms: in reality, one often finds different uses within national contexts. The tendency in the United States is to use the terms 'multiculturalism' and 'multicultural education'. In Canada there exists a Ministry of Multiculturalism and Citizenship, created following the adoption in July 1988 of the Law on Multiculturalism. In the United Kingdom, the Swann

Report 'Education for All' (1985) insists on the term 'cultural pluralism' and on a 'pluralist approach'. In France, on the other hand, one prefers to speak of 'intercultural education'. In fact, the terminological differences do not always correspond to a diversity of meaning: the Swann Report (1985) and the recommendations of the Council of Europe express the same idea of a pluralist society.

However, the preference for the expression 'intercultural' is to reflect the notion that intercultural education is by nature constructive and also that the intercultural society is an objective of society. The prefix 'inter' underlines the inter-connection, the exchange, whereas 'cultural plurality' or 'multicultural' evokes the idea of one culture standing next to the other. 'Cultural plurality' and 'multiculturality' express a sense of 'fact', of a common human experience, which does not just concern our complex urbanised societies but also, from a modern anthropological view, all of human society. In fact, the difference between complex societies and simple societies, with regard to multi-culturalism, may be well only a difference of degree and not of type (Goodenough, 1976; Garcia-Castano and Pulido-Moyano, 1992). Cultural homogeneity is thereby reduced to a definition, an ideological construction, functional to a political vision, whereas all human society is a multicultural society.

Multicultural societies are not however intercultural: interculturality is indeed a perspective of action, of reciprocal exchange between cultures and groups, for the enrichment of social experience and strengthening of democracy. It was an ideal, even though fragile, which fuelled the anti-racist movements and which inspired particular commitments from the left, seeking alternative programmes to replace the gap left by the diminution in the centrality of social class in the socio-political debate, and requires reconsideration of the concept of citizenship, of political and social citizenship, of the relationship between social rights and political rights, the modes of integration; in truth, exactly the same existing dichotomies of community and society.

Anthropology and education

In relation to the multicultural nature of human interactions, anthropology questions the ideology of cultural homogeneity, which is at the basis of the Nation State. In fact, the intercultural problematic was developed in cultural anthropology long before it arose in education, initially in America some forty years ago (Franz Boas, Ruth Benedict, Margaret Mead, Melville J. Herskovits,

Robert Redfield, Clyde Kluckhohn, Jules Henry and Georges Spindler). It is the epistemology of relativism and of democratic humanism to which Claude Lévi-Strauss referred in Structural Anthropology II (1973) which constitutes the implicit theoretical basis of intercultural education.

As long ago as 1947 the American Association of Anthropology submitted to the United Nations Commission on Human Rights, then preparing its text for the Universal Declaration, a criticism that it only contained definitions founded on the dominant concepts of the countries of Western Europe and America. It proposed a Declaration of Human Rights which would be applicable to all human beings, and recalled the damage done by western imperialism which, where it did not lead to the total extermination of peoples, affirmed their cultural inferiority: 'The history of the expansion of the western world was signalled by the humiliation of the human person and the decay of the human rights.'

The Association then presented as its contribution to the Universal Declaration:

'1.   The individual achieves his personality through his culture; the respect for individual differences implies the respect for cultural differences;

2.   Respect for differences between cultures is given value by the fact that no scientific technique for the qualitative evaluation of cultures is available ...   The goals which determine the life of a people are of significance to those people and cannot be supplanted by some other point of view, including some pseudo eternal truths.

3.   Standards and values are relative to the culture to which they belong, in the sense that, all the attempted formulations which contain assumptions based on the beliefs or moral codes of one culture must be withdrawn from this measure so that the application of the Declaration of the Human Rights is addressed to humanity as a whole.' (cited by Liauzu, 1992)

A few years later, American anthropology has also developed a commentary on the points of contact and of conflict between anthropology and education, questioning those central figures in the debate on intercultural education. Education, from an anthropological viewpoint, is cultural transmission - a process which explains how a child becomes an adult, whether it be in the

80

Pacific Islands or in New York. In this way it interprets the concepts of socialisation and education, whether through the formal institutions of schooling or through similar social processes. The transmission of cultural patterns is therefore central to the understanding of educational processes. A comparative approach must take into account the 'fashions' at the time of transmission in the selection of knowledge which is seen as imperative to transmit to new generations, the values and educational techniques apparent in the transitions from infant to adolescent and adolescent to adult. It moves us away from the supposed universality of transmitted knowledge in western educational patterns (whether they are academic, technical, or other), and leads precisely to the essential need to understand other cultural codes.

It is in particular through Melville J. Herskovits (1948) that we are appraised of the problem of enculturation, which contributed to the convergence of educational and anthropological theory. In defining enculturation as a process of cultural conditioning, conscious or unconscious, formal or casual, exercised in a context restricted by a given body of agreed actions, by which people tend to feel that their perceptions and judgments must be better than others,

> 'Herskovits' single greatest contribution to the convergence of educational and anthropological theory is the degree to which he has pointed out that ethnocentrism is implicit in curricula, in the attitudes of teachers toward members of minority groups, and in the widespread, but mistaken, assumption that other cultures are somehow inferior to our own because of our technical superiority.' (Nash, 1974)

Herskovits maintains that the main task of the anthropologist is to convince educators that truth is dynamic, 'that it develops patterns in a generation or for one people, and is not the same at other times or in other places.' (Herskovits, 1947, p. 217).

On the other hand, Robert Redfield (1962) raises the difficulties of universal elements of education, which exist in all cultures - folk or urban, simple (oral) or complex. Kluckhohn (1962) maintains that educators, like anthropologists, should concentrate on universal human skills, common to all cultures, containing significant human values. It exists in the origins of anthropological humanism, theorised by Claude Lévi-Strauss (1973), which constitutes, as we have already indicated, a foundation for intercultural theories.

'After the aristocratic humanism of the Renaissance and the bourgeois humanism of nineteenth century, ethnology marks therefore the beginning of the world which eventually became our planet, of a doubly universal humanism. It seeks its hopes within the humblest and most despised societies, it proclaims that nothing human would know how to be foreign to man, and also discovers a democratic humanism which opposes that which preceded it: created for the privileged, to maintain privileged civilisations.' (Lévi-Strauss, 1973, p.322)

Spindler (1959) looks at how the educational process reflects the conflicts of values in the context surrounding the school and clarifies the role of the teacher in cultural transmission. In defending the anthropology of education, he maintains the necessity that the educator should be conscious of how his values originate, of the relationship of his values to a larger cultural context, of the manner in which the value judgments of teachers are transmitted to students. It is the application of cultural relativism to class.

Why in Europe, even more than in the United States, have the suggestions of anthropology - in spite of the powerful thoughts of Lévi-Strauss - been taken on board so reluctantly by education? The answer lies in the nature of European educational thought (a universal encyclopaedic curriculum model) and in European educational systems whose history is mainly determined by the development of Nation States.

The emergence of interculturality in Europe: local and global

During the 1970s, intercultural education had focused on the education of migrant children, considered as a separate group, requiring special provision. For some years now that has not been the issue: intercultural education is now about education for all, changing from a problem of immigration to a mission for the future (Berque, 1985). It was necessary to develop a theoretical basis, which at the time attacked the traditional principles of curricula in European educational systems and the hopes of a progressive pedagogy inspired by Marxism (the critique of schools and social class). Reconsidering this debate around notions of modernism and post-modernism, it questions the existence of a global culture, casting doubts on the epistemology of knowledge, ending grand theories, leading to a lack of confidence in progress. The certainties of Marxist thought - fundamental to progressive education - in the centrality of social class, the valuing of revolution, the relationship between wealth and the means of production, were also at stake in the discussion.

On the other hand, the socioeconomic and political processes encouraged a return to an educational model which identified the Nation State and national culture, culture and language, State and society: it was the effect at that time of a collection of phenomena called 'globalisation' - that is, 'the intensification of worldwide communications between places some distance apart, which leads to some local events being determined by events several kilometres away and vice versa' (Giddens, 1990), and, more specifically in the case of European countries, the process of European integration and of regional separatism. The analysis of globalisation shows how social sciences, in the first half of this century, were structured around the idea of national homogeneity and of independent states, now clearly out of date.

Some institutions, intended to form the character of the nation, worked in accordance with the wishes expressed at the beginning of nineteenth century by Madame De Staël, calling on proud citizens to identify their borders and be ready to defend them; some institutions which, through generations have promoted love of the homeland and of the flag and hatred of the enemy, learned through folk tales and songs. It was often other European countries against which the homeland was to be protected (the English and the Germans for the French, the French for Spaniards, the Austrians for Italians). These institutions were now required to look both farther afield and more closely within the nation: towards the world, towards Europe and toward its regions.

The development of a system of Nation States in the West and its diffusion to the whole world are a part of modern reality. In their turn, Nation States have developed an interdependent structure which is expressed in international relations and intergovernmental organisations. This process, even though it was often interrupted by wars, marks a general movement towards a more or less distant 'single world'. The Nation States would be less and less sovereign in the control of their own affairs, and lose control of their own economy. An element of their legal and political expertise would also be delegated to some intergovernmental organisations, as is already the case for the European Union. In fact, it is to the formation of several foci, economic and political, that one looks to now, rather than to the formation of a 'single world', although it has to be recognised that States are now internally disturbed by local and regional demands.

Although, in cultural terms, globalisation has some specific characteristics (the role of mass media, 'the global village', the fragmentation of languages), the possible translation into education of the 'single world', international or global education, remains pure rhetoric, in spite of the efforts of international organisations.

The development of local and regional demands coexists, or, rather, is a consequence of the social, political and cultural processes which characterise globalisation and which encroach upon national and local identities. According to Giddens (1990), the development of global social relationships probably serves to weaken some aspects of nationalist sentiments in countries (or in some States in particular), but it can occasionally lead to the support for more localised 'nationalistic' feelings:

> 'In some circumstances of increasing globalisation, the Nation State becomes too small for the big problems of the life and too big for the small problems of the life.' (Giddens, 1990, p.13).

According to Alain Touraine (1987), it is in fact the phenomenon of economic and cultural trans-nationalisation which has raised the question of patriotism, to understand the identity of the State and of society which is transmitted by historic consciousness.

At the same time, the end of the polarisation of the world into two after the fall of the Berlin Wall in 1989 also marked the end of ideological and political styles of memberships and favours a return to communitarianism, to nationalism and to ethnicity, especially in Eastern Europe: 'Trans-national amalgamations in the shadows of the new international order, together with Eastern Europe's ideological and territorial transformation, have created the background for an identity crisis in both an individual and collective sense.' (Alund, 1994)

Regional and local demands, both cultural and political, which have appeared in Europe in the course of the last twenty years, have returned cultural homogeneity to some territorial regions and to some ethnic and social groups whilst at the same time denying the homogeneity of the Nation State. The emergence of these demands could not be considered favourable to intercultural experiences; local demands are often intolerant of outsiders, of immigrants from the southern continents. Imposing new patterns of relationship between State and community, these demands have, however, at least in some countries such as Spain for example, deeply modified the educational systems. Minority languages and cultures have been introduced (as first or second languages) and texts relating to history and citizenship altered.

We have dwelt upon the question of the Nation State, around which is structured the idea of a homogeneous culture and the educational system. The term nation, whose etymological origins lie in the Latin 'natio' meaning 'birth', contains the idea of being born into a community and was derived from two different concepts, French and German. The first emerged during the French Revolution, taking a universal vision and implies a conscious political will on the part of the members ('the collection of participants, all governed, all subject to the law, work of their free will, all peers with rights and freedom.' Sieyès, 1789). The second concept, on the other hand, is one of a nation as an ethnic community, related by blood or culture, a nationalistic German approach rigorously formulated by Herder.

It is the extension of these original differences, toward the end of nineteenth century which produced, in most European countries, what Taguieff (1995) calls the racialisation of nationalism, an ideo-political phenomenon, which identifies as a decisive consequence the emergence of several categories of excluded groups:

> 'The essential norm of cultural homogenisation within the modern Nation State (developing or already created), the nationalistic norm, allows therefore three distinct solutions to the problem of internal minorities; that the traditional groups absorb the different cultural groups, that it finds a solution through a system of specific inclusion (annexing and hierarchical subordination), or it ignores the problem.' (Taguieff, 1995, p. 38)

Thus there are three approaches: total cultural assimilation, incorporation, extermination. In the French concept of the 'nation', assimilation corresponds more closely to the ideal of an open egalitarian society.

Intercultural education and European education

> 'The appeal for a European direction in the educational systems of member States came from the Council of Europe and the European Commission, as a path towards the social and cultural integration of Europe. Since the 1970s, questions of culture and of identity and their role in education was one of the preoccupations of the European processes. If, in the seventies, it was the education of the migrants' children which opened the door to the teaching of languages and mother-cultures, the preoccupation since the beginning of the 1980s, has been to question more closely the meaning of intercultural education and

the European dimension of education (European Union, 1976)'. (Hansen, 1995)

Now, if it is in fact true, that there was no actual impact on the curriculum (Batelaan and Gundara, 1993) and that 'No European educational system has managed to realise the goals contained in the different recommendations put forth by the Council of Europe', then conferences on these topics, educational experiences, the production of a considerable material and pedagogic debate have had an influence. It means that the work of the Council of Europe and of the European Union in matters of intercultural education was not purely rhetorical. 'A number of pilot projects and educational experiments have been carried out across Europe, where, although to a lesser extent, the European Union has also played a part.' (Hansen, 1995, p.3)

The total absence of concrete applications in the educational systems can, alternatively, be ascribed to inability of Council of Europe to legislate (De Witte, 1990), and to the absence of educational questions in the Treaty of Rome and in the Single European Act. The situation is a little different now, since Articles 126 and 127 of Chapter 3 of Treaty of Maastricht consider the jurisdiction over education by the Union (Commission of the European Community, 1993). So, as affirmed by the Commission, there is now 'new competence for the Community in the field of education' and 'the new possibilities offered by Article 126 (which) calls for a comprehensive and coherent approach to complement action taken by the Member States.' (Commission of the European Communities, 1993)

The position held by education in European processes, European education, European identity, and intercultural education are not devoid of ambiguities. Hansen (1995) reflects on the construction of Europe and of the European in European speeches on culture and on education: 'Can one detect efforts to changes a relationship such as the one Paul Gilroy points to when he claims that the terms 'black' and 'European' remain categories which mutually exclude each other? (Gilroy, 1990, p.74)'.

While making the link between intercultural education and the politics of migration, intercultural education and the dismissal of racism and xenophobia, Hansen remarks how there exists a contradiction between the condemnation of racism and of xenophobia, the affirmation of the necessity of imposing tolerance, and the presentation of immigration as a 'problem', which could be resolved through the reduction of immigration and a stronger control on refugees (Miles, 1993). The intergovernmental groups which consider questions of migration are mainly directed politically towards the control and closing of boundaries to immigrants coming from a third country: 'The meaning of the categories "immigration" and "immigrant" do not refer to all people who are mobile across national boundaries' (Miles, 1993), but only to immigrants proceeding from a third country, illustrates very well where racism and exclusion are now located. As Alund maintains, 'a discriminatory programme at the borders will legitimate racism within the country'. (Alund 1994)

There is therefore a kind of paradox in relation to European political education. On the one hand is the insistence on 'the value' attributed to 'the contribution which immigrants make to diversifying and broadening the learning experience of all pupils', whereas on the other immigration/migration is considered a problem in relation to questions of security and seen in a negative manner. This dramatically negative perception of immigration is not proportional to the actual numerical presence of immigrants in Europe (Palidda, 1992a; Stolcke,1992); a little less than eight millions, which is 2.4% of the total European population of about 324 millions, which includes all non-community immigrants (including, North American, Canadian, Japanese, etc.). For particular countries the percentage varies from 1% in Spain to 7% in Germany.

There is no ambiguity in the evidence that European politics are favourable to the integration of populations and closed as regards new immigrants. Integration is then considered possible provided illegal immigration is ended. From the point of view of intercultural education, the two facets are difficult to hold together: you cannot be open and closed at the same time, especially when one considers the social and cultural dynamics of the contemporary world. It is precisely at this moment in the intercultural debate, as much a debate about the nature of society (and ideology), that thought is needed on the relationship between Europe and the rest of the world. The processes of decolonisation and the emergence of a 'Third World' are a significant points of political and cultural reference, and it is also right to raise in discussion the social structures created during the colonial period and the reemergence of historically dominant societies. (Liauzu, 1987, 1992)

It would certainly be an exaggeration to deny the positive aspects of European proposals for education and culture, intercultural education and the European dimension of education, and to see only eurocentrism. A discussion of educational patterns which will correspond more to the realities of cultural plurality in Europe has begun. It is at the same time important to denounce the ambiguities, the contradictions, still found in the documents produced by the Council of Europe and by the Commission of the European Communities. Intercultural education is not always presented in this manner. Sometimes it is associated only with the teaching of migrant children as distinct from the

European dimension of education. The European dimension of education, 'based on the cultural inheritance of the Member States,' having the aim 'to develop the European dimension in education at all levels so as to strengthen the spirit of European citizenship, drawing on the cultural inheritance of each Member State' (European Union, 1976), is not very clear on genuine European citizenship of the future. In the best approaches to the European dimension of education, (see, for example, a recent publication under the auspices of the Commission, The Sources of European Identity) there is an insistence on exchanges, reciprocal influences, cultural interchange, and an unveiling of the dis-homogeneity in cultures from the same origin within the structures of the European State, at the risk of the exclusion of some of the pupils belonging to the same European home.

The ambiguities arise in fact at a time when political perspectives and ideology (which underpin the educational projects) are developing a critical view of European knowledge, of its paradigms and, generally, of the values assigned to the products of one culture compared to another. The application of cultural and epistemological relativism could help to establish all cultural practices and products as having the same value and validity, whereas in the curricula used in European educational systems, selections are made from one national culture, or, at most, from a generic European culture (Colby, 1992). Now, clearly, henceforth that selection cannot only be made from European culture. There must also be work on the reinterpretation of non-western cultures and the misrepresentations of them made by the West. This reflection on intercultural education resonates with present uncertainties about the ideas and the values around which Europe is to be constructed and of the destiny of western culture.

Europe: multicultural societies and xenophobia. The intercultural challenge

With dramatic emphasis, Ernesto Balducci, theologian, anthropologist and Italian pacifist, wrote in 1989, a few years before his death: 'The Europe that one prepares with such spirit and style, will it be a Europe with walls erected against the third World, - naturally with some draw-bridges to lower in order to permit to the armies of some multinational feudal Lord to leave for their enterprises of depredation - or will it be a Europe determined to help the process of integration between the two worlds?' (Balducci, 1989, p. 10). The future of intercultural education and of intercultural society depends on the answer that one gives to Balducci's question. As underlined by Batelaan (1992), speaking of intercultural education in Europe obliges one to consider above all the basic values on which the process of European integration is constructed and negotiated. Few authors who write and work on the problem of interculturalism are optimistic that it will be Balducci's second kind of Europe which will prevail.

> 'The construction of Europe gave impetus to a renewal of eurocentrism which appears today to have been founded on the defence of the privileges of developed society, combined with the defence of idiosyncratic regional societies and interest groups.'(Palidda, 1992b, p.1)

Palidda proposes different patterns which related European unification to political strengths and interest groups: European regions, Mediterranean Europe, Atlantic-Europe, etc. But the different patterns contain a poor view of the Southern world. Once the East-West confrontation is ended, it is the North-South confrontation which will become central in the structure of European integration: and the South is presented most often as a threat by portraying it creating international migrations and raising the challenge of Islamic fundamentalism.

We have already made reference to the negative view of immigration developed by the European Union (Ministerial meetings at Trevi, Schengen, etc.), and the association in official documents of immigration with other factors which disturb the public order (terrorism, drugs, prostitution, etc.). Such an approach to the question of immigration - at the level of political initiative - corresponds to a totally negative social representation, which certainly does not encourage the development of harmonious intercultural relationships. Without any doubt, this negative approach of the European Union authorities and governments encourages hostile attitudes on the part of European populations (that, elsewhere, the E.U. and governments actually positively condemn). The developing upsurge in the phenomena of racism, xenophobia and intolerance unfortunately characterises many European societies. Does the ideal of the intercultural society constitute a strong answer to these phenomena? Is it carried forward by significant social support? Could it counter all the national traditions, including the French 'republican pattern'?

The ideal of the intercultural society can in fact be reduced to pure rhetoric. Bastenier (1992) recalls that intercultural relations are social constructs, known to have uncertain outcomes. Intercultural relations cannot be conceived in terms of the rhetoric of exchange, when it is related to domination. The setting up of intercultural practices must also be translated into political compensation, in order to help the underprivileged groups, who are often immigrants (Reyneri, 1992). The intercultural approach, in order to be credible, must be placed at the heart of collective action which offers affirmation of the values on which should be founded an effective democratic society and respect for human rights - equality and solidarity (Palidda, 1992c).

In fact, the actual precursors of the intercultural society are in practice absent from national and European politics. Where 'multiculturalism' is recognised at an official level, it means the recognition of self proclaimed communities within the general public, with, sometimes, a risk of 'ghetto-isation' of these particular communities. Against this policy of integration by 'communities' and their representatives, there is also the French pattern of integration, by individual citizenship, a universalist claim. The two policies do not correspond to the ideals of an intercultural society. The social movements, in their turn - anti-racist, pacifist, ecological, feminist - which share the ideals of the intercultural society, are far from being powerful facing the dangerous rise of the xenophobic right in most European countries. These groups, having abandoned the 'biologic' version of racism, have focused on cultural differences as criteria of inclusion/exclusion, new ideologies of domination. Exactly as in fact noticed by Taguieff (1995), racism operates with or without reference to 'race' in the biological sense (variety of a species) and that 'cultural racism' has emerged as a successor of biologic racism.

> 'Biological racism is founded on somatic characteristics (colour of the skin, size, shape of skull, etc.) in order to establish categories of human beings who are placed in a relationship of inequality or discounted. 'Cultural racism' - pseudo racism or neo racism - finds its explanations from the course of history or of social functions and categorisations drawn from cultural traits (manners, language, religion, etc.). Its frontier with ethnicism, in truth with certain kinds of 'communitarianism', is indeterminable.' (Taguieff, 1995, p.36)

In analysing the present socio-political context, Stolcke (1992) speaks of a 'cultural fundamentalism' which has emerged beyond racism as a specific political language in which anti-immigrational feelings are rationalised:

> 'In the global village, crossed by multiple national conflicts, cultural identity and diversity are invested with a new symbolic and political significance. However, cultural fundamentalism is not simply a new disguised racism. On the contrary, cultural fundamentalism, which is

90

essentially based on a notion of culture, is a specific ideological answer to a specific problem, the one posed by the 'strangers among us'. And, in the last analysis, this doctrine is structured by assumptions implicit in the modern concepts of the Nation State, of national identity and of citizenship.' (Stolcke, 1992, p.38)

The question is, according to Stolcke, that in spite of social and economical processes characteristic of globalisation, the political and ideological pattern remains that of national integration, with its dynamics of exclusion, whereas new forms of social integration, new identities and new citizenship should be possible. If the old dies, the new still doesn't manage to be born. Certainly, it took time and work, and preliminary activity to structure a model of an intercultural society which is, not just rhetorically, precisely the delivery through discussion of our paradigmatic visions of the world (Liauzu, 1992).

The land of the setting sun (Sunset Land) : the other in the western culture

In denouncing the lack of effort invested in the question of eurocentrism, Liauzu (1992) analysed the changing definition of difference in European culture from the time when modernity is defined as beginning, the end of eighteenth century, to the present day: the savage, the barbarian, the men 'of colour', the 'traditional societies', the Jew, the immigrant.

In this work, he browses through pictures of 'outsiders', as they appeared in the writings of Mirabeau, De Holbach, Rousseau, Voltaire, the Abbot Gregory and Bernardin of Saint Pierre, and in our times Taguieff and Edgar Morin. It is in these images that the beginning and end of the 'conqueror of the west' can be seen. Criticism of the European 'civilisation' (elsewhere the significance of term 'civilisation' is determined by the beginning of modernity) is as old as it modern:

> 'Instead of counselling the invasion of this magnanimous nation (the country of the Houyhnhnm), I would hope that it decides to send a large number of its inhabitants to Europe to be civilised, through the teaching of the fundamental principles of honour, of justice, of truth, of temperance, love of the public good, strength, chastity, friendship, benevolence and fidelity.'

So wrote Jonathan Swift in 1726, and he added that of these fundamental principles there remained in Europa only the name, the empty name, the exercises having been for a long time forgotten or ignored.

It is precisely the ambivalence between generous and convenient principles of domination which creates the strongest general criticism of European and western culture. Condorcet wrote at the end of the eighteenth century:

> 'Perusing the history of our enterprises, of our establishments in Africa and/or in Asia, you will see our trade monopolies, our treasons, our bloodthirsty contempt for the men of another colour or of another belief, the insolence of our usurpations, the extravagant proselytism or the schemings of our priests, destroy those feelings of respect and of kindliness that the superiority of our visions and the advantages of our dealing had first contained(...) But without doubt the moment approaches when, ceasing to make evident the corruptors and tyrants, we will appear to them as useful instruments, as generous liberators. (...)' (*Sketch of a historic tableau of the progress of the human mind*, Condorcet, 1864, cited by Liauzu, 1992)

The ambivalence of the West, which knew how to be colonialist and anti-colonialist, racist and anti-racist, eurocentric and universalist, is at the nexus of the intercultural debate today. The West could be, according to Balducci, compared to the god Janus, who was truly double-faced.

> '... the genocides, racism, not only related to irrational and accidental decisions, are inherited tendencies in European history. Against this, the only resort was the affirmation of universal values and of solidarity which over-rides the national and religious, ethnic and cultural, affiliations.' (Liauzu, 1992, p.13)

But are these universal values sufficient? It is not by chance that this question assumed a particular dramatic importance after the Second World War, in consequence of the processes of decolonisation, and, especially following the end of the Communist utopia and the crisis in Marxist thought. Where universal values cannot any more be taken to be the basis of humanism, then anthropology could bring a fundamental contribution to the reconstruction of relationships with strangers and outsiders, as we have underlined already in mentioning

Lévi-Strauss and his proposition of democratic humanism through coming to terms with the most humble and despised societies (Lévi-Strauss, 1973).

Anthropological humanism is also theorised by Balducci (1992) in his work, *The Land of the Setting Sun (Sunset Land)*. Balducci sees in the meeting between the West and other cultures, finally on a basis of parity, the possibility of finding a world-wide culture:

> 'Assimilation or subordination: thought until recently to be the destiny of others in relation to western man. Modernity did not know of any other outcomes. The new times bring us face to face with a vision never before imagined and which is only made possible today, and which indeed is obligatory, because of the structural unification of the planet and of the nature of interdependence, which joins the one ethnic group to another in the variety of which the world is rich. It is the road of equality in diversity and of diversity in equality.' (Balducci, 1992, p.73)

The possibility of arriving at an 'earth conscience' (Gelpi, 1992) is made possible through globalisation, which, even if it means domination by the oligarchic multinational groups, also means the development of an environmental sensitivity, which reveals the limited resources of the planet and the impossibility of exporting western-like patterns of life everywhere.

However, according to some authors, globalisation has already meant the westernisation of all cultures, the diffusion of patterns of life and western institutions to all corners of the planet (Asor Rosa, 1992), exactly at the moment where the westernisation of world is seen as questionable. The problematic of interculturalism, which puts theoretically dominant cultures and humble, despised cultures on a level of parity, is created in the same body of western thought as previous Marxist ideas which attracted so many of the revolutionaries in the Third World. However it is evident, in the contribution of other cultures, that there would become essential a new relational modality with 'others'.

In what then can one trust? In the pessimism of those who maintain that the West, carrier of death, is already everywhere and that all flight is impossible, or in the optimism of those that sees in radical critical modernity, a possibility of renewal of democracy and of social relationships, in every society and in all the planet?

Escape from the west and intercultural education

A literary version of the criticism of European civilisation and of the tension in humanism of which Claude Lévi-Strauss speaks, a result of the interaction with the humble and despised cultures, is also found in the work of the Cuban writer - of French origin - Alejo Carpentier.

In the novel, *Los Pasos Perdidos* (The lost country) written in 1953, Alejo Carpentier invokes the life - in the period between the 30s and the 40s - of a Cuban musician, living in New York, searching for Europe and an idealised European culture - the smile of Erasmus, the discourse on the method, the humanistic spirit, the Faustian tension and the soul of Apollo - symbolised by Beethoven's ninth symphony - as expressed in music. It ends in 1945, when, in a Nazi concentration camp, torturers and guards, stopped by the American army and locked up in a hut, sing the hymn 'Las estrofas de Schiller me laceraban a sarcasmos...'

The 'hombre sin esperanza' (man without hope) returning to the New World will recover, for one short period, the courage and the joy of life in a village lost in the Venezuelan forest, alongside Rosario, an Indian in hair and cheekbones, Mediterranean in forehead and nose, black in the solid plumpness of his thighs. Rosario, who knows all the secrets of the plants and help the hero's need to remember the words with which Don Quixote begins...

Search of identity, multiplicity of affiliations (the hero is the son of a Swiss musician and of a Cuban woman, born and raised in Havana, lived in New York, journeying twice to Europe), encountering cultures: *Los Pasos Perdidos* is not at all a flight from 'civilisation' into the world of nature, a very well known literary genre. Carpentier does not want the 'naturalisation' of Native-American cultures. In the subtle game between the old and the new world, and the nostalgia of a world outside of time, *Los Pasos Perdidos* is especially a flight from a West which has lost its myths and indirectly its principles. Rosario is compared to the 'Parisian' of Crete who reads the history of Genevieve of Brabant as if was a history of present, faits divers; the Odyssey is one of the books that is found in the village of the forest. In the West, the deep sense of the works which made western culture has been forgotten and in order for the West to recover these noblest of values, it is necessary to leave it and seek interactions with other cultures through which process life could be returned to the myth and to the principles that the West once produced. But this research is located outside of time, because the present time is dominated by the Lords of the Apocalypse. The themes raised by Carpentier in 1953 appear absolutely central to the problem of interculturalism.

94

And, as Carpentier's hero shows, escape from the West is quite impossible: what is possible is to provide the instruments by which to understand the painful and uncertain social process by which the new can emerge. The deconstruction of the paradigms of our vision of the world, presented as universal, in order to take hold of that which is relative, eurocentric, is an essential stage of this understanding. It requires now the construction of knowledge and ideology: it is in this work, that the intercultural pedagogy finds its place and makes its way.

References

Alund, A. (1994), *Activity in Modernity: Youth, Culture and Identity*, paper given to the XIII World Congress of Sociology, Bielefeld.

Asor Rosa, A. (1992), *Fuori dall 'Occidente ovvero ragionamentosull' Apocalissi*, (Torino, Einaudi).

Balducci, E. (1989) "E l'Europa alza le mura", citato in *Avvenimenti*, no.6, p.10.

Balducci, E. (1992), *La terra del tramonto*, Edizioni Cultura della Pace, San Domenico di Fiesole .

Bastenier, A. (1992), *Les relations interculturelles sont des rapports sociaux et donc des conflits à issue incertaine*, comunicazione presentata al Convegno, 'La Pluralité Culturelle dans les Systèmes Educatifs Européens', Nancy, 29-31 gennaio.

Batelaan, P. (1992), *Education interculturelle en Europe*, comunicazione presentata al Convegno, 'La Pluralité Culturelle dans les Systèmes Educatifs Européens', Nancy, 29-31 gennaio .

Batelaan, P. and Gundara J. (1993), 'Cultural Diversity and the Promotion of Values through Education', *European Journal of Intercultural Studies*, vol.3, no.2/3, 61-80.

Berque, J. (1985), *Éduquer les enfants de l'immigration*, Ministère de l'Education Nationale, C.N.D.P., Parigi.

Carpentier, A. (1979), *Los pasos perdidos*, Editorial Letras Cubanas, Ciudad de la Habana, (prima edizione 1953).

Colby, D. (1992), 'Cultural and Epistemological Relativism and European Curricula', Bath College of Higher Education, U.K., *European Journal of Intercultural Studies* (in press).

Commission des Communautés Européennes, (1993), *Green Paper on the European Dimension of Education*, COM(93) 457 final, Brussels, September.

Condorcet, J-A. N. de Caritat, marquis de (1864), *Esquisse d'un tableau historique des progrès de l'esprit humain*, nouvelle édition, Parigi .

De Witte, B. (1990) 'Cultural Linkages' in Wallace, William (ed.), *The Dynamics of European Integration*, (London, Pinter Publishers for The Royal Institute of International Affairs).

Di Carlo, S. (1994), *L'educazione interculturale*, (Rome, Tecnodid).

European Union (1976), 'Resolution of the Council and the Ministers of Education, meeting within the Council on 9 February 1976 comprising an action programme in the field of education', *Official Journal of the European Communities* (No C 150) , 15.6.92, pp. 366-70.

Garcia Castano, F.J. & Pulido Moyano R.A. (1992), *Educacion multicultural y antropologia de la educacion*, comunicazione presentata al Curso de Verano, Universidad Antonio Machado, Racismo y Educacion: Hacia una educacion multicultural, Baeza, 31 agosto-4 settembre 1992, pp. 1-45.

Gelpi, E. (1992), *Conscience terrienne, Recherche et Formation*, (Firenze, Mc Coll Publisher).

Giddens, A. (1990), *Le conseguenze della modernità*, (Bologne, Il Mulino).

Gilroy, P., (1990), 'The end of anti-racism', *New Community*, vol.17 no.1, pp.71-84.

Goodenough, W. (1976), 'Multiculturalism as the Normal Human Experience', *Anthropology and Education Quarterly*, vol.7 no.4, pp.4-6.

Hansen, P. (1995), *Schooling a European identity: locating immigration, culture and difference within the education policies of the European Union*, paper presented at the ERASMUS Seminar: Intercultural Education and Curricula, Girona, 10-14 July, 1995.

Herskovits, M.J. (1948), *Man and His Works*, (New York, Alfred A.Knopf, inc.).

Kluckhohn, C. (1962), *Culture and Behaviour*, (New York, The Free Press).

Lévi-Strauss, C. (1973), *Anthropologie Structurale II*, (Parigi, Plon).

Liauzu, C. (1987), *L'ecole et l'immigration: enjeux interculturels d'une société plurielle. Dossier critique. Essai Bibliographique 1975-1987*, I.R.E.M.A.M., Aix-en-Provence.

Liauzu, C. (1992), *Race et Civilisation, L'autre dans la culture occidentale*, (Parigi, Syros/Alternatives).

Miles, R. (1993), *Racism after 'race-relations'*, (London, Routledge).

Nash, R.J. (1974), "The Convergence of Anthropology and Education", in Spindler, G. ed., *Education and Cultural Process toward an Anthropology of Education*, (New York, Holt, Rinehart and Winston Inc).

Palidda, S.,(1992a): *Pour une approche des réalités effectives des migrations*, working paper I.U.E.

Palidda, S. (1992b), *Pour la reconnaissance universelle de la liberté d'identification collective comme continuum entre citoyennetée et cosmopolitisme*, comunicazione presentata al Curso de Verano Universidad Antonio Machado, Racismo y Educacion: Hacia una Educacion Multicultural, Baeza, 31 Agosto - 4 Septiembre 1992, pp. 1-20.

Palidda, S.,(1992c): *L'integrazione degli immigrati difronte all'opposizione tra relativismo culturale e universalismo come problema di risanamento della democrazia*, working paper I.U.E.

Reyneri, E. (1992), *Politiques d'intégration économique et sociale des immigrés*, comunicazione presentata al Seminario: Sciences Humaines et Migrations, sotto la direzione di S. Palidda, Instituto Universitario Europeo, Novembre.

Redfield, R. (1962), *Human Nature and the Study of Society: the Papers of Robert Redfield*, University of Chicago Press, Chicago.

Sieyès E.J. (1789), *Qu'est-ce que c'est le tiers état?*, Parigi.

Spindler, G. (1959), *The Transmission of American Culture*, (Cambridge, Mass., Harvard University Press).

Stolcke, V. (1992), *The 'right to difference' in an unequal world*, dattiloscritto, Istituto Universitario Europeo, San Domenico di Fiesole.

Swann Lord (1985) *Education form All: Report of the Committee of Inquiry into the Education of Children from Ethnic Minority Groups*, (London, HMSO.

Swift, J. (1933), *I viaggi di Gulliver*, Biblioteca Romantica Mondadori, Milano (prima edizione l726).

Tagueiff, P. A. (1995), 'Racisme/Racismes: Eléments d'une problématisation', in *Magazine Littéraire*, Juillet-août 1995, pp. 35-39.

Touraine, A. (1987), *Les scientifiques parlent*, (Parigi , Hachette).

8 Language diversity and intercultural education

Kanka Mallick

Cultural and linguistic diversity has been a fact of life in many parts of the world for many centuries. However, the recognition of the value of cultural and linguistic diversity and its educational implications is more recent. Most countries are now demographically pluralistic, characterised by the presence of two or more distinct groups of communities. They are differentiated in terms of language, religion, ethnic characteristics and cultural heritage. In spite of such diversity, many countries have failed to recognise and support the heterogeneity of their citizens.

As an agent of society, the educational system has an important role to play in helping to produce citizens who can live relatively harmoniously in a multicultural society. Each individual, family, community and society shares this responsibility. Unfortunately the educational response to ethnic, linguistic, cultural and linguistic diversity in many western countries has not always been positive. For example, surveys of historical development within mainstream provision over the last thirty years show a sequence of assimilation, integration and pluralism in the political and educational response to Britain's increasingly pluralist society (DES, 1985). This pattern is also apparent in the response to linguistic diversity. Martin-Jones (1984) identifies three types of educational response to linguistic diversity. Each of these reflects the different educational philosophies as well as the different views about language and the nature of language learning as they evolved in the last three decades. In all of these phases there is an implicit view of the status of the linguistic minority language itself.

Significant support for an educational model which advocated an intercultural philosophy in language education was provided by the publication of the Bullock Report, *A Language for Life* (DES, 1975). This Report was a turning point in the development of official attitudes to minority languages. It stated that:

> 'No child should be expected to cast off the language and culture of the home as he crosses the school threshold and the curriculum should reflect those aspects of his life'.

Thus the recommendations by the Bullock Report made a significant and positive shift in thinking towards bilingualism and linguistic diversity as part of cultural pluralism and intercultural education.

Language issues

Language is a complex, multi-faceted phenomenon. It is about communication and social interaction. Language plays an important role in the maintenance of a given culture. The acquisition of language develops out of the physiological, psychological and social needs of the individual growing from infancy through childhood into adulthood.

Language and culture construct a framework in which individuals come to form their identity. On the one hand, it is a process which goes on within the individual and, on the other, it is a social process which through the vehicle of language and culture operates not just on the individual but also on those around him or her. Language is not only a means of achieving identity but also a means of developing self-esteem (Romaine, 1995).

A child's language development is an important issue within the context of a multicultural society. The first language of the child should be his/her traditional cultural language. The mainstream language, the lingua franca, should be introduced when formal schooling begins; but the onset of schooling should not imply the subordination of the child's native language - that too should be fostered in the educational system and incorporated into the syllabus, formal and informal, of the multicultural school. This leads us to consider the concept of 'bilingualism'.

During the past few decades contributions to the theoretical and empirical knowledge bases related to an understanding of bilingualism have reshaped our view of bilingualism. At the turn of the century, bilingualism in children was regarded as a linguistic, cognitive and academic liability (Hakuta, 1986). Today's understanding of bilingualism clearly shows that bilingualism is not a linguistic liability and may even serve as a cognitive and academic advantage.

The concept of bilingualism is firmly established in the mind of the lay person as the ability to speak, read or understand two languages equally well (Richards et al., 1985). In other words, in everyday use a person is called bilingual when he or she knows and uses two languages perfectly. Unfortunately, it is difficult to describe what speaking one's mother tongue 'perfectly' means. Contrary to the everyday use of the term, educationists have attempted to arrive at a comprehensive and scientific concept of bilingualism, although their definitions are sometimes vague and even contradictory.

Bloomfield (1933), who had studied the foreign-language learning process among immigrants in the United States of America, holds the view that an individual can be classified as bilingual only when he or she has a 'native-like control' of two languages.

Saunders (1988) points out that:

'Such a definition leaves more speakers of more than one language unaccounted for, people who do not have 'native-like control' of one (or even in some cases) both of their languages'.

Haugen (1953) has put forward the following definition:

'Bilingualism is understood ... to begin at the point where the speaker of one language can produce complete, meaningful utterances in the other language'.

This view raises the question as to how proficient a person needs to be in the second language in order to be classified as bilingual? Some writers define bilingualism as practice of alternatively using two languages.

Mackey (1970) regards bilingualism as the alternate use of two or more languages by the same individual. Such a view seems to be more popular because it does not try to specify the level of competence in the second language and does not require equal knowledge of both languages. Stern (1983) addressing the issue from an educational point of view writes that:

'.... the light-hearted use of the term 'bilingualism' to describe the objective of language teaching can arouse exaggerated expectations if it is not understood that the modern definition of bilingualism does not necessarily mean 'full' and 'equal' command of two languages'.

This view is widely acknowledged in the educational circle since it is extremely rare to find someone who has equal command in two languages. Some writers are of the opinion that the distinction between 'bilingual' and 'monolingual' is arbitrary.

A broader and more flexible definition regards bilingualism as the situation where an individual can use either of the two languages irrespective of the level of command or judgement of the range of quality of linguistic skills. It is quite possible that in such cases one language will be dominant and the other subordinate. However, the practicability of using language as a medium of communication ought to be the criterion of judging whether one is bilingual or not.

Many educators today regard bilingualism as a great linguistic and social advantage. Bilingual children should not be stigmatised as incomplete monolinguals. The ability to speak more than one language, however imperfectly, should be encouraged. This should be regarded as an asset of invaluable importance for those who speak, for the community in which they live, and for the nation as a whole. For example, native British children who learn the languages and cultures of their bilingual schoolmates are likely to develop more understanding and tolerance towards them.

Within the label 'bilingualism', there is always variability. Some children read and write in two languages equally well; others read mostly in one language or the other.

As language is used within a social context, it must also be seen in terms of the use bilingual speaker makes of his/her two languages within the context of a bilingual community. The bilingual child is the one who functions in two language environments regardless of fluency or literacy. Bilingual education is a system of education which maintains or develops skills in both of those languages. Evidence shows that the type of educational experiences children typically receive differs considerably according to the socio-economic status of their community and the languages spoken in their homes.

For the average English-speaking Briton, the probability of being fluent in a second language is relatively remote. The educational system in Britain has a deep monocultural and monolingual orientation. There are countries which have two or more official languages, where the majority of people are bilingual. In those countries bilingualism is regarded as normal and unproblematic. This is the situation in parts of Canada, Singapore, Switzerland and India. There are more than 6,000 languages in the world, many of them not written. Yet, in many Western countries, cultural and language diversity is frequently seen as a negative element within the educational context. Research conducted in the

1950s and 1960s did not seem to be positive about bilingualism. However, over the past 20 years, research on bilingualism has shown that it has benefits for *all* children.

Yet, there still exist myths about bilingualism in education circles of many western countries. There is also a misconception that one language leads to a cohesive society. All the Arabic speaking states do not form a cohesive area. Many people seems to believe that bilingualism confuses children and has negative consequences which leads to underachievement. Some argue that minority children do not need to have support for their first language at school, they should get it at home. Many teachers in Britain hold the attitude that ethnic minority parents do not want their children to use their first language in the classroom, and that they want them to learn English. Such ethnocentric assumptions cannot be substantiated or justified by research evidence. The promulgation and co-existence of many languages are considered barriers by some educationists as this is considered inconvenient as well as expensive. This is an attitude of covert language imperialism in so far as one or two languages seek to suppress many. It is now accepted by all educationists that the mother-tongue is the best medium for the early education of the child.

Bilingualism can be a positive resource in classroom activities if teachers are willing to accept different conceptions and knowledge, and stimulate children to share them. Pupils' family life, their cultural background and their experiences can be important resources for teaching. This approach stimulates children's self-esteem and can help them to overcome shyness and discriminatory feelings by developing mutual understanding between children from different linguistic backgrounds.

Pupils' language development is a fundamental educational issue in multicultural societies. Children who have limited capacity in learning language will have many difficulties in achieving the necessary levels of language proficiency. Too often teachers and policy makers in Britain have assumed that language differences are synonymous with *language deficiency*, a view which has led many to devalue and reject non-standard English languages and those who use them. Over recent years, much has been written in this field, although it can be said that relatively little change has taken place.

Bilingualism has been and still is a topic of both interest and debate in many parts of the world. In fact, the issue has been put on as one of the top items of political agendas in North America, Europe and Australia. It is also clear from debates, discussions and media reports that the issue of bilingualism is often centred around the rights, needs and expectations of minority groups in society. This has a marked impact on education, primarily because of the gradual awareness among minority groups throughout the world that their identities are being eroded. It should be remembered in this context that the native language of minority groups is not the same as the language of the majority group in any society. Thus, the concept of bilingualism has become synonymous with the education of minority ethnic groups. Many countries (e.g. United States, Britain, Canada, Australia) are seeking, through the school curriculum, to assert a national language which is always the language of the dominant group and thereby implicitly giving monolingualism a high priority. This not only restricts the development of minority languages, but creates a false sense of superiority of a specific language in the minds of the dominant group.

The ethnic, linguistic, and cultural minority groups in most societies are at the lower end of the economic continuum. They have no access to either resources or power and therefore are unable to influence any educational policy at the local or the national level. In Britain for example, people who make decisions and control resources are, on the whole, standard English speaking monolinguals and see no need to change it. Speakers of English as a first language see themselves as speakers of a high status language. Language imperialism is still quite powerful in Britain.

Language has been the focus of educational debate for a very long time in Britain. This debate got momentum and broadened its scope in the 1960s when large numbers of children arrived from the New Commonwealth speaking a wide range of languages and dialects of English (Edwards, 1984). Although a number of initiatives were taken to treat linguistic diversity as a classroom resource there has been little guidance from the government. A few local education authorities adopted strategies to treat linguistic diversity as a positive element.

The strength of the mother tongue teaching has been greatly advanced by arguments from other quarters. The 1976 draft EEC (European Economic Community) Directive on the 'Education of Migrant Children' provided further impetus to the need for mother-tongue teaching based on both linguistic and cultural grounds. According to the Directive, member states were charged to promote mother tongue teaching in accordance with their national circumstances and legal systems (Council of Europe, 1977). Unfortunately, the British government has given very low priority to this area. The potentiality and positive aspects of bilingual education programmes have failed to merit serious attention.

Language diversity and intercultural education

Few would deny that the most obvious cultural difference between ethnic groups is that of *language*. This is the cement which readily binds that intricate patterns of customs, attitudes and belief that we call *culture*. Language itself is a part of culture; every language provides an index of the culture with which it is most intimately associated. Unfortunately, there are many ethnic minority groups in Britain who no longer cultivate their own language because of social pressures or a lack of provision in school.

For centuries the English authorities suppressed and persecuted speakers of Gaelic and Celtic in parts of the U.K., and even penalised those who spoke their native language in school. The result has been a tragic alienation of cultural identity. Now only a minority of Welsh people can speak their ancient language.

Welsh is experiencing something of a revival, this being recognised in National Curriculum provision. It cannot have been a matter of 'generosity' on the part of government. It must have been responding to the political reality in Wales. Welsh language learning even has support among English settlers in parts of Wales where the language has strong roots.

However, the situation of the Welsh language is different from that of many other 'minority' languages in the U.K. It is a language which has cultural and historical roots in Wales and is a language which has developed, evolved and adapted in that setting. A number of other minority languages used in Britain do not have the same local traditions. This is an important difference and one that cannot be overlooked.

In a democratic society for each child the opportunity to develop his or her native language is a precious birthright. It is tragic that in Britain many minority ethnic parents under the pressures of assimilationist educators have spoken only English to their young children. While this may ensure that children will speak English by the time they enter infant school, it is a form of alienation which robs the child of birthright, and cuts him/her off from a great many intimacies of culture. It is a denial of identity and affects the child's self-esteem.

Parents should speak to the child in their native language until the child enters infant school. Then the lingua franca, whatever it is, can be learned. There is no good evidence that such practice is in the long run educationally harmful. There is some evidence that it has a positive impact on learning.

There has been a great deal of debate around the world about bilingual, multilingual, culturally pluralistic and intercultural education as a response to growing demands by ethnic minority groups for the recognition of their culture and language. For example, English-speaking countries including the United States, Britain and Canada do not provide education in languages other than English. Those desiring 'mother-tongue' teaching in those countries have to provide their own.

It must be recognised that to introduce the teaching of languages other than the language of the country (which is often the language of the dominant group) within the context of intercultural education involves quite major changes within the education system. This is because the teacher in most countries has traditionally been a generalist classroom teacher.

Another important consideration in the successful introduction of languages other than the language of the dominant culture school curriculum is the climate of opinion regarding such an innovation. The questions to be considered are:

a)   Is there sufficient knowledge available about appropriate teaching methods, and are there the necessary resources to back it up?

b)   Are classroom teachers, and the community in general, convinced of the desirability and the advantages to be gained from introducing languages other than the mainstream language?

c)   Are there successful models of such practice which can be referred to?

Positive responses to these questions would create a favourable climate for the introduction of minority languages particularly in the primary school.

The question we must ask: how far is existing educational provision in schools appropriate for the *aptitude and ability of* a bilingual child? In making generalisations it is recognised that there are *variations in curricular patterns* and that certain schools have been able to make limited use of two languages within the classroom.

There seems to be a number of *prevailing assumptions* which underlie the kinds of curricular experience which are provided for bilingual children in English primary schools:

a)   There is a tendency to treat children of Asian or African origin as a broad but rather homogeneous group. The effect of this assumption is to minimise cultural and religious variation and to ignore the potential relevance of different languages, dialects and patterns of bilingualism which exists in schools.

b)   The second assumption is the belief that effective control of English as a mean of access to educational opportunity depends on spending the whole or even the bulk of each school day learning through the medium of English. This is not to dispute the usefulness of English within the larger British society while still questioning the curricular strategy which convention assumes is needed. International experience and research does not support this assumption.

c)   Finally, it is often said that many Asian parents in Britain have no wish to see their home language introduced into the school and that they want their child to use only English there.

While this may have been true at one time (perhaps in 1960s and 1970s), recent research in Britain suggests that this is no longer true. There is clearly room for parent and teacher understanding of the issues involved in the use of more than one language within the school.

While it would be fair to say that not all schools or all teachers in Britain can be regarded as making all these assumptions, or of making them as points of principle rather than of practicality, it seems that in practice this is broadly the case.

At primary school level and in terms of general educational policy, there has been a willingness to recognise cultural distinctions between indigenous children and those from minority groups. These distinctions are however cultural rather than linguistic. Such distinctions have been selected for their compatibility with the idea that intercultural education involves a curriculum which is experienced equally by children of all backgrounds. While this may be desirable in itself, the logical extension of this process to linguistic aspects of a child's cultural identity and to his/her bilingualism is not compatible with the widely held idea that equality of opportunity consists in providing for all children within the same basic curriculum. This apparently desirable principle leads to a curriculum compatible with the aptitudes and abilities of children from the majority ethnic group and an education which is monolingual and mainly monocultural, rather than intercultural. The importance of 'mother-tongue' teaching in this respect has been shown by many studies in the U.K. and Canada. Mother-tongue teaching aims to:

a)   promote cognitive and social growth;

b)   increase children's confidence;

c)   have children's full potential developed;

d)   enhance the value of children's culture and the language itself as part of that culture;

e)   promote children's own identity through his/her language;

f)   facilitate communication between parents and children;

g)   enrich the cultural life of the country as a whole by means of a diversity of linguistic resources.

Most of the European nations are bilingual or even multi-lingual. This is also true of African, Latin American and Asian countries, as well as other places throughout the world. There is an increasing awareness of the need for programmes to education through the use of bilingual approaches. Sweden has undertaken to provide for *every child* an education in the mother-tongue as well as in Swedish. But there is persistent monolingualism among indigenous British people - including most teachers. There is no denying of the fact that command/competence in English language is essential to equal participation in British society. It is also important to acknowledge the facts of linguistic diversity. Minority languages need to be given equal status, and not made marginal to mainstream education.

During the past two decades, findings from various parts of the world have confirmed that bilingual children compared with monolingual children show definite advantages on measures of 'cognitive flexibility', 'creativity' or 'divergent thought'.

In primary school, the child's mother-tongue should be used as a medium of instruction alongside the dominant and official language within the normal school time-table. Thus, bilingual education should be seen as essential for the identity development of the child. Bilingual education and mother-tongue maintenance should be included in intercultural education policy and practice (Ghuman, 1994).

It is essential for the bilingual child's self-esteem that his/her bilingualism is recognised *positively*. Bilingual children develop skills in switching from one language to another and they feel proud in acting as interpreters and translators when they are grown up. This also provides positive self-esteem for the child. Bilingual children provide a link between home, school and the community.

The presence of bilingual children in the school raises language awareness and enhances awareness of cultural diversity. There are positive effects of bilingualism for *all* children. It offers access to different types of relationships with different kinds of people. It raises the language skills of monolingual children and offers access to the literature and languages of different cultures. There is also research evidence that children whose first language is valued in school are likely to feel happy and confident, and as a result are motivated to learn.

Although education for a multiracial Britain has made some progress in the last 20 years, the multilingual nature of British society is still far from being acknowledged. The linguistic diversity of British society has so far been either ignored or viewed as a liability rather than as a national resource.

In a multicultural, multiethnic society, even if bilingual children constitute a small percentage of the total school population, each individual has a right to a broad and balanced curriculum and work at the appropriate conceptual level. The goals of educational equality, equal rights and social justice for millions of children and young people in inner cities, urban and rural areas, in democratic countries have not been realised. Schools and teachers can play an important role in the process to bring these goals to fruition.

The school should adopt a positive response to a multilingual and multicultural society. Such a strategy will strengthen school and community links. It will also increase staff knowledge and understanding of bilingualism. It will provide all children equal access to the curriculum which is the fundamental philosophy of 'Education for All'.

References

Bloomfield, L. (1933) *Language.* New York: Holt, Rinehart and Winston.
Council of Europe (1977) *Council Directive on the Education of the children of Migrant Workers*, 77/48b/EEC, 25 July.
Department of Education (1975) *A Language for Life (The Bullock Report).* London: HMSO.
Department of Education and Science (1985) *Education for All: Report of the Committee of Inquiry into the Education of children from Ethnic Minority Groups (The Swann Report).* London: HMSO.

Edwards, V. (1984) *'Language issues in school'* in *craft*, M. (Ed.) Education and Cultural Pluralism. London: The Falmer Press.

Ghuman, P. A. (1994). *Coping with Two Cultures.* Clevedon: Multilingual Matters.

Hakuta, K. (1986) *Mirror of Language: The Debate on Bilingualism.* New York: Basic Books.

Haugen, E. (1953) *The Norwegian Language in America: A Study in Bilingual Behaviour*, 2 Vols. Philadelphia: University of Pennsylvania Press.

Mackey, W.F. (1970) *'A typology of bilingual education'*. Foreign Language Annals, Vol 3, pp. 596-608.

Martin-Jones, M. (1984) *'The newer minorities: literacy and educational issues'* in Trudgill, P. (Ed.) Language in the British Isles. Cambridge: Cambridge University Press.

Richards, J., Platt, J. and Weber, H. (1985) *Longman Dictionary of Applied Linguistics.* Harlow, Essex: Longman.

Romaine, S. (1995) Bilingualism (2nd edition, in series: *Language in Society*, Vol. 13). Oxford: Blackwell.

Saunders, G. (1988) *Bilingual Children: From Birth to Teens.* Clevedon: Multilingual Matters.

Stern, H.H. (1983) *Fundamental concepts of Language Teaching.* Oxford: Oxford University Press.

Part III

Interculturalism and multicultual education

9 Multicultural education and the concept of culture: a view from social anthropology

F. Javier Garcia-Castano and Rafael A. Pulido-Moyano

Introduction

In our view, discussions on multicultural education arise when some aspects of culture, as the 'macro-variable' which embodies diversity, enter the classroom. As soon as the presence of clearly differentiated (by differences related to skin colour, mother tongue, values, religious behaviour and so on) ethnic groups is detected within schools, the need to pay attention to such differences by using 'special' education is acknowledged and a new conceptualisation for discrimination exerted through school has appeared, discrimination by cultural difference. Traditional Western schools, which used to produce gender and class differences, now discriminate among those who belong to culturally different groups (i.e. those which differ from the dominant group). Needless to say, cultural discrimination has always existed, being intertwined with 'classical' gender and class discrimination.

Multicultural education arises from reflection on the presence of children from minority groups in western schools. It was assumed that they required special treatment in order to solve academic problems supposedly related to the 'distance' between their original cultures and the dominant culture presented in, and represented by, the school. Based on a great variety of methodological and theoretical presuppositions, many educational programmes were theoretically designed to reduce the failure of these children in school, to make them appreciate their own culture, to integrate them into the 'host' culture, to promote 'cultural pluralism', etc. This clearly represents a diversity of goals, methods and curriculum strategies, their rationale being that of coping with the diversity of the school population.

In this paper we eschew one particular approach to the understanding of multicultural education through social anthropology (particularly from the anthropology of education, one of its sub-disciplines). This approach is based on a concept of culture, the core concept of social anthropology. We feel obliged to 'denounce' this fact, and to reflect upon multicultural education from our own anthropological framework. We hold that a concept of culture lies behind each model of multicultural education, though it is most often implicit. The concept of culture underlying the diverse models of multicultural education constitutes an obstacle in defending equality among individuals, which is - in principle - a desirable goal within each model. We doubt that schools by themselves can reach any of the goals mentioned above; indeed we think that the very relationship between schools and states should be central to discussions on multicultural education. However, we will not focus on that issue in this paper. What we want to emphasise is that the hidden (we might say 'taken for granted') concepts of culture in multicultural education models encourage the idea that individuals are not only different but also unequal. The recognition of the 'difference' within schools leads - most often unintentionally - to the idea that some cultures are not valid for school and social success, hence they must be replaced by dominant cultures.

Models of multicultural education

Elsewhere (Garcia and Pulido, 1992), we have reviewed the diverse conceptions of multicultural education. We used the categorisation made by Margaret Gibson (1984). In her article, Gibson analysed different approaches to multicultural education in the USA and we extended her review to include other bibliographical sources and databases. We will summarise the four models she described, indicating some correspondences between her typology and those developed by Banks (1986) and Sleeter and Grant (1987).

- *Cultural assimilation:* This perspective was triggered by the recurrent academic failure of pupils from minority groups, and also by the rejection of genetic and cultural deficit hypotheses about the cause of this failure. It coincides with some works from the group Sweeter and Grant called 'Teaching the culturally different', as well as with Banks' 'assimilationist' and 'cultural deprivation' paradigms.

114

- *Cultural understanding:* Advocates of this model hold that an education about cultural differences is necessary, not an education for the culturally different pupils. The goal is to value the cultural richness of diversity, thus conceiving cultural peculiarities as an educational content. Here we can include literature on 'human relations' (Sleeter and Grant), and three paradigms in Banks' typology: 'ethnic additive', 'self-concept' and 'racism'.

- *Cultural pluralism:* Preservation and extension of pluralism. This approach stems from the rejection of acculturative and assimilative practices by ethnic minorities. For these groups, neither cultural assimilation nor cultural fusion are acceptable social goals. It coincides with what Sleeter and Grant called 'multicultural education' and with two paradigms in Banks, 'cultural pluralism' and 'cultural difference'.

- *Bicultural education:* In this model, multicultural education is intended to make individuals competent in two cultures. It also rejects assimilation, claiming that the original culture must be preserved and mainstream culture is to be acquired as a second or alternative culture. 'Language' paradigm (Banks) and most literature about 'single group studies' (Sleeter and Grant) can be included here.

- *Social transformation:* This model did not appear in Gibson's article. Here we group (a) some works she considered to belong to the pluralist model (b) 'multi- cultural education that is social reconstructionist' (Sleeter and Grant), and (c) 'radical' paradigm (Banks). From these perspectives, multicultural education is understood as a process designed to develop the awareness of students, parents and communities about socioeconomic conditions, in order to enable them to engage in social actions based on a critical understanding of reality. Here we find literature categorised by Delgado-Gaitan (1992) under the label 'empowerment model'.

There are many other categorisations of literature in multicultural education. Lynch (1986:37), has collected eight typologies:

Gibson (5 educational categories) :
   Culturally Different
   About Cultural Difference

Cultural Pluralism
Bicultural Education
Multicultural Education for All
Willians (3 approaches)
Technicist
Moral
Socio-political
Nixon (5 broad organisational curriculum approaches with 3 phases)
Accretion
Optional Extra
Common Core
Piecemeal Development
Permeation
a. Small-scale Innovation
b. Co-ordination and Development
c. Consultation and Evaluation
Lynch Model 1 (6 curricular tactics)
Parallel
Additive
Permeation
Materials Production
Consultancy
Action Research
Lynch Model 2 (3 ideologies)
Purposive-Economic
Egalitarian Inter-dependent
Gay (4 stages)
Simultaneous variety
Refined, Broadened and Definitive
Gestalt Holistic
Process Approach
Watson/Stephan (8 dimensions)
Political
Social
Economic
Cultural
Socio-psychology of Multicultural Societies
Amalgamation
Assimilation Quasi-immigration

Banks (10 paradigm changes)
    Ethnic Additive
    Self Concept
    Cultural Deprivation
    Language
    Assimilationist
    Genetic
    Cultural Pluralist
    Cultural Difference
    Racist
    Radical

Given that almost all the literature on multicultural education has been written by and for educators, it is not surprising that the underlying concept of culture was never a parameter upon which to elaborate typologies or categorisations of diverse multicultural education approaches. The very concept of culture has never had a central position in the construction of theoretical discourses on education, neither has it represented a crucial 'variable' on which educators' thought could be grounded. There existed - and there exists - a great variety of implicit concepts of 'culture' behind discourses on multicultural education, though we are not going to elaborate a new typology using the criterion of its presence. What we want to emphasise is, firstly, that the fact of not making the concept of culture explicit has been an obstacle in the development of investigations of the phenomena of multiculturalism in schools, and secondly, that there has never existed any model, paradigm or approach to multicultural education which was based mainly on an anthropological conceptual framework, and that is why they lack a solid concept of culture. As pointed out by Moodley (1986:69):

> 'A somewhat static conception of 'culture' is implicit in most views of multicultural education. Culture is seen as a set of more or less immutable characteristics attributable to different groups of people. They are used to identify people and often produce stereotypes, contrary to intention (Rosen, 1977). The notion of culture which the Royal Commission's Book IV (1969:11) espouses as an afterthought under the heading 'The cultural contributions of ethnic groups' reveals a lyrical fiction that bears little resemblance to minority reality. 'Culture', the Commission waxes, 'is a way of being, thinking and feeling. It is a

117

driving force animating a significant group of individuals united by common tongue and sharing the same customs, habits and experiences.'

Bullivant (1993) is one of the authors who has stressed with most effect the need to borrow from the anthropological concept of culture in designing multicultural education conceptions. He contrasts that type of wrong or distant usage from the scientific treatment that current anthropology makes of such a concept :

> 'The Committee [on Multicultural Education] also adopted a view of the concept of culture similar to that of the Galbally Committee, based on the well known, but theoretically outmoded, definition of Tylor (1871). However, it is inherently limited for far-reaching policy-making to adopt 'the most common, popular usage in education which equates culture with social group's heritage, i.e. traditions, history, language, arts and other aesthetic achievements, religious customs and values'

As we said before, the emergence of multicultural education was related to the presence of differentiated ethnic groups in classrooms, that is, the introduction of the concept of culture as a key to understanding the diversity within schools. Hence we cannot grasp the full significance of the meaning of multicultural education unless we engage in an effort to clarify the concept of culture. Anthropology can make a great contribution and, in this sense, we think that Wilson (1992) exaggerates when in trying to justify his indiscriminate usage of the terms 'race', 'culture', and 'ethnic', he said that " 'Culture' is worse still: I have seen no definition of this term with any serious pretension to clarity" (p.299).

We find various definitions of 'culture' within the literature on multicultural education. Thus, Lynch et al. (1992:9) pointed out that "of course, each [political] structure has its own distinctive culture, including the shared norms, values, ideologies, assumptions, symbols, meanings, language and other cultural capital which hold it together and enable it to function as a coherent unit, without disintegrating". Garcia (1992), borrowing from Kroeber and Kluckhohn, defines 'culture' as "the totality of learned beliefs, tools and traditions shared by a group of humans to give continuity, order and meaning to their lives; it consists of a group's accumulated experiences and products" (p.106). For Strivens (1992) culture consists of:

118

' ... those phenomena which create a sense of common identity within a particular group: a language or dialect, religious faith, ethnic identity and geographical location. They are underlying factors which give place to shared understandings, rules and practices which govern the everyday life. Cultural behaviour is learned behaviour, but so profoundly and completely learned that it becomes, to a great extent, unconscious.'

Another author who has encountered the concept of culture in her positionings within the multicultural education domain is Taboada (1992) for whom Anglo-Saxon anthropological tradition presents culture as:

'an homogenised functional whole, identically transmitted from one generation to next. It is this 'ideal'-type concept of foreign culture which comes from literary and artistic works, as well as from stereotyped folklore, that acts as a referent for debates about education of immigrant cultures.

It is necessary to problematise this concept, to the extent that what concern us are their aspects of continuity, unity and functionality.

... Thus, culture should be whatever, except a definitive gift that individuals receive in a group ... It appears rather as a collective elaboration, in perpetual transformation, and in this sense the culture of immigrants is only a specific aspect of the modalities of change of societies and individuals.

... [In its anthropological sense] culture is something determined to a great extent by environment and material conditions.'

In the same vein, Donald and Rattansi (1992:4) talked about a redefinition of the concept of culture in the light of some critiques on the concept which underlie multiculturalism:

'This suggests a definition of culture that is closer to what many social scientists and cultural theorists would have in mind when they talk about culture than the versions associated with either multiculturism or antiracism. This is not limited to religious beliefs, communal rituals or shared traditions. On the contrary, it begins with the way that such manifest phenomena are produced through systems of meaning, through structures of power, and through the institutions in which these are deployed ... culture is no longer understood as what expresses the identity of a community. Rather, it refers to the processes, categories and knowledges through which communities are defined as such: that is, how they are rendered specific and differentiated.'

We think there exist some theoretical co-ordinates within socio-cultural anthropology which have served to generate a concept of culture able to sustain a new model of multicultural education. Let us describe some of this conceptual basis before characterising it.

A concept of culture

Generally speaking, social sciences have assumed that 'culture' emerges as a generalisation in describing a supposedly homogeneous human (sub)organisation. Thus, we anthropologists used to think - making other people think - that many societies are monocultural and it is only recently as a result of anthropological research into post-industrial urban societies that we begin to refer to them as multicultural. However, differences between 'complex' and 'simple' (or primitive) societies in relation to their multiculturalism is held to be just a matter of degree, not of type (Goodenough 1976).

It is obvious that, in telling 'others' how 'we' are, we use some referents which define ourselves which makes us appear as homogeneous, but we would never use those referents if we were to define 'us' to ourselves (perhaps we never undergo such a process of self-definition). Those homogenising referents would be useless, and probably the members of our group would not feel comfortable to see themselves reflected in those references. When we define our group as opposed to an 'other' group, we do not invoke the differences actually existing within our group, differences which generate diversity within it. Instead of that, we invoke similarities and shared characteristics among us, thus constructing an homogenising discourse in which we merely select those themes which are more relevant for the maintenance of our social group (Garcia-Garcia 1988).

When asked for a definition of the Spanish, Andalusian or Granada culture, responses do not go beyond generalisations and stereotypes, because such statements ease the task of defining the 'other'. Needless to say, we can indeed talk about such and such a culture of any group; what we want to defend is that, in trying to 'project' a culture onto all its members, we find serious obstacles in recognising the replication of this culture in the real behaviour of each member. Each individual has a particular version of all her/his physical and symbolic environments, a personal view of the culture which we say she/he

120

belongs to (if it is possible to talk about belonging to a single culture). Her/his behaviour often diverges to a varying degree with respect to the norm established in the homogenising discourse.

Each individual has her/his own, personal, subjective version of the 'culture' which others - the social scientist among them - attribute to her/him, each version being different in some degree from the ones held by the rest of the group members. Each member has a personal view of how things function within the group, that is, of his/her culture. What has traditionally been presented as the culture of any group is nothing but the organisation of its constituting diversity, of the intragroup heterogeneity inherent in every human society. The idea of an organised 'diversity' points to the existence in any group of as many versions of the world and of life as there are individuals belonging to that group, different but 'equivalent' versions in a such a manner that the differences do not prevent the identification and recognition among members that they are holders of mutually intelligible schemata.

A realistic comparison between what people do and what people say they do would lead us to the idea we are defending: we listen to a homogenising discourse but we observe a plurality of heterogeneous behaviours. Much of the anthropologist's task consists of combining both kinds of information in order to make explicit and to explain culture, as well as to interpret the meaning of what people say they do in relation to what they do. That is precisely the difference between writing a report of facts and looking beneath them to understand how people cope with them and how the probability of their recurrence increases or decreases (Wolcott, 1985). Thus, we should infer the nature and meaning of culture (composed by concepts, beliefs, and principles for action and social interaction) from words and behaviours displayed by members of the group under study. Our assumption is that what actually constitutes culture is not an internal homogeneity but an organisation of internal differences (Garcia-Garcia 1991), and that cultures have a 'spoken' uniformity rather than a real unity (Garcia-Garcia 1988). That is why the anthropologists' task is not completed until they contrast the uniformity reflected in discourse with the actual intragroup diversity, the organisation of which is ultimately the culture of that group.

Human society as a multicultural reality

These first conceptual guidelines, borrowed from sociological anthropology, are crucial in our approach to multicultural education. Stemming from them, we think that human beings, wherever they live, are living in a multicultural world. This idea is supplemented with a second one, all members of any group develop competences in various cultures (some authors prefer to call them microcultures, in order to use the same root concept at different levels). Each individual has access to more than one culture, that is, to more than one set of knowledge and patterns of perception, thinking, and action. No culture is ever fully acquired by any individual, only some parts are acquired of each (micro)culture to which she/he has access throughout her/his own experiential background. The sum of all those parts constitutes a private, subjective view of the world and its contents; it is her/his 'propriospect', to use a term coined by Goodenough (1981).

Because we have competence in various cultures we are in this sense multicultural, like an immigrant child who after some time in the new settlement develops competence in, e.g.:

- The culture of her/his household group, both in native (pre-migration) and modified versions - adapted to the new environment - (though we think that most likely both versions will construct themselves mutually once a migrant family is settled in the host community).

- The culture of the ethnic group to which she/he belongs, both in relation to the manifestation of its traditions and customs (and being competent does not mean here to accept or behave according to them, but to know or to recognise them), and - linked to the former - in relation to its difference with respect to other ethnic groups living in the new environment.

- The culture of diverse peer groups, ranging from the closest circle of friends with the same ethnic origin to that (the school classmates) with a greater diversity and created in an institution with universalistic purposes.

- The classroom and school cultures, in which children learn those apparently non-biased contents (not only from text-books) required to give access to privilege and power positions.

This child becomes competent in many cultures, all of them presenting different information out of which she/he will actively (and both individually and collectively) construct her/his own version of the world, her/his own version of 'her/his' culture, her/his 'personal culture theory' (Kessing 1974), her/his propriospect (Goodenough 1981), a multicultural version.

In order to formulate an initial profile of an anthropological approach to multicultural education, in which education is understood as the process of culture transmission-acquisition, we want to add further considerations on the treatment of the concept of 'culture' in establishing those of 'difference' and 'identity'. To begin with, we think that in current Western contexts, where culturally justified inequalities are very common, to emphasise differences without assuming inequalities is really quite complicated. Once again, boundaries among cultures are understood as something easy to identify. Perhaps this boundary-making was useful in the past, if ever, when anthropology made one-to-one correspondences between geographical regions and cultures. The 'other' was far away from us, and this distance facilitated the construction of relativist discourses on cultural differences. But nowadays, the 'other' is among us, and those one-to-one correspondences are not useful any longer. Differences have been constructed from a very static concept of culture, and the teaching of differences is a new way to reify cultures and to encourage the assumptions of inequality.

Western cultures are not the only cultures in which members self-perceive themselves as different from those who do not belong to 'them'. Usually it is assumed that every culture establishes a distance from other cultures and situates itself in a position of superiority. This construction of difference through 'distance' prepares the way for systems of inequality. It is true that every group engages itself in the definition of differences as a self-identification procedure. We can easily observe, however, that within a system where 'we' dominate the 'other', then differences (whether exposed by 'us' and the 'other') have distinct weights, distinct degrees of recognition. Generally dominant groups 'inform' the biggest number and diversity of people that they are different, and expose with the best 'quality of communication' which are the differences that separate them from other groups. This propagandistic game makes minority groups believe that the only existing right way is that of eliminating differences by getting closer and closer to the dominant group. To indicate differences is to establish a hierarchy, because cultures differ in the degree of recognition.

Some authors have made one-to-one correspondences between culture and ethnic groups, using interchangeably the phrases 'plurality of ethnic groups' and 'cultural pluralism'. Again within this approach we find the idea that it is possible clearly to identify where each culture starts and ends, and that our society is a cultural mosaic. Culture is not only identity, that is a reductionistic idea. Identity is most often the 'meeting point' for members of any group, i.e. their better version of homogenising descriptions of their own group. The analysis of cultural practices demonstrates that such identity is coined, maintained and transformed through an endless series of tensions and conflicts, and that it is constructed precisely in the comparison with the 'other'. This anthropological analysis demonstrates that mechanisms of identification used by group members are only a part of culture. If we forget that, we are close to admitting that culture is nothing but an instrument for otherness-based processes of differentiation.

Antecedents of an approach to multicultural education based on anthropology of education

It is crucial to understand the meaning of culture in studying social interactions within the school community, and anthropology provides the best way to reach such an understanding (St. Lawrence and Singleton, 1975). Both general anthropology and each of its subdisciplines make essential contributions to multi-cultural teaching and learning (Johnson, 1977). Anthropology can provide multicultural education with a wide and diversified range of research strategies and methods well suited to coping with the complex realities it faces. The anthropological contribution to educational research is evident in works such as Trueba et al.'s (1981), with a series of micro-ethnographical studies on minority children in the classroom, showing the validity and importance of ethnography for bilingual education. In their study of Indian children, Foersters and Little Soldier (1981) also defended the use of ethnographical models to analyse, compare and locate conflicts and/or discontinuities between home and school cultures. From the 1950s onwards, cultural anthropologists in the U.S. have engaged themselves in curriculum development for public schools (Dynneson, 1975; Dwyer-Schink, 1976). Ethnographers have demonstrated their ability to propose practical ways to reduce the 'culture clash' in a multicultural classroom (Clark, 1963). Apart from the methodological contribution, the implication of anthropology is necessary in action programmes, as we can see in Jordan's (1985) work, in which anthropological knowledge guides a bicultural education programme, or in Koppelman (1979), who poses the need to evaluate these programmes from anthropological conceptions.

However, where is the anthropological view of multiculturalism as the normal human experience, as propounded by Goodenough (1976)? Previous models or conceptions of multicultural education have a partial and biased scope in engaging with the extremely wide and heterogeneous spectrum of existing factors whilst from an anthropology view we can think about the multiculturalism/school dyad holistically. London (1981) said that cultural anthropology constitutes an adequate framework for obtaining such a perspective in combination with other disciplines, enabling us to go beyond the analytical deficiency of assimilationist and cultural pluralist models.

Basic assumptions of a model founded upon an anthropological conception of culture

As Carlson (1976) said, multicultural education is, to a great extent, a sort of applied social anthropology. This means that we can project the theoretical and analytical corpus of anthropology on to the development of (more or less formal, institutional or 'calculated') processes of transmission-acquisition of diverse cultural repertoires. We want to point to the different assumptions or principles of procedure guiding the construction of an anthropology-based multicultural education. Let us begin by remembering the advantages, described by Gibson (1984:112-113), carried by a definition of multicultural education as the process whereby a person develops competences in multiple systems of standards for perceiving, evaluating, believing, and doing, i.e. in multiple cultures:

> 'First, we no longer are restricted to the view that equates education with schooling or multicultural programs with formal education ...
> Second, we no longer are restricted to the view that tends to equate culture and ethnic group ...
> Third, since the development of competence in a new culture usually requires intensive interaction with people who already are competent, we can see even more clearly that efforts to support ethnically separate schools are antithetical to the purposes of multicultural education ...
> Finally, the possibility, and indeed likelihood, that education (both in and out of school) promotes awareness of and competence in multiple cultures leads us away from the notion of bicultural education and dichotomies between native and mainstream culture.'

Our earlier assumptions are supplemented by important appreciations emerging from this perspective on the idea of a multicultural education. Some of them are related to the causes that provoked the appearance of multicultural education programmes, others to the reasons for the maintenance of these programmes. Thus, for example, multicultural education is no longer understood as that demanded by groups of poor migrants who originated these programmes. Certainly, much of that demand points to assimilationist models, intended to gain access to the levels of welfare held by 'non-marginal' members of dominant cultures. These poor migrants left their respective original cultures in very difficult socio-economic conditions which they intend to ameliorate. In some cases they consider school success to be a fundamental requirement to enable future generations to improve their life conditions. Some groups are even willing to suffer processes of assimilation and - consciously or not - they accept the risk of losing their original cultural identity. (A different issue, though related to this, is that of the 'identity' problems of second generations).

Henceforth, when we refer to multicultural education we do not mean programmes designed for minority groups, but for all groups (though we must recognise that from our theoretical position it may make no sense to speak in terms of majorities and minorities.) Minorities, by the way, are usually conceptualised as those groups with a deficit. If we think of those who formulate the deficiencies of any one culture in comparison with any other, we will become aware that the very fact of that formulation is not a practice directed towards the promotion of equality. It is true that certain groups have not adapted themselves to their new contexts, but this does not legitimate any discourse on 'deficit'. In other words, when we talk about 'deficit' we are denying a crucial ability of groups to generate new adaptation strategies in new contexts. The only thing we can say is that those groups have not put in practice, for the moment, strategies for adaptation to such contexts. In fact, differences among cultures are also a matter of particular ways of adaptation to distinct contexts. Such parameters of difference (not of inequality) can be a good base for the comparison and the encounter of cultures.

If we say that there exists a separation between a dominant culture and minority cultures, we are implicitly recognising that we can clearly establish the boundaries between and/or among them. Needless to say, we do not deny the existence of domination relations, but we think that it is very difficult to delineate in a precise way the distribution of 'weights' in those relations. In a few words; 'cultures' themselves are not fighting to appropriate regions of power within societies, the true fighters are certain groups invoking in their discourses a presumed culture which they utilise in order to legitimate their actions.

Bearing in mind these last ideas, it is clear that a multicultural education programme should not disappear because of change in migratory fluxes.

Multicultural education is not an education designed to/for a given group amenable to quantification and to be labelled as 'disadvantaged', 'minority' or 'marginal' in comparison with other groups. Multicultural education is an education which even questions the very idea of the relationship between school (as an apparatus for social and ideological reproduction and legitimation) and state. Schools transmit the dominant culture within geographical frontiers of the state, but we cannot go on maintaining the idea of a presumed homogeneity in the dominant culture (such an homogeneity never existed). Now we should ask 'what culture, within which frontiers?' Multicultural education must develop itself in society as a process of cultural production and cultural critique, a process characterised by:

- diversifying the cultural contents of transmission (a diversity often leading to contradictions among them);

- diversifying the transmission methods, adjusting them to different students to facilitate an equal possibility of gaining an access to knowledge;

- promoting students' greatest levels of awareness about cultural diversity, which does not consist of 'giving information about specific systems, but of presenting them in order to get a definition of what culture is borrowing from current cultural anthropology ... showing that the model emanating from a culture cannot be judged with reference to another, because they are options of philosophy of existence which, seen as a whole, cannot be placed in a particular hierarchy on the basis of the rational argument' (Camilleri 1992:144);

- providing students with the necessary cognitive resources in order

    (a) to know diversity and cultural differences existing in their environments;
    (b) to perceive and to analyse social inequalities, which through the utilisation of diversities and differences become inequalities in the distribution of power and resources in society;
    (c) to criticise such conversation and to construct proposals for transformation; and
    (d) to employ themselves in critical and active ways in social action;

- fighting against the idea of an inevitable mutual exclusion between on the one hand, the preservation of ethnic and/or cultural identities or peculiarities of disadvantaged minority groups, and on the other, access to high-powered positions within society. However, whenever the dilemma arises it will be for members of affected groups to make this decision, a process in which they could apply abilities such as those aforementioned;

- elaborating programmes by combining the analysis of specific communities (in which they will be implemented) with the commitment to a global, universalistic conception of the culture reality.

From transmission-acquisition of a culture to development of a cultural critique

Our conception of multicultural education is founded upon our theoretical positions within the anthropology of education, the subdiscipline which studies the processes of transmission and acquisition of culture. Culture is transmitted through a variety of mechanisms and agents. Part of culture self-transmits in the function of its own dynamics, while part of it (especially in western or westernised societies) is transmitted in privileged institutions which emphasise those formal or academic aspects of culture, to a certain extent because they are only useful for academic activity.

It is in the domain of social relations in which culture is produced, preserved, or modified. Transmission and transformation, i.e. continuity and change of its forms, are basic processes of any culture. When we speak of multicultural education we do not mean a process of transmission of culture, as much as a process of promotion of (critical) knowledge about it. Human groups, creators and transmitters of culture, have their own distinctive rationality. They project this particular logic on to their own cultural forms, they develop an implicit knowledge on it (a 'know how'), as well as an explicit, speakable knowledge on it (a 'know that'). In other words, members of cultures are not only culture users but they are able also to explain and interpret it.

However, sociological and anthropological studies on different human societies and/or cultures demonstrate that native discourses on their own cultures do not coincide with the discourses elaborated by social scientists. There are various reasons for such divergence, including a different selection of relevant facts for interpretation, the management of different kinds of data,

128

methodological strategies specific to theoretical intentions in social sciences, the use of interpretive models alien to the logics of social actors, the existence of different cognitive processes which obey different rationalities and, of course, the fact that cultural forms and knowledge of them have divergent social functions.

Multicultural education should be aimed at transmitting, fostering and facilitating a critical understanding of culture, of cultures. Though we make this reflection after contrasting 'native' discourse and its rationality with those of social scientists, we are not predisposed to favour the latter. Indeed it makes no sense to talk about any 'victory' of scientific views, insofar as socio-anthropological science has developed its rationality precisely through the close examination of native logic and of behaviours based on it. We must clarify this point in order not to fall into an epistemic ethnocentrism in which any rationality, including the one we want to spread to generate critical knowledge on culture, would be dominated by the scientific rationality.

The term 'critical' has different meanings in this context. On the one hand, it is close to scientific knowledge, in the sense that it is a systematic knowledge which goes beyond that spontaneous or folk knowledge held by native users (or social scientists who do not follow the scientific method and research techniques of social sciences). This kind of knowledge is not produced exclusively in academic circles. On the other hand, as a consequence of the former meaning, 'critical' means 'relativist' concerning its own culture. In current societies, a trend exists to 'make absolute' local, regional and national cultures. This trend has political, nationalistic, or separatist objectives, or simply it is aimed at reinforcing cultural identities, within a framework of political struggles and redistribution of power. At the same time, there exists an opposite trend, which can be seen in processes of homogenisation and standardisation of culture under the influence and interests of trans-national industries of communication, producers and administrators of cultural goods. Both phenomena, contradictory and/or complementary as they can be considered, are central characteristics of current societies. These two trends become more acute with the crisis of Eastern countries, but their roots come from far away, being connected with the internationalisation of both capital and division of labour, shaping of new states, nationalistic battles, crisis of traditional oligarchical power, and emergence of new social groups in the distribution of political and economic privilege.

A critical-relativist knowledge with such characteristics is not one that exalts its own values and scorns alien ones. On the contrary, it is a knowledge that defends only what can/must be defended from its own cultural forms, and that respects the alien ones in the same way. Here we remember the slogan in an antiracist demonstration in Barcelona (February 1992): "Igualtat per virtue, diversitat per conviure" ("Equality for living, diversity for living together"), which reflects the fundamental insight underlying our discourse. This second meaning of 'critical' as 'relativist' with respect to its own culture comes from evidence of cultural diversity and of the fact that every human group historically decides and shapes the characteristics of their cultures so as to adapt to a great variety of ecological, demographical, political, social, and ideological conditions.

However, these two meanings do not address the crucial issue of the function of knowledge about culture. Any knowledge is a social discourse, that is, a social practice. That is why 'critical' has a third meaning, that of 'alternative knowledge'. Multicultural education should be an empowerment of a social reflection (encouraged by schools and other educational agencies) on self-comprehension by human groups and of self-criticism about their own cultural forms, both traditional and modern, in order to improve their life conditions, and to strengthen their cultural identity through the recognition and acceptance of cultural diversity.

At this point, we can instrumentalise the experience offered by the process of making of anthropological knowledge, a process of observation and continuous questioning about realities under observation. We construct this knowledge by describing observations carried out which in turn are complemented by what is told about them, i.e. the said and the done together. We arrive at this critical knowledge through the process of understanding our being in comparison with 'alien' being. Thus, if we are to produce a critical knowledge of our own culture, then this knowledge must be made through a contrast with other cultural forms. The very epistemological principle held in anthropology related to 'distance' (which is not a matter of physical separation) clearly reflects this need of comparison as the best base for mutual respect and recognition of multicultural reality.

Perhaps we are going to need such a 'distance' to realise that to differentiate is not the same as to discriminate, and that diversity is not the same as inequality. To educate from and for multiculturalism consists of promoting an awareness of these distinctions which structure the perception of human beings and their presence in the world. Perhaps a 'distance' will be necessary again to consider if schools, any schools in the western sense familiar to us, can really promote an education seen as a development of a cultural critique. In the end, a just and realistic distance can put everything in its proper place, so that we do not forget what can be expected from schooling: a place for cultural production, which is not the same as a place for cultural critique.

Acknowledgement

An earlier version of this paper was published in Revista de Education no.302 (1994). The authors wish to thank CIDE and DGIYT (Ministry of Education and Science), DGM (Ministry of Social Affairs), DGBC (Department of Culture of Andalusian Government) and MED-Campus program (European Commission) for various research funds.

References

Banks, J.A. (1986) 'Multicultural Education: Development, Paradigms and Goals' in Banks, J.A. & Lynch, J. (eds.) *Multicultural Education in Western Societies,* (London, Holt, Rinehart and Winston).

Bullivant, B.M. (1993) 'Culture: Its Nature and Meaning for Educators' in Banks, J.A. & Banks, A.M. (eds.) *Multicultural Education Issues and Perspectives,* (Boston, Mass., Allyn and Bacon).

Camilleri, C. (1992) 'From Multicultural to Intercultural: How to Move from One to the Other' in Lynch, J., Modgil, C. & Modgil, S. (eds.) *Cultural Diversity and the Schools. Education for Cultural Diversity: Convergence and Divergence, Vol.1* (London and Washington DC., The Falmer Press).

Clark, K.B. (1963) 'Clash of cultures in the Classroom' in *Integrated Education* vol.1, no.4, pp7-14.

Delgado-Gaitan, C. (1992) 'Destacando la cútura en la educacion multicultural' in Garcia-Castano, F.J. (ed) *Hacia una Educacion Multicultural* (Granada, Universidad de Granada).

Donald, J. & Rattansil, A. (eds.) (1992) *'Race', Culture & Difference* (London, Sage).

Dwyer-Schick , S. (1976) *The Study and Teaching of Anthropology: An Annotated Bibliography* (Athens GA, University of Georgia).

Dynneson, T. (1975) *Pre-Collegiate Anthropology: Trends and Materials* (Athens GA, University of Georgia).

Foersters, L.M. & Little Soldier, D. (1981) 'Applying Anthropology to Educational Problems' in *Journal of American Indian Education* vol.20, no.3, pp1-6.

Garcia-Castano, F.J. (1991) 'En busca de modelos explicativos del funcionamiento de la transmision/adquiscion de la Cultura' in Diaz De Rada, A. (ed.) *Antropolgia de la Educacion* (Granada, F.A.A.E.E).

Garcia-Castano, F.J. & Pulido-Moyano, R.A. (1992) 'Educacion Multicultural y Antropolgia de la Educacion' in Fermosa, P. (ed.) *Educacion Intercultural: la Europa sin fronteras* (Barcelona, Narcea).

Garcia Garcia, J.L. (1988) 'El tiempo cotidiano en Vilanova d'Oscos' in *Enciclopedia tematica de Asturias* (Silerio Canada, Gijon).

Garcia Garcia, J.L. (1991) 'Que tienen que ver los espanoles con lo que los antropologos saben de ellos?' in Catdera, M. (ed.) *Los espanoles vistos por los antropologos* (Jucar, Gijon).

Garcia, R.L (1992) 'Cultural Diversity and Minority Rights' in Lynch, J, Modgil, C. & Modgil, S. (eds.) *Cultural Diversity and The Schools. Human Rights, Education and Global Responsibilities* Vol.4, (London and Washington DC, The Falmer Press).

Gibson, M.A. (1984) 'Approaches to Multicultural Education in the United States: Some Concepts and Assumptions' in *Anthropology and Education Quarterly* vol.15, no.1 pp 94-119.

Goodenough, W. (1976) 'Multiculturalism as the Normal Human Experience' in *Anthropology and Education Quarterly* vol.7 no.4 pp 4-6.

Goodenough, W. (1981) *Culture, Language and Society* (Ca., Menlo Park).

Grant, C.A (ed) (1977) *Multicultural Education: Commitments, Issues and Applications* (Washington DC, Association for Supervision and Curriculum Development).

Grant, C. et al. (1986) 'The Literature on Multicultural Education' in *Education Studies* no.1 pp 47-71.

Johnson, N.B. (1977) 'On the Relationship of Anthropology to Multicultural Teaching and Learning' in *Journal of Teacher Education* vol.28, no.3 pp10-15.

Jordan N. C. (1985) 'Translating Culture: From Ethnographic Information to Educational Programme' in *Anthropology and Education Quarterly* vol.XVI, no.2 pp 105-123.

Kessing, R.M. (1974) 'Theories of Culture' in *Annual Review of Anthropology* vol.3 pp 73-97.

Koppelman, K.L. (1979) 'The Explication Model: An Anthropological Approach to Programme Evaluation' in *Education Evaluation and Policy Analysis* vol.1, no.54 pp 59-64.

London, C.B.G. (1981) *Anthropology of the Classroom: Cultural Diversity, Its Meaning and Significance for Human Understanding, Communication and Student Interaction* (Resenado en RIE de Julio 1983).

Lynch, J. (1986) *Multicultural Education. Principles and Practice* (London, Routledge).

Lynch, J. (1986) Multicultural Education in Western Europe in Banks, J.A. & Lynch, J. (eds.) *Multicultural Education in Western Societies* (London, Holt, Rinehart and Winston).

Lynch, J., Modgil, C. & Modgil, S. (eds.) (1992) *Cultural Diversity and The Schools. Prejudice, Polemic or Progress?* (London and Washington DC, The Falmer Press).

Moodley, K.A. (1986) 'Canadian Multicultural Education: Promises and Practice' in Banks, J.A. & Lynch, J. *Multicultural Education in Western Societies* (Holt, Rinehart and Winston).

Sleeter, C.E. & Grant, C.A. (1987) 'An Analysis of Multicultural Education in the States' in *Harvard Educational Review* vol.57, no.4 pp 421-444.

St. Lawrence, T.J. & Singleton, J. (1975) *Multiculturalism in Social Context: Conceptual Problems Raised by Educational Policy Issues* paper presented at Symposium: Toward a Definition of Multiculturalism in Education, 74th Annual Meeting of the American Anthropological Association, San Francisco, Ca.

Strivens, J. (1992) 'The Morally Educated Person in a Multicultural Society' in Lynch, J., Modgil, C. & Modgil, S. (eds.) *Cultural Diversity and the Schools. Education for cultural Diversity: Convergence and Divergence* Vol.1 (London and Washington DC., The Falmer Press).

Taboada Leonetti, I. (1992) 'From Multicultural to Intercultural: Is It Necessary to Move from One to the Other?' in Lynch, J., Modgil, C. & Modgil, S. (eds.) *Cultural Diversity and the Schools. Education for cultural Diversity: Convergence and Divergence* Vol.1 (London and Washington DC., The Falmer Press).

Trueba, H.T. (ed) et al. (1981) *Culture and the Bilingual Classroom: studies in Classroom Ethnology* (Illinois University, Urbana. Midwest Organization for Materials Development).

Wilson, J. (1992) 'Moral Education, Values Education and Prejudice Reduction' in Lynch, J., Modgil, C. & Modgil, S. (eds.) *Cultural Diversity and The Schools. Prejudice, Polemic or Progress?* Vol.2, (London and Washington DC., The Falmer Press).

Wolcott, H. (1985) 'On Ethnographic Intent' in *Educational Administration Quarterly* Vol.21, no.3 pp187-203.

10 Intercultural education in the United Kingdom

Nigel Grant

The United Kingdom of Great Britain and Northern Ireland

The United Kingdom is, and always has been, multicultural in population; this is true of the indigenous population, in spite of widespread perceptions that this has recently changed. This is partly because there is little understanding of the State itself, and how it came into existence. We are frequently hearing of Britain 'becoming multicultural', as if it were culturally uniform until the first black Britons settled in the 1960s (Canter et al, 1993; Grant, 1994). The intercultural composition of the population certainly changed in the 19th and 20th centuries, but the state was already multinational, multilingual and multicultural right from the start. This is not always recognised widely, in England and abroad, as there still is a confusion of the terms 'the United Kingdom', 'Britain' (or 'Great Britain') and 'England', which are widely used as synonyms. Just to give one recent example, we recently saw a young English cricketer, who seems to have done quite well in a match against Australia, posing before the TV cameras flourishing a United Kingdom Union Flag; he was playing for the English team. This solecism is astonishingly common; the vast majority of football fans apparently think that the flag is the British or English flag, and we even see English fans waving Union Flags when supporting England against Scotland. Indeed, the majority of fans (and maybe of the population at large) seem to believe that this is the banner of Britain or England. At the risk of becoming pedantic, we need to sort this out, something which in my own childhood every youth knew from school, for these terms are not the same.

The United Kingdom of Great Britain and Northern Ireland consists of four countries; in order of size, England, Scotland, Wales, Northern Ireland.

They came together at different times and in different ways [see note 1]. They are very different in population; England has about 55 million people, Scotland five million, Wales about three million, and Northern Ireland about one and a half million. They have at different times been joined with England. The first was Wales, which was conquered, annexed and incorporated in 1536. England tried to conquer Scotland, but was finally defeated in 1314 (Bell and Grant, 1977); it was united with England by a union of the Crowns in 1603, and the parliaments were joined in 1707. Constitutionally, it was supposed to be a union of two sovereign kingdoms, while Wales was a principality. Together, they make up Great Britain, the English and Scottish flags being combined to form the British flag. The 'Great' of Great Britain has never been a grandiloquent title, in spite of the constant (one suspects) misunderstanding of many politicians; it was simply to distinguish it from Little Britain, or Brittany. The Union did not affect the churches of Scotland or England, which were and are still separate and both established, (Presbyterian and Episcopalian - Anglican - respectively), or the legal systems, which remain separate. That is what Britain is [see note 2]. In 1801, after the failure of the Irish Rising in 1798, the Parliaments of Britain and Ireland were joined, and the Irish Parliament was abolished. Since this was confined to Protestants and the vast majority of the people were Catholic, there was little protest. For the flag (the Union Flag, often miscalled the Union Jack), a new cross was invented to add to it. The cross of St. Patrick, red diagonal on a white ground, was devised to lie alongside the cross of St. Andrew of Scotland, with an additional narrow white stripe to separate the red and the blue, thus saving the colour-scheme of red, white and blue for the overall effect, while producing a rather messy flag, which almost no one can draw accurately.

The English flag is a simple red cross on a white field; the Scottish flag is a white diagonal cross (a Saltire) on a blue field; the Irish flag was deemed to be a red diagonal cross on white (the modern Irish flag is a tricolour of green, white and orange, and is used in the Republic), and the Welsh flag was never incorporated at all as Wales was not a kingdom, and anyway a green and white flag with a red dragon in the middle would not fit the colour-scheme of the United Kingdom of Great Britain and Ireland. The Union Flag is not, and never was, the flag of Britain, or England.

The last change in the country's name required no changes to banners, for it became the United Kingdom of Great Britain and Northern Ireland. Even here, there is some confusion. Northern Ireland is not British; it broke away from the rest of Ireland and stayed in the UK after 1921, having the area with a Protestant majority, which happens to be six of the nine counties of the province of Ulster - not the whole of Ulster, but part of it. Three counties of

Ulster are part of the Republic, including Donegal, which contains the northernmost part of Ireland (Kee, 1976).

The other entities, aside from the Republic of Ireland, are the Isle of Man and the Channel Islands (more accurately, the Bailiwicks of Jersey and Guernsey, which do not form a political entity, but which are totally independent of each other). These are not part of Britain or the United Kingdom at all; they are not subject to the Westminster Parliament, to which they send no members or taxation. They are Crown Dependencies, and pay towards defence and foreign policy, which they then leave to the United Kingdom government. All other powers are in the hands of the Tingwall (Man) and the States of Jersey and Guernsey. Their powers over education are limited not for any lack of autonomy or legal control but because of their scale and dependence on England, in effect, for models and example (Bell and Grant, 1977).

The various countries have their own languages. England has English, as do many other countries - the United States, Canada, Australia, New Zealand and the Caribbean and of course Scotland, Wales and Ireland, apart from any other languages that may be current. It is also widely used as a lingua franca in many other countries, including India, Pakistan, Bangladesh, and much of Africa.

Scotland has two native tongues, apart from English. Gaelic is spoken by very few, some 60 thousand according to the last census in Scotland, though in some areas (like the Western Isles) it is spoken by about eighty per cent; the majority, however, live in the Lowlands of Scotland (MacKinnon, 1974 and 1991; Grant, 1985, Grannd, 1984). The Scots language is a Germanic tongue, close to English; like English, it developed from one of the 'Anglo-Saxon' dialects. It created a rich literature, particularly in the 15th and 16th centuries, culminating in the work of Burns in the late 18th century, by which time it was much penetrated and corrupted by English, which had taken over the role of the official and cultivated language (Kay, 1988; Grant, 1987). There are no census figures (unlike for Gaelic) to give us any idea how many speak it. Many believe that they are speaking 'bad English', which many certainly are not, in spite of the repressive attitudes of many schools. It is widely said that Scots is 'just a dialect', but that is ignorant and confuses similarity with dependency; Scots is a language with dialects, but developed from Anglian separately while exchanging vocabulary with English (Ballard and Grant, 1977; McClure, 1986; Kay, 1988). Most Scots can and do speak English of one kind or another, often shading into Scots. Gaelic, of course, is quite different, being a Celtic language, related to Gaelge or Irish.

Welsh is widely spoken in Wales, by about 20 per cent of the population, and is widely used in education, the churches and the media. The actual number of young speakers is rising, but the overall picture is of general decline, largely because of people coming in from the outside. It is stronger in the north and centre than in the urbanised south, and immigration has been weakening the currency of Welsh, especially in the border areas. Most Welsh nowadays speak only English, but notably also with a distinctive accent (Bell and Grant, 1977).

In Northern Ireland, most of the inhabitants are Anglophone. There is a little Irish, but to a very limited extent, since this is associated in the minds of most with the Republic. Actually, there is very little in the Republic either, and an absolutely minuscule presence in Northern Ireland. There is also a small but unknown number of speakers of Ulster Scots, as the Protestants who settled from the time of James VI (who became James I of England, and therefore of Britain, in 1603) were either English or Scots and some of the latter brought their language with them. The English of Northern Ireland is also spoken with a distinctive pronunciation.

The United Kingdom, therefore, is a multinational State, with different cultures and to some extent different languages. No other country is part of England (though Wales was for a while, and in some ways still is, treated like one. Wales has an educational system legally tied up with the English system, while Scotland has a totally autonomous one, except politically.) It is not quite a unitary state, not (so far) federal; it is an accretion over time and thoroughly untidy in that it lacks any theoretical framework to let its citizens decide who they are. The English are, of course, the vast majority, but they are not the whole of the UK, although some of them think they are. If the United Kingdom means anything, it will have to decide what kind of State it is, because it has now become more plural, 'racially' as well as linguistically. This is so not only of the various peoples who make up the Kingdom, but of any more coming into it. It is also true of our European neighbours.

Immigrant-descended groups in the UK: European settlers

There have, of course, been settlers in the UK from almost every imaginable source, but there have been certain patterns since the 19th century which still leave their marks. The first settlers in numbers were the Irish, at a time when the whole of Ireland was still part of the UK. The Great Hunger of the 1840s devastated the West of Ireland and led to massive emigration from which Ireland is only now recovering (Kee, 1976). The potato blight killed thousands from starvation, and millions of others fled for survival - to Glasgow, Liverpool, London, New York, Boston, and many other parts of America, Australia - with marked effects on the populations of these countries. The language was allowed to die, as were some other cultural 'markers', but two were clung to: the Catholic Church, and, more vaguely, an attachment to the values (or at least the rhetoric) of Irish Nationalism, or more minimally, support for radical causes. The Catholic population of Glasgow and the massive support for the Labour Party are partly linked with this. It is also worth remembering that the immigrants were extremely poor, and were willing to work for what they could get. This led to strike-breaking and undercutting, which encouraged anti-Irish and anti-Catholic feeling for many years and which still makes itself felt at times everywhere in the UK. Most of the Irish, however, do not now experience direct discrimination, though memories can be long. Many Irish people tend to come to and fro across the Irish Sea to work in Britain, though this is less obvious with America and Australia, for obvious reasons.

The Italians began coming in the 19th century, at first as workers for the padroni (patrons, bosses), who organised seasonal workers to come to Britain for agricultural or unskilled manual work (Colpi, 1991; Dutto, 1986). The padroni profited and the traffic continued. The earliest (about 1861, according to the Census) came from the North and Centre of Italy, Liguria, Tuscany, Emilia and Lombardy. This continued, but expanded and extended to develop presence in particular trades, like the Lucchesi who virtually constituted the figurinai, the makers of statuettes, or the brickworkers and metalworkers, who settled mostly in Bradford. The attachment of the principle of campanilismo, or devotion to the region, reinforced the tendency for people from one region to favour one area, like Liverpool in the 19th century when most Italians came from Genoa or Naples, Glasgow (mostly from Lucchesi or Ciociari), or Edinburgh in the 1930s (mostly from Frosinone in Lazio). In 1871, when the population had come mostly from Tuscany, Emilia and Fronsinone, the earliest Southerners settled, making up 20 per cent of the total. This tendency for people from particular regions to settle in particular areas militated against the formation of a single Italian-language community, for there was very little mixing of people from different regions; they kept to their own dialects, which was normal in Italy too.

The pattern of occupation began to change as far back as the 1850s, when there was a drastic reduction in the number of beggars and casual labourers, organ-grinders and street-entertainers, and the establishment of regular occupations. Padronismo, which had begun about 1880 to 1890, lasted to some extent until the 1920s, by which time it had virtually died out. One successful development was in catering - restaurants, cafes, fish-and-chip shops, and ice-cream shops, which not only profited but were rescued in 1905 by the invention of the 'ice-cream biscuit' (wafers and cones), which helped the Italians to offer the dish in a more acceptable vehicle than the 'licking-glasses', which were widely-condemned as unhygienic. The Italian population had more or less successfully integrated into British societies, and had also found a gap in the market which they could exploit.

Then came the rise of Mussolini and Fascism, building up to and then being involved in war. Up to 1940, there was already some suspicion, and many Italians were active Fascist supporters. On the outbreak of war, there was much action, official and informal, against them. The London and Glasgow fasci were banned, there were anti-Italian riots in many cities against property and people (being anti-Fascist did not help), and many Italians were interned. Some were shipped off to Canada in the Arandora Star, which was sunk by a torpedo, with great loss of life; many others were sent to Australia, and brutally treated and robbed on the way. Many of the few Italians who were left experienced bullying and harassment. The 1920 Aliens Order was invoked to intern any citizen of an enemy power, regardless of his or her views, including anti-Fascist Italians and anti-Nazi Germans and Austrians. All of the United Kingdom experienced anti-foreign sentiment, some of which is still obvious enough.

It took time, but the United Kingdom did, eventually, recover from this particular episode of anti-Italian hysteria. The main element was time, and by the 1960s, Italian cafes were once again reappearing, but with cappuccino and espresso coffee, the restaurants were deliberately emphasising their Italianness. The trattoria was becoming popular and was edging out the 'greasy spoon' and even the fish-and-chippy. This has a great deal to do with the rise in popularity of foreign package holidays and the greater prosperity in the UK, and the growth in liking for foreign food. Other nationalities have benefited from this too. But the figures of Italian residents in the UK - just under 100,000 in 1981 - are almost certainly wildly inaccurate. The Census counted as Italian only those born in Italy; and the numbers of those who changed their names at the time of the war in the 1940s or after are, of course, not known. This applies to most 'immigrant' groups in the UK.

The early settlement of Europeans did not stop there. There were refugees from Eastern Europe, of Jews from Russia and the Baltic States and Poland. Most of them came in the 19th century, and some settled in identifiable 'Jewish' areas (Krausz, 1972; Kuper, 1981; Wistrich, 1992). Many were in professions associated with wealth - banking, finance, jewellery, some were successful in academia or, later, the media and publishing, but others were too poor to enter banking or lacked the education to enter academia, and had to make do with tailoring or the garment industry. Jews in the UK have assimilated to various degrees; most have let their language fall out of use, whether Yiddish or another, and the extent to which they keep up their religion depends largely on the sect they belong to, all the way from Hasidim to atheist. Some, of course, arrived with nothing, from Lithuania or Latvia, and had to make their own way, some successfully.

Their numbers were added to, slightly, by the Nazi Endlösung. Few escaped, fewer were admitted, but a handful of German and East European Jews, survivors of the Holocaust, did come here. They are mostly elderly by now, naturally, but some of them have children, some of whom still retain Jewish identity, to some extent or another.

There are also other groups of European origin, though most of them came later, after 1950. There are Portuguese (many from Madeira) and a few Spaniards; there are Ukrainians, mostly post-World War II, and Greeks and Turks, mostly in fact Cypriots, dating back in most cases to the 1950s. They seem to reflect the relative proportions of the population of Cyprus and, since Turkey invaded Cyprus, tend to use their ethnic description to indicate their nationality. They overlap considerably with the later arrivals, mentioned in the next section (Krausz, 1976).

Immigrant-descended groups in the UK: The later groups

Most of the Poles came after the Second World War, largely as a direct consequence of the war and the political changes thereafter (Krausz, 1976; Graham, 1989). They have not assumed any particular occupational pattern, but have one special characteristic which makes them particularly vulnerable multiculturally. Because of their military connections, they were nearly all men. Very few marriages took place between two Poles, as most of them have married UK women. The extent to which they have wished or been able to assimilate is partly due to their own cultural identity and the strength with which it is maintained. Some have maintained their Polish identity, and are keen that their children assume it too; for very many others, Polish identity is kept for the father, and the learning of Polish is maintained by complementary classes run by Polish institutes at evening sessions or on Saturday mornings. The attitude of the wives also varies, ranging from complete supportiveness to rejection or embarrassment. Learning Polish can be a burdensome load for a child, especially for one born locally; it is a grammatically complex language, and not one readily used; using it, requires support from the Polish community to provide opportunities for practice, which a father is often not well-placed to supply. The absence of Polish-speaking mothers is a particular problem for UK Poles. How far a woman has taken on Polish identity can sometimes be told by the form of the name. If a mother or daughter ends her name in -ski, she is probably Anglicised; if she ends it in -ska, the feminine form, she is probably Polonised, or trying to be (Krausz, 1976; Graham, 1989).

This range of populations experienced a further change about the 1960s. One of the earliest of the Chinese immigrant groups came to the UK in the 19th century, but remained extremely few (Krausz, 1972). The earliest records go back as 1814, and Hong Kong did not became a colony until 1843, extended in 1860 and again in 1898; it has grown and prospered, and is due to be handed back to China at the expiry of the lease of the New Territories. The original immigrants to the UK were settled seamen, overwhelmingly from the southern provinces of Kwangtung and Fukien, then overwhelmingly from Hong Kong up to the present. Occupational patterns tend, even now, to stress the catering trade, attributable to the growing popularity of Chinese restaurants, in which the Hong Kong Chinese have established a dominance; but by no means all of them are in catering, contrary to widespread belief. The languages are Cantonese and Hakka almost entirely, but it is extremely difficult to find out what they actually speak. Cantonese has social prestige among the Chinese, Hakka has not, and this tends to colour their self-reporting of language. They learn Chinese characters for writing, which are the same for all forms of Chinese, however they pronounce it, as Chinese is essentially ideographic rather than phonetic; but their pronunciation is radically unlike that of Putonghua or 'Mandarin'. Most are also fluent in English, especially the young (Pan, 1990; Chen, 1990). More recently, there have also been settlements of 'Vietnamese', many of whom are actually ethnic Chinese from Vietnam, who are either bilingual or simply of Southern Chinese provenance.

The Afro-Caribbean or West Indian population is descended from slaves who, after liberation, were inclined to emigrate to the United States, but this was stopped in 1952 by the McCarran Act and they switched their attention to the UK at a time when job opportunities were tempting (Krausz, 1972). It seems hard to imagine now, but in the 1950s there was a shortage of labour, especially in jobs that the British were unwilling to do, such as public transport or nursing. Ironically, the earliest immigration of black nurses to service the National Health Service was started by the then Minister of Health, Mr. Enoch Powell, who later became notorious for his public denunciation of the Government's policy in letting immigrants into the country. This agitation fuelled a great deal of racism then and later.

Practically all of the West Indians come from Jamaica, Barbados, Trinidad, Bermuda or Tobago; islands where there is a strong British tradition but serious overcrowding, where almost everyone speaks English (though some in their own way), where most are Christian (usually of the charismatic sects), but where there is unemployment and problems of poverty. There is also, in

Jamaica for example, an acceptance of single parenthood, and education has a low priority. They have had to adapt to the realities of life in contemporary Britain, where there is no longer a surplus of jobs, and where racism reinforces the negative stereotypes. Not surprisingly, many find the social climate hostile, and education does little to improve things, no matter how successfully the children may try to cope with it (Krausz, 1972).

Unlike most 'immigrant' groups, the West Indians are not evenly distributed through the UK. There are very few, for example, in Scotland, and a large concentration in London. This is partly because they have tended to settle in areas with links with their original areas - Jamaicans, Barbadians and so forth. The host population tend to regard them simply as 'West Indians', to whom they are inclined to attach the stereotypes they happen to have come across, be they positive or negative. The West Indians, however, do not think of themselves as simply one undifferentiated group.

The Indian sub-continent has been the source of the most prominent groups to add to the multicultural population in the UK. It is hard to be precise exactly where they all come from, as some of them came before India and Pakistan were created in 1947, and reinforced when the East African Asians were forced to leave in 1967 (Krausz, 1972). The areas they came from varied, but with an emphasis on Gujerat and the Punjab (the latter both for Indians and Pakistanis) and Bengal, particularly since the independence of Bangladesh in 1971. In fact, the Punjab is a major area for emigration to Scotland; both Indians and Pakistanis tend to come from there (Maan, 1992). Gujeratis are more common in England. The Indians, Pakistanis and Bangladeshis are sometimes referred to as 'the Indian community', 'the Pakistani community' or even 'the Asian community'. This is a misnomer, for they are not a community in any real sense; possibly, they constitute several communities, varying hugely in nationality (Indian, Pakistani, Bangladeshi), religion (Hindu, Muslim and Sikh, again with varying degrees of observance and commitment), in language (Gujerati, Punjabi, Bengali, Urdu, Hindi, and some others).

There are other areas of uncertainty as well. The question of prestige, as with the Chinese, applies here too. Take the case of Punjabi, spoken by most of the Asians in Scotland. Among Indians, especially Sikhs, Punjabi is a sacred and literary language, and therefore has high status. Among Pakistanis, it has not, but Urdu has (which most Pakistanis speak to some extent, and some even write Punjabi using the Urdu script, while Sikhs use the Gurmukhi script for Punjabi, and some Hindus use the Devanagari script for Punjabi as all do for Hindi). This is therefore likely to colour the self-perception of Muslims, Hindus or Sikhs about their real or aspired to language, whatever their actual competence in it may be.

Another complication is the passing of time in the host country, for primary immigration has now been slowed down to a trickle whereas children continue to be born. Consequently, a majority of Asian children in the UK have been born there, and grow up speaking English (and sometimes other tongues as well), often with unmistakable local pronunciation. This is true of other 'immigrant' groups in the UK as well; the young were born locally and were schooled locally. Some have visited the home countries, and some have not. Some have learned about the home country from their parents' memories, which may be things as they were but no longer are.

This is particularly obvious among Muslims, but not confined to them. The young people may well meet different sets of values among their contemporaries, and some may find them less limiting than the traditional values of their home. There is a widespread belief that Asian girls will inevitably submit to arranged marriages; some do, but this is by no means guaranteed. This is a western perception, often based upon myth. It is, in fact, a common occasion of generational conflict in some Asian families.

Indeed, there is no uniform pattern for second- or third-generation children and their value-systems. The extent to which they pursue their parents' personal values, language, religion and so forth varies enormously. The use of complementary schools and language and religious schools are the like, and the motivation for using them, are impossible to predict. Surveys have suggested that Muslims are the most likely to set a high value on religion, Sikhs least likely, but one has to be careful (Corner, 1984). Most Muslim children use the ordinary schools, though in Scotland, where there are Catholic schools as part of the public system, many Muslims use these, apparently liking the religious emphasis, even if it is of the wrong kind; but they are still a minority. There is also a high preference among Muslims for single-sex schools, especially for girls, because the atmosphere is more reassuring for parents. The low priority apparently given by Sikhs to religious affairs, according to surveys, may be misleading as well. They are less likely than some Muslims to press for religious instruction or language lessons, but that may be because they prefer to leave that responsibility to the Gurdwara rather than the school.

The occupational patterns of the Indian and Pakistani groups range from unemployment and unskilled work to professional careers, with a high demand for education, especially among the young. Indians and Pakistanis tend to do quite well at school, and the support for education among parents is high (Maan, 1992).

But they have also identified successfully a new slot in the market, as have the Italians and the Chinese. In catering, the first Indian settlers in the UK were seamen, who found that there was a demand for their cooking among their own countrymen, and like the Italians and the Chinese came to dominate a portion of the market. It proved popular, and remains so, partly because it is different and relatively cheap. There is another factor; these groups, like the Greeks (or at least the Cypriots), have noticed that the British have a habit that they have been able to profit by. The Italians, the Chinese, the Indians and Pakistanis and the Cypriots have recognised that not only is their food quite inexpensive, but that the British have developed a taste for it. It has also spread to the specialist as well as the general retail trade. A few other nationalities, Thai for example (though unlike the others there is no historical connection with the UK), have got in on the market, to the great enrichment of the British cuisine.

This has implications for young people in settled groups. There is a widespread and often-repeated belief that employment is taken care of: 'They can always go into the restaurant or shop'. Alas for this comforting belief, most young people have no intention of going into the catering or retail trade if there is anything else available; they may use this as a standby, if necessary, but have their eye on qualifications and a profession just as much as anyone else. Their expectations of the schools are not likely to be markedly different from anyone else's (Corner, 1984).

Nor are they likely to shrug and accept a lower performance from the school system. Some at least will expect the same chances as anyone else to compete with their compatriots, and are as likely as any to react negatively if this is being denied them. We will return to this presently, but have to recognise that any minority groups, whatever their achievements, are all too likely to find that the real problems of growing up are compounded by two factors - being part of a cultural minority, and widespread racism. Growing up is difficult enough without being hindered by the view taken by others on the basis of your appearance or the colour of your skin.

How many 'immigrant' people are there in the UK at present? Estimates range from just over three million to well over five. There are many problems, including one of definition. For one thing, the majority of 'adventitious' populations were born in the UK, and some of them have lost their own language, or have modified their cultural identity to some extent. How do you classify a young woman, born in London, who is working as a lawyer, whose parents came from Jamaica, who speaks English, and who happens to be black? How do you classify a young man, who was born in Birmingham, speaks English, and also Punjabi and Urdu, who is a teacher, and whose parents came from Pakistan? Can these be called assimilated, or have they integrated while keeping their own cultures along with the new one?

It seems that we have an ethnic minority population of several millions all over the UK, with concentrations in several areas - London, Birmingham, Glasgow, Coventry, Bradford, Manchester, Newcastle, Edinburgh and elsewhere. The biggest groups seem to some from the West Indies (though as has been pointed out West Indians themselves do not generally describe themselves as one group), India, Pakistan, Bangladesh, East Africa (or at least Asians or their descendants from Kenya, Tanzania and Uganda), China (especially Hong Kong), Ireland, Italy, Poland, the Ukraine, Cyprus, plus much smaller groups from elsewhere (Mann, 1992; Khan, 1985).

This gives us well over 100 languages, spoken by substantial numbers in the UK. We have to include Gujerati (with Kutchi), Punjabi, Bengali (with Silheti), Hindi, Urdu, Pashto, Polish, Italian, Ukrainian, Portuguese, Greek, Turkish, Cantonese, Hakka, Chinese (Putonghua), and smaller groups speaking Arabic, Thai, Serbian, Croatian, Maltese, Finnish, and of course the West Indian variants of English, Welsh, Gaelic, Scots and Gaelge. All of these languages are to some extent being maintained, and the schools have to give more thought to which ones they can pay attention. The 'native' population is, as has been pointed out, already multicultural to an extent not fully appreciated; and it has to cope with the demands and needs of this extraordinarily diverse mixture of peoples.

The tasks that this population faces the UK with are extremely complex. They have to cope with two areas: the availability of, and access to, the learning of their indigenous languages and other developments in their cultural field, like religion and cultural norms. The other is racism and similar phenomena such as xenophobia or religious bigotry. Both of them have many complications, and a great deal more research is needed in both fields.

Problems: language use and availability

We do not yet know with any certainty either the extent of language maintenance among the various minority groups. We do not even know with any accuracy how many they are, both for reasons of distrust of official-seeming enquiries, and because some of the groups may have ambiguities about their own identities.

There are a great many studies of particular minorities, such as Terri Colpi on the Italians (Colpi, 1991) or Bashir Maan on the Scottish Asians, (Maan, 1992) but very few studies covering several groups. There is The Other Languages of England (1985), by the Linguistic Minorities Project, based in London University (Khan, 1985). It is a good study, but limited by its terms of reference. As the title suggests, it only deals with languages used in England. The others are not dealt with. One has to look carefully to confirm that it does refer to England only, for the authors use the term 'Britain' in the careless way already alluded to. (It is like the ESRC Centre at the University of Coventry for research into ethnic affairs, which has a great deal of impressive documentations, based on England entirely, but designated as a national centre of excellence.) The case studies deal with London, Coventry and Bradford, thoroughly and extensively; there are no studies of Scotland, Wales or Northern Ireland at all, not in this study nor in the ESRC Centre. The picture is seriously distorted in that no data take account of the multicultural nature of the indigenous population. Further, it ignores the languages of the West Indians who, although they all speak English, have a number of varieties in the spoken form.

What we do learn from this study is something of the enormous variety in the degree of language retention or switching, the variations in use between generations, something of language revival or decay, and the use of mother-tongue teaching in the schools or complementary classes. The complexity of the tasks is daunting, as this and other studies makes clear, because English has its claims too.

No one is suggesting that English should be neglected; it is the normal language of the country and the normal medium of communication. Many children still need some help with it, especially linguistic minorities, but not only these. There is little evidence to suggest that bilingualism carries a 'deficit' (Haugen et al., 1981; Khan, 1994).

Secondly, there is a need for the acceptance of the other languages - their own or someone else's - not just for conversational use, but for study if so desired. This could take some time, for one of the reasons for scepticism on the part of some minority parents and pupils is the notion that their language will have no currency in society or in education. It also has to be available to children from other groups. If Punjabi or Chinese are taken only by children from these groups, as has happened in some places, it will be seen as inferior to French, Latin, German, Italian or Spanish. There is no need for any language to have to be in competition with any other, Gaelic with French or Latin with Punjabi; there is more room for languages than is normally accepted in the UK. Some will find it hard to cope with, but is should at least be possible to learn English, a European Union language and another language or so. If the Dutch and the Danes can do it, so can the UK, if our attitude to what is possible undergoes some revision.

A basic problem is a UK suspicion of languages, an assumption that they are extremely difficult and that everyone speaks English anyway. One is reminded of the mother in Yorkshire who withdrew her daughter from school when she discovered that her child had actually learned a few words of Punjabi (she called it 'Pakistani'), and saw this as a threat to 'English civilisation' or even 'Christian civilisation'. Punjabi was not needed for communication, and would get in the way of mastery of English. There are cases of teachers actually forbidding Asian children to speak their own languages to each other, or even mocking them. There is at least one local authority which collects figures of children 'whose first language is not English', and set them out in a way which suggests little understanding of languages or even of geography [see note 3]. This kind of reaction to bilingualism is not, in fairness, universal, but is still far too common. Intercultural education requires a major change in our attitude towards not only pedagogy but the curriculum, for everyone.

This is not to decry the work being done by many local authorities in mother-tongue teaching, in language-development courses, and of course the immense difficulty of the tasks in terms of resources, teachers, materials and books. Much good work is begin done, and in many schools the attitudes of teachers towards ethnic minorities cannot be faulted. But the negative attitudes are still there, parents still sometimes object to attention and resources being diverted. In England and Wales, the 'National Curriculum' concentrates on relatively few subjects, and languages are almost limited to the European Union and, in Wales, Welsh. There are certificated courses in Chinese, Punjabi, Urdu, Gujerati, Polish and so forth, but they are not defined as EU languages, which puts not just these languages in an awkward position, but also casts a question-mark over the position of Latin, Greek and Russian. These are not banned from classroom use, but the degree of prescription marginalises them. In Scotland, where Gaelic figures in examinations, it suffers in some schools from being offered only as an alternative to French and the Scots language does not figure at all, except in some lessons in literature, usually under 'English' (Kay, 1988; McClure, 1986).

It would be ungenerous to discount the work being done for languages in the schools, but it is important that it is realised that the negative attitudes already mentioned survive, and that pressure on resources and time is a general problem, and that the devolution of finance to schools, under the pressure of accountancy, militates against policy initiatives anywhere in the multicultural area. There remains colossal work to be done, and much more research to guide it. Until education is given the resources required to undertake its tasks, unlikely in the present or likely political environment, intercultural education will remain an 'extra' for educational priorities. Where is it now in the 'national' curriculum, or the 5-14 guidelines in Scotland, stated as urgent?

It has to be realised that the study of languages, religions, history and cultures cannot be left as a matter for the minorities. There can be no future for the country if intercultural education is viewed simply as a kind of remedial course. Every child needs to be introduced at least to the cultures (languages and the rest) of the people among whom we live, and spread cultural understanding beyond this as well. Intercultural education has to be for everyone.

Problems: racism and xenophobia

It is widely recognised that one of the problems facing the UK is racism, usually of the white-on-black kind. Every reasonable person should accept that racism is stupid and evil. Quite apart from the social analyses of the irrationality of racial discrimination, its effects on the people who suffer from it and its effects, the social waste and distortion of social living, the potential for racist attitudes and actions to build up trouble and even danger, there is a more fundamental objection to it. It is supremely irrational to discriminate against or to despise people on the grounds of 'race', which usually constitutes a limited number of personal characteristics which our society recognises as making people 'different' in some biologically identifiable way, and to attach to these differences intellectual or moral differences which are held by some to be inborn. There were even 'schools of thought' in the 19th and early 20th centuries, which did a great deal to inform colonial and domestic policy (Grant, 1992; Gould, 1984); we are not alone in this, as we mark and remember the 50th anniversary of the liberation of Auschwitz and celebrate the fall of the apartheid regime in South Africa.

But we are too early to rejoice at the relegation of racism to the history dustbin. We are witnessing murderous 'ethnic cleansing' in Bosnia, the rise of nationalist right-wing groups in Germany, France and Russia, and in Britain too. Few (at any rate publicly) advocate 'scientific' racism, but the publications of Professor Richard Lynn of the University of Ulster are just one indication that attempts to generalise about the mental ability of blacks are not altogether gone (Lynn, 1972).

We must recognise that many members of minorities in the UK experience discrimination, insult, even physical attack. This is bound to militate against their chances of success in education. But it goes far beyond victimisation of West Indians or Pakistanis. Racism is not all that precise in its selection of victims. The victims of racism are often not all that different, as the horrors of the Holocaust should remind us, as should the anti-Italian discrimination of war-time. This is still true today: the millions of victims of genocide in Rwanda were essentially Watutsi being killed by Bahutu, whose main difference is height. Those who have suffered from 'ethnic cleansing' in Bosnia were different in religion and nationality, but were 'racially' identical with the Serbs. The Irish, who have received a great deal of victimisation are, myths notwithstanding, rather hard to distinguish visually. The Turks, who receive such negative treatment from young Germans of the extreme right, are little different in most cases. There are many instances of racist persecution which seem based on no more than a perceived difference; yet the intensity of the hostility is just as intense. This is what happened to the Jews in the Third Reich.

This is why racism and xenophobia are linked. They are very often connected with conspicuous physical characteristics, but need not be so. Essentially, the necessary characteristic is to be perceived as basically different. If it is there conspicuously, the generalisations can follow easily; if not, diagnoses are required, and 'polite' people can have some difficulty before exercising their prejudices (Evans, 1993).

Prejudice is insidious, and not confined to 'races'; women meet it quite often (complete with generalisations), and so can working-class people. Just as Broca tried to justify racial discrimination by arguing from brain-size, he also used the same arguments to justify prejudice against women and the lower classes. Human prejudice is much more widespread then most of us realise; it can distort relationships by intruding curiosity, distaste, dislike, fear, contempt, hatred and so on down the scale to discrimination. Racism has been often defined as 'prejudice plus the power to discriminate'. This is incomplete as a definition, but power certainly reinforces prejudice, as happened until recently in South Africa (Modgil et al., 1986).

The 'outgroup' may seem to be a threat, to the social structure or the economy, to housing or jobs, or may simply be inclined to be there and not subservient, and may actually demand particular attention to language or religious or cultural needs in education or anything else. If the outgroup is obviously different, it is easy to scapegoat its 'members' for all kinds of threat, real or imagined, whether there is any evidence or not. If they are not, it is still possible to generalise about what they are, even just in 'character', even on the basis of imagined threats to the integrity or even the basic survival of the nation or race.

We may as well recognise that some people are lazy, unpleasant, stupid, dirty, noisy, bigoted and anti-social. These can be found in any group. We must also recognise that some people are, by something in their culture, made even more uncongenial. But any generalisations would be valid only for individuals. The point could be made by tossing a coin and asking for guesses on the odds of heads or tails each time; the odds are of course exactly the same. That is why predictions of educational prowess based on race do not work; predictions may be valid for individuals, not for populations. Yet in the past, the race of an individual was often used in just this way, and class and sex as well (Gould, 1984).

So what are the possibilities of using education more effectively to combat racism? Much has been written on 'multicultural education' and 'antiracist education', as if they were essentially opposed. It should be recognised that some multicultural education, known as the 'three Ss' approach (saris, samosas and steel bands) to emphasise the picturesque or quaint is fairly ineffective if it does not attack racism. But surely any multicultural education that does not deal with racism is a contradiction in terms. 'Antiracist' education that starts off, as some kinds do, with an assumption that any white has to be racist by definition will not do either (Ashrif, 1986). There is plenty of evidence that people of any 'race' can be racist, and the victims can be of any 'race' too. As it happens, most people in the UK are 'white', and most of the depressed groups are black or brown; and the whites have most of the power. In this country, also, the majority have experience, if only vicariously, of being dominant, and may react against threats to this with hostility. But to say that whites must be racist, and that blacks must be victims, is to take the whole argument to a deterministic level, beyond the exercise of reason, let alone free will.

If people are open to education in dealing with racism, what can it do? Education has not an impressive record in shaping attitudes when the pressures in society are strong the other way. We can perhaps deal with the myths and superstitions, and we can do something to make children more familiar with other peoples. Familiarisation is possibly a step to international understanding. But international understanding is not a specific against conflict. There is no way in which we can ensure that a child can be made to love his Chinese or Pakistani classmate, but it is possible to get him to treat him right, or at least to avoid kicking him or insulting him. The ultimate justification of multicultural education is a sense of fairness and justice. If need be, there are certain things we can prevent as unacceptable. Some attitudes are to be encouraged, and we know how they should seem. They may not be internalised, but at least the expectations will be known.

But it is an illusion to expect that 'getting to know' other peoples will guarantee that all will then be well. Beyond question, prejudice can be aggravated by ignorance, sometimes in spectacular fashion, but it is easy to forget how fragile knowledge can be. At present, the two communities in

Europe who can be assumed to know each other very well are the Bosnians and Serbs in former Yugoslavia and the Protestants and Catholics in Northern Ireland. They lived next to each other, even with each other, in recent times. In the latter case, they have just stopped killing each other, at least for the time being, and in the former are still at it. In neither case was the great majority involved, but the fear and the hatred exacerbated it and enabled the active forces to continue. 'Knowing' what the others are 'like' was open to distortion in either case, and at least provided an acceptance of hostility. 'Knowing' the other people will never be enough.

All one can say is that it may help, if all forces are pulling together in the same way and at the same time. Education has to be broad-based, working together with social and political policies. Then something might be achieved, but it will be a long and uncertain process. Anti-racist education, or multi-cultural education, cannot possibly work if it is a mere addition to the curriculum. It cannot rely on having one panacea to solve the whole question of racism. It is an extremely complex phenomenon, and will have to have complex solutions in education, and anything else.

The prospects of effective anti-racist or multicultural education (essentially the same thing) are not great, for the forces behind racism are deep-seated in our society, and serious mistakes are bound to be made. This is one reason why some authorities tend to marginalise the whole issue as 'trouble', and concentrate on areas where the population is such as to make it a local issue. But the alternatives are horrifying, as we can learn from the news bulletins from Sarajevo or any of the depressing large number of places where racism or bigotry flourish yet again.

In principle, the issues of racism and language availability and encouragement are closely linked. It is essentially about accepting people's right to be themselves, as themselves, as valuable in their own right, however different they may be in the way they look or the way they speak. It will be a fearsome job, but we have to try.

Concluding note

Two points have to be remembered about intercultural education in the United Kingdom. As has been mentioned already, the UK is already multicultural in composition, ever since it was founded, and the peoples that compose it have their own needs and demands as equals. Secondly, it is part of the European Union, which is also multicultural in its very structure. We all, majorities and minorities alike, have to start thinking more plurally.

If we mean it when we say that the EU is important to us, we have to remember that all of us - not just the Danes and the Luxemborgers, but the Germans and the French and the English - are themselves minorities now. Some are not used to this. We do not know our neighbours well enough, and make few attempts to adjust our way of thinking to the fact that the world has changed.

Most of us expect foreigners to speak the same as we do, even to have the same practices in business or administration, even food and dress. We have been spoiled rotten by the world. We expect everyone to behave as if we were still a powerful people, rich, cultured and civilised, and pay little attention to the evidence of the past, let alone the present. And other peoples - whether abroad or in our midst - can be tolerable, or amusing, or an exasperating nuisance. We do not study our own history enough to know that our perception of our own past is seriously flawed.

A nation which does not know where it has been, cannot know where it is going. A great many of us have been seriously at fault in understanding this for years. The Scots, the Welsh and the Northern Irish are not exempt from this any more than the English, though at least they have some idea who they are, though not a great deal about each other, let alone the people who live in our midst. Scotland, for example, must be the only country where its children learn more of another people's history than they do of their own (Bell and Grant, 1977; ACAS, 1989).

The plurality of the population of the United Kingdom is an actual potential advantage. The non-English nations have several hundred years' experience of being a neglected minority, and the English have a great deal to learn what it is like to being in a similar position in Europe. This can cut both ways. They can learn what it is like to be in this position - the Danes, for example, know this already - and what it is like to be distinctive and maintain self-respect, in language or anything else. The Danes know that too (Rφrdam, 1972). No one imagines that this will be easy, for the urge to make everyone the same is deep-seating. The Scots, Welsh and Irish have long been at the receiving end of this (Bell and Grant, 1977; ACAS, 1987). As a country and as Europeans, we have to learn that we cannot expect everyone to accept that 'British is best' will do any longer, if it ever did; the imperial era is long past. We have to get used to this idea, deep down.

Obviously, there must be limits, but we must start. Children - all children, not just those in areas where there are ethnic minority pupils - will have to study more of their own culture and that of their European neighbours and those of the minority groups within their own society. Languages will have to figure too, and so will history, geography, art, music and literature. It is an enormous task for the whole curriculum, not just for an add-on bit. No one expects that children can learn more than a little. Few will learn more than their own language and perhaps some of another, no one expects expert knowledge of any culture, including their own. But something could be done to introduce children to something of their own cultures and those of others, on which they can build later. We can give them some of the elements, and then encourage the development of lifelong learning, for one childhood will never be enough to progress through all the field of study that will be necessary.

So: children must be taught on a broad base, must be introduced to the skills of reasoning, and must have study available throughout life. That at least will be an advance for intercultural education in the UK, and for education anywhere.

References

Advisory Council for the Arts in Scotland (1989), *Scottish Education: a Declaration of Principle* (Edinburgh, Scottish Centre for Economic and Social Research).

Ashrif, S. (1986), Paper presented to In-Service Teachers' Course , Strathclyde Region, November. (Mimeo).

Bell, R.E. and Grant, N.D.C., (1977), *Patterns of Education in the British Isles* (London, Allan and Unwin).

Carter, B., Green, M. and Sondhi, R, (1993) 'The one difference that 'makes all the difference?': schooling and the politics of identity in the UK.' *European Journal of Intercultural Studies*, Vol. 3, No. 2/3, 1993, pp.81-87.

Chan, A. (1990), *The Chinese Community in Britain* (Glasgow University Department of Education, Glasgow).

Colpi, Terri (1991), *The Italian Factor: the Italian Community in Great Britain* (Edinburgh, Mainstream).

Corner, T.E. (1984), *The TEEM Project* (Glasgow University Education Department).

Dutto, M. (ed.) (1986), *Gli Italiani in Scozia: la loro cultura e la loro lingua* (Consulato Generale d'Italia in Scozia, Edimburgo).

Evans, B. (1953), *The National History of Nonsense* (London, Michael Joseph).

Gould, S.J. (1984), *The Mismeasure of Man* (Harmondsworth, Penguin).

Graham, Y., (1989), *The Polish Community in Scotland* (University of Glasgow M.Ed. thesis).

Grannd, N. (1984), 'A'Ghaidhlig agus forhlam air a'Ghaidhealtachd's a'Galldachd an Alba.' *Gairm*, 127, an Samhradh 1984, 205-211.

Grant, N. (1994) 'Multicultural societies in the European Community - the odd case of Scotland'. *European Journal of Intercultural Studies*, Vol. 5, No. 1, 1994, pp.51-59.

Grant, N.D.C. (1985), 'Gaelic in education: needs and possibilities.' *Modern Languages in Scotland*, 25 January 1985, pp. 141-150.

Grant, N.D.C. (1987), 'The education of linguistic minorities in Scotland. ' *Aspects of Education*, 36, 1987, pp.35-52.

Grant, N.D.C. (1992), 'Scientific' racism - what price objectivity?' *Scottish Educational Review*, Vol. 24, No. 1, May 1992, pp.24-31.

Haugen, E., McClure, J.D. and Thomson, D.S. (eds.), (1981), *Minority Languages Today* (Edinburgh University Press).

Kay, B. (1988), *Scots - The Mither Tongue* (Edinburgh, Mainstream).

Kee, R. (1976), *The Green Flag* (Three volumes), (London, Quartet).

Khan, S. (1994), 'Bilingualism and the curriculum.' *Multicultural Teaching*. Vol. 13, No. 1., Autumn 1994.

Khan, V.S. (ed.) (1985), *The Other Languages of England* (London, Routledge and Kegan Paul).

Krausz, E. (1972), *Ethnic Minorities in Britain* (London, Paladin).

Kuper, L. (1981), *Genocide* (Harmondsworth, Penguin).

Lynn, R. (1972), 'Intelligence in black and white.' *Daily Telegraph*, 20 May 1972, p.14.

Maan, B. (1992), *The New Scots* (Edinburgh, John Donald).

MacKinnon, K. (1974), *The Lion's Tongue* (Inverness, Club Leabhar).

MacKinnon, K. (1991), *Gaelic: a Past and Future Prospect* (Edinburgh, Saltire.)

McClure, J.D. (1986), *Why Scots matter* (Edinburgh, Saltire).

Mirza, Mrs. (1989) former Head Teacher, Glasgow Language Training Centre; personal communication.

Modgil, S. et al., (eds.) (1986), *Multicultural Education: the Interminable Debate* (Barcombe, Falmer).

Pan, Lynn (1990), *Sons of the Yellow Emperor* (London, Mandarin)

Rørdam, T. (1972), *Schools and Education in Denmark* (København, Det Danske Selskab).

Wistrich, R.S. (1992), *Anti-Semitism* (London, Mandarin).

Notes

1. Edward I of England attempted to conquer Scotland at the end of the 13th Century. The Scots defeated his son at the Battle of Bannockburn in 1314, and signed a treaty with his son in 1328. In the meantime, the Scots sent a letter to the Pope in 1320, declaring their right to nationhood and making the point that this did not depend on the King. The Declaration of Arbroath is as famous as the Magna Carta in England, even now. See Prebble, K. (1973), The Lion in the North (Harmondsworth, Penguin) and Ferguson, J. (ed. and commentary), The Declaration of Arbroath 1320 (Edinburgh University Press); also Barrow, G.W.S. (1981) Kingship and Unity: Scotland 1000-1306 (London, Edward Arnold).

2. England is bounded by the Tweed, the Severn, the Channel, the North Sea and the Irish Sea; it is not, therefore, and never has been an island. Britain=England+Scotland+Wales. It is an island, and does not include any of Ireland. The United Kingdom= Britain+Northern Ireland (but not Man, Guernsey or Jersey). That should be clear to all, but seems to evade the understanding of many.

3. Strathclyde Regional Council collects the figures every year, but often lists India, Indian, Pakistani, Punjabi, Hindi and Urdu separately; similarly China and Hong Kong and Cantonese. Gaelic speaking pupils in the Western Isles seem to be excluded, apparently on the grounds that they speak English as well.

11 Intercultural education: the reality in Italy

Attilio Monasta

Introduction

The presence of persons of different cultures and languages within the same community (society, work environment, school, and so on) is a catalyst of the contradictions which lie, usually unknown to most of the people within that community. It is evident that all those who are in a dominant position and who wish to hide those contradictions and preserve the status quo, will consider the 'others' as potential enemies. Vice versa, all those who wish to reveal these contradictions and use them for positive changes to community life and organization, might consider the 'others' as potential or real allies. As far as inter-cultural relations are concerned, I believe that the emphasis on inter-personal relationships and the psychological and sociological instruments for the analysis of a multicultural society is insufficient for understanding and solving the problem. In my opinion, if change is to occur, it is necessary to engage, on the one hand, in political action for a positive change of the society as a whole and, on the other hand, in a wider educational effort, based not only on behavioural and psycho-sociological learning issues, but also on cognitive and political learning issues.

Problems

The selective function of schooling was made evident from the early Sixties as a consequence, if not a conscious instrument, of the class structure of society. It is now almost irrelevant to know whether the 'teacher' has the main responsibility for pupil marginalization and drop-out (see Scuola di Barbiana, Lettera a una professoressa, LEF, Firenze, 1967) or whether the teacher himself is a simple and perhaps unconscious instrument, therefore a victim himself of the selection system of the society. It is a matter of fact that school drop-out is closely related to the social status of the pupil. However, this problem seems to have been forgotten during the last twenty years or so. In many countries, the main problems of school education, according to the largest number of educational studies, seem to be, on the one hand, the lack of job opportunities for teachers as a consequence of the falling birth rate and, on the other, the relationship between school and work in a period of recession and growing unemployment.

It appears to me that the relationship between education and social stratification (a nice way to define the discrimination process against children and youngsters of a lower social status which happens within the school age) is no longer seen as important. However, the inability of education and school to cope with the real needs of the clients and their passive reproduction of social stratification become evident as soon as new and different 'clients' enter the system. The inability of teachers to teach their own national language to their own compatriot pupils becomes evident only when they have to communicate properly with 'foreign' pupils. The rigidity of school organisation (timetable, number of pupils per class, division between disciplines, lack of rooms, lack of equipment, etc.), which prevents teachers from giving more attention to the needs of the less privileged, is not put in question until the moment in which a particular type of 'problem child' comes into the classroom: the representative of another culture.

In the same way, the organisation and division of work within the industrialised society, has not been under discussion for the last twenty years or more and is not even now, in a period of growing unemployment and economically and socially disastrous effects of the industrial policy of the leading western (and far- eastern) countries. What is currently blamed is 'the recession' and 'the crisis', as if they were the causes and not the effects of the economic and financial policies. However we discover again that the wealth of the wealthy is a direct function of the poverty of the poor only when some new poor people, coming from another culture and unexpectedly entering into our society, accept to play in it a role that millions of national workers, all the fathers of the present unemployed working class, used to play some years ago. When migrant workers, once living in very poor countries, because of the exploitation of the world resources by the more industrialized and wealthier countries, now expect to be exploited directly within the system, this system reveals itself for what it is. One could furnish further examples.

I think that it is ideological, a deformation of analysis, to believe that migrants and migrations are the real problem: they are the catalyst of our problems. Their presence within our society reveals the main problems which existed before and without their arrival. Moreover, they reveal what many of us, even progressive and open-minded, find hard to understand, that the wealth of the so-called developed world would not be possible without the exploitation, sometimes the starvation, of the great majority of human beings. This is why 'they' are so disturbing. The Italian case could be taken as a paradigm for this type of analysis. When Italy had to 'export' a large number of Italian migrants to other countries, the system was not questioned (it was even forbidden to question it during the fascist regime); or when large internal migrations made millions of southern Italians go North in search of jobs, and live (as the 'extra-community' workers of today) 8 persons to a room in the poor periphery of Milan, the system was not questioned. The Unions concentrated their struggle on better salaries and an improvement in the working environment. A real movement for change was not undertaken until the late Sixties and early Seventies, and this was defeated by terrorism and murder. Already in the late Seventies, the progressive forces of society led Italian people to defend and sustain democracy, rather than to change it because of the terrorist strategy. It is now evident that the simple defence of a democratic system ended it, rather than reinforced it.

Recent racist attacks against migrant workers in Italy (as elsewhere in Europe) are now considered to be related to unemployment, marginalization and 'boredom' of Italian youngsters. However, a student of mine wisely put forward the following observation: "Do you really believe, Professor, that young people beat to death a black man, just because they are bored, because they have nothing else to do?" We seem to forget that the philosophy of competition and 'do it yourself', on which the present cultural hegemony within the industrialised world is based, is 'educating' people for violence. We should perhaps be more surprised that these cases are, for the moment, relatively few in number in our society.

The same can also be said about school. Italy is the only country in the world that does not have professional preparation of its teachers. Probably the teachers of other countries, though prepared in Colleges, Écoles Normales or Pädagogische Hochschulen, are equally unable to solve the problems of intercultural education. However, the absolutely original situation, of lack of educational studies for teachers in Italy, becomes evident only when they have to teach a Chinese child and they are astonished that he or she does not understand them. Some interesting studies (Formosa, 1992) undertaken in schools in Prato (the industrial area west of Florence) have shown that the traditional form of summative assessment, which is already discriminatory against a significant section of Italian pupils, prevents the teacher even from assessing the knowledge and abilities of Chinese pupils. It was enough, during the experiment, to change the form of assessment to reveal that the average performance of the Chinese child was within the norm and sometimes better than the class average. This research not only revealed that Chinese children are no 'different' in learning, but also that the teachers in question lacked essential competences, since they were cognisant only of the 'social' situation of the pupils and unable to check their 'cognitive' development. I wonder how many Italian children have suffered equally because of the same lack of preparation of the teacher which only the Chinese catalyst has revealed.

Moreover, the intercultural challenge calls into question an entire education system based on the positive qualities of Italian teacher competence: personal commitment, creativity, the resistance to scientific approaches, standardization and routine. It is not by chance or by political ignorance that Italy is still the only country in the world that does not provide professional and educational preparation for its teachers. The alliance between neo-idealistic philosophy and catholic tradition, which also absorbed and Italianized the post-Deweyian activism from the Fifties, had and still has the effect of marginalizing any scientific approach to education and it has put the emphasis on inter-personal relationships, moral values, family centred education, charitable ways of problem solving. I am not saying that these paradigms should be considered as a negative educational approach; on the contrary, wherever education and teacher competence lack them the full education system is a simple institutional machine of ignorance and, again, marginalisation (Illich, 1973). The negative aspects of the Italian educational tradition are that these paradigms have been, and still are, used to deny any scientific approach and to prevent any professional preparation of teachers. There is also the ideological use of these paradigms, i.e. when they are used to hide the political and economical hegemony of a large part of the organization of Italian culture which has profited from them.

Realities

As far as this approach is taken into account, the main instrument for understanding the problem and for the development of a reasonable educational strategy is a political one, in the proper sense that 'politics' can be used: power - where the power lies, who has the decision making power, how power for change can be correctly acquired and used, how much and in what ways is education power, power for whom, etc. It would be naive to think that all those whose power is threatened by the simple revelation of the contradictions existing within their society, identified by the growing presence of different cultures and national identities, should not consider this growth dangerous and the 'others' as potential enemies. They will try to divide and split the power of different social and ethnic groups, putting one against the other, the white working class against the coloured workers, the working people of any colour against the unemployed, one ethnic minority against another, the poor of one single ethnic group against the wealthy (or even the less poor) of the same group, and so on.

The present trend in intercultural studies seems to presume that multiethnic societies are societies at risk and conflicts arise more easily within these types of societies rather than within the monocultural ones. Some scholars (Gundara, 1993) are aware that the so-called monocultural societies are artificial constructions, as are the effect of domination, destruction or at least marginalisation of the variety of cultures, languages and traditions that always characterize any social community. However, it seems to me that the origin of conflict is found by many within the psychological, social and anthropological paradigms of interpersonal relations. Poverty and marginalisation generate frustration, and frustration generates aggression. National identity is not only an instrument to define yourself within your community, but is also an instrument to define yourself as different from the 'others', to defend yourself from the others and against the others. History seems to be full of examples of ethnic conflicts, national conflicts, religious conflicts.

Even if it is hard to question this kind of argument, mostly for the early stages of history or for the less complex societies and inter-national relations, I would rather question "who writes history books"? The story we know is that which has been told by the 'rulers' and by the intellectuals who are 'related' to them. The most recent developments in inter-national relations show clearly that multiethnic societies, which were able to live in peace for generations, have been forced to divide and then (sometimes against their local history and tradition) to attack and destroy each other, for the sake of the economic and political interest of powers which the combatants do not even know.

If wars were fought between traditional armies, following 'gentlemanly' rules, drawing fronts, strategies and tactics on maps, people could believe in history books. But when war is used to kill babies, to rape women, to destroy day by day life and reduce anybody to the original condition of an animal (either a prey or a predator), it is evident that national fights and national identities are a banal pretext, are only ideological tools to hide the real history which is going on at the expense of people. And it is false to compare the apparent madness of the present war in the Balkans with the inter-ethnic aggression of 'these people' throughout history, and even with the ancestral tribal wars, where the club, the sword and the knife were in use. The cost of only one machine gun is higher than all the knives and clubs we could collect in the whole region. The modern organisation of war is qualitatively different from the usual human conflicts. Modern arms are not the instruments of war; they are one of the causes of the wars. The budget of the international arms trade is not the effect of conflicts, but rather the cause of them. And war is a great pedagogical instrument to persuade people that their lives are in danger if they do not fight against the 'others'. Modern war is not irrational. We have to understand the different rationality of modern wars if we want to prevent them before they start, since it is always too late to try and stop them.

I do not know the real reasons for the social and international conflicts of centuries ago. But I feel that present conflicts have almost nothing to do with inter-personal and inter-ethnic relations. They rather use, of course, the human 'aggression' (after having stimulated and nursed it with an intelligent and rational 'educational' policy) for political and economic goals which will remain hidden.

Instruments for positive change

I turn now to consider how change can be initiated within the multicultural society. The educational strategy which might be derived from the above analysis is based on a wider concept of education. Educational sciences have to include the analysis of the mechanism for consent and reproduction of consent which is used not only (and not mainly) within school education. Most of the political decisions, almost the entire world of media communication and, in general, the organisation and diffusion of 'culture', should be the object of attention and analysis as educational instruments. Therefore the role of intellectuals should be the centre of our analysis and the main field of the educational strategy within a multicultural society. Intellectuals are the producers of ideological or critical thought. As far as the intellectuals do not take part in favour of the oppressed (Said, 1993), there is little chance of creating a multicultural society with any human dimension, any acceptable pattern. Intellectuals, however, are not only the so-called traditional intellectuals (scientists, scholars, writers, opinion makers, journalists, teachers, etc.); they are also found among the leading officials of political parties, professional associations, unions and employers associations, etc. They are all producers and vehicles of education, which could frequently mean the ideological use of information and culture.

As far as school education is concerned, I feel that most of the emphasis of present intercultural education, and of education for peace, is placed upon the socio-affective and behavioural learning issues. This approach is based on the concept that collaborative education leads children to understand each other, to accept and help each other. The development of positive inter-personal relations is meant to educate children to become peaceful adults, open minded persons, ready to understand and accept other adults within society.

Whilst I feel that this approach is important and is necessary I strongly believe that it is not in itself sufficient. It will not prevent the destruction by those in power of these efforts to make children and adults more co-operative and understanding of each other. This disruption is achieved through political decisions, using cultural messages intentionally designed to inspire feelings of aggression and to cause the animality of human beings to swell and explode. Within our society, the psychological strength of the individual is a thin paper barrier against the perverse rationality of power.

Beside the socio-affective and inter-personal relational learning, school education needs to achieve clear, strong and new cognitive and intellectual issues. It must enable people gradually and from childhood to come to know, understand and detect early enough the political, economic and cultural signals of exploitation, discrimination, organized violence and conflicts. The study of history should be one of the main concerns of school; though history and history books have to be substantially revised, to promote the point of view of intercultural education. Everybody knows that the study of history in schools, even within the most progressive approach, is heavily eurocentric, nationalistic, if not imperialistic. The language used within history books is heavily ideological and usually racist: the equation between people and their rulers is generalized ("the Germans declared war ..."). History for the youngest pupil, should start from the present and look to the recent past for understanding the present. Ancient history for children is either non- understandable or mythological. The main educational issue of school should be critical thought (if not even 'diffident' and 'inquisitive' thought). Any cognitive issue can be either ideological or critical, according to whether or not we educate ourselves to ask these questions: "who said that?", "when and why this has been said, written, discovered?". Intercultural education, in my opinion, starts from the critical questioning of the ideological use of culture and, therefore, from the questioning of the legitimacy of our own culture.

References

Formosa S. (1992) *La variabile valutazione in situazione scolastica multiculturale,* unpublished dissertation, Università degli Studi di Firenze.

Gundara J. S. (1993) 'Multiculturalità, secolarizzazione e educazione', in Tassinari G. et al. (eds) *Scuola e società multiculturale,* (Firenze, La Nuova).

Illich I. (1973) *Deschooling Society,* (New York, Harper and Row).

Said E. (1993) *Culture and Imperialism* (London, Chatto and Windus).

Part IV

Interculturalism, curriculum and teacher education

12 Intercultural education in Portugal
Ana Paula Cordeiro

Abstract

The concept of intercultural education is relatively recent in Portugal. Many political decision makers, experts, researchers, academics and other professionals within the education sector, are still not completely aware of the importance of this educational strategy.

In this vein, this study pursues a double objective: to put into context the emergence of intercultural education and ascertain its state of development in this country. This is achieved through a first part that examines the social and political context which lends support to this educational strategy and a second part in which the political measures taken are analysed together with the action taken to put them into effect.

Section I

The social context of emergence

The intensification and diversification of immigration flows

One of the factors most closely connected with the recent advancement of intercultural education in Portugal has been, without doubt, the *broadening of the multicultural nature of Portuguese society as a result of varying waves of immigration that have occurred since the mid-seventies.*

The geographical positioning of the area now constituting the Portuguese state has always been favourable to the interaction and settlement of different peoples. In reality the existence of various ethnic groups in the national territory dates back to the pre-Christian era, and indeed has continued throughout the centuries. The historical evidence of this reality is to be found in the presence of Iberians, Lusitanians and Phoenicians, Celts, Visigoths and Moors and, in much later times, Jews, Gypsies, Africans and Europeans.

However, despite the fact that the population residing within Portuguese territory has long shown a multi-ethnic nature, the cultural heterogeneity of the population has only become significant in Portugal in the last decades of this century.

Various economic and political events at a national and international level have given rise to a new dynamic within migratory movements towards Portugal. These have had profound repercussions on its demographic make-up and structure.

Among such events is the world economic crisis resulting from the OPEC oil crisis that strongly affected the European economy. It caused the collapse of many industrial organisations and thus brought about a restriction in employment opportunities, which had been available in the more developed northern European countries, to the large numbers of people in the South. Such occurrences resulted in a significant decline in immigration in these countries as well as the return of significant numbers of emigrants to their respective countries of origin.

Such a situation came to be seen in Portugal, traditionally a country with large numbers of emigrants. In reality, the state of social and economic under-development that the country experienced until the middle of this century included a number of 'push' factors (namely low employment and unemployment, poverty and various shortfalls in the areas of health, education and social security provision). This led to the abandonment of village birthplaces, especially in those regions considered more backward from the point of view of access to goods and services. Because of this, many Portuguese, motivated primarily by economic reasons, have shown a strong propensity to leave the country in search of better living conditions. Proof of this are the 4,500,000 Portuguese currently scattered around the world.

Although Portuguese emigration had been, until the middle of this century, essentially to overseas destinations - above all centred on Brazil and the United States - from this point onward it was directed predominantly towards the interior of Western Europe, with France and Germany as the main destinations.

Faced with serious economic crises from the beginning of the seventies, these countries took measures to restrict the entry of foreigners and give them incentives to return to their respective countries of origin. This led to an increase of the number of *emigrants returning to Portugal*, which until then had been insignificant. The Population Census of 1981 reveals that since 1973, 200,000 emigrants had returned to Portugal, and that half of them came from France.

However, the change of régime in Portugal (1974) and the consequent swift decolonisation process which followed played a crucial role in the process of intensifying the cultural heterogeneity of the population living in Portugal.

The civil instability in the newly independent African states led to the flight of many refugees and the *repatriation* of more than 500,000 Portuguese who, until then, had been living in the former overseas colonies. If 60% of the returning nationals had been born in Portugal, the remainder, including their descendants and at the same time people with Portuguese nationality but of African birth and descent, brought with them manifest and deep-rooted cultural differences.

For their part, the increasing number of foreign citizens arriving in Portugal from the beginning of the eighties enjoying the status of *immigrants*, *asylum seekers* and *refugees* added even more to the heterogeneous nature of the society. We are talking about individuals of very diverse geographical and cultural origins, coming from extremely dissimilar social and economic situations.

Among the foreign citizens with permission to live in Portugal, the nationals of the Portuguese-speaking African nations - Cape Verde, Angola, Mozambique, Guinea Bissau and São Tomé e Principe - have clear prominence.

The struggle for power which unleashed civil war in many independent African countries and the difficulties relating to the state of social and economic underdevelopment that they had been kept in, led to thousands of people leaving their places of origin.

Given the affinities resulting from centuries of common history, many people sought stability and basic living conditions for survival in the ex-colonial power.

In a different legal situation, but also worth mentioning, are the groups of people coming from East Timor and Macao.

However, amongst the foreigners legally based in the country, the Europeans also show a high profile. The underlying reasons for their presence appear to be connected to the social and economic situation resulting from the consolidation of Portuguese democracy which attracted new foreign investment, channelled principally into tourism, commerce, agriculture and services.

Of the total number of foreigners of EU origin, citizens from Great Britain and Spain account for the largest percentage. Such a state of affairs is explained, in the British case by centuries-old strong commercial relations, and in the Spanish case by physical proximity. The flow of immigrants from France, Italy and Germany is also important and shows significant increases.

In the overall picture of foreigners who have legal immigrant status in Portugal, the numerical weight of those from the American continent is worthy of note as well. Of this group, the Brazilians stand out without doubt as they constitute, in the totality of foreigners, the second largest nationality in numerical terms. The growth observed in this current of immigration is connected, among other reasons, with the existence of cultural affinities, namely linguistic ones. In addition, there is the social, economic and political instability that has affected Brazil for some time.

The new geopolitical composition of Europe has contributed in the same way to the relocation of foreigners in Portugal. The country has become, like many others, a host for citizens from Eastern Europe who have fled the newly independent states of that region due to the problems and difficulties experienced there after the break up of the old political régimes.

In relation to the total number of legal foreign residents - according to the Foreigners and Frontiers Service 131,593 in 1993, close to 2% of the resident population - those enjoying the status of refugee or asylum seekers have lately shown a substantial increase as well as a growing diversity of origin. The most important groups in numerical terms are nationals from Zaire, Romania and Angola.

Inequality and social instability

Linked with the *confluence of the migratory flows* is a *growing complexity in social relations*. The *coexistence of diversified cultural communities* in Portugal has led to the increasing need to learn how to deal with and manage this diversity, and consequently to the interest for intercultural education.

The settlement of migrant communities over a period of general economic crisis has drawn attention to *inequality* and *social exclusion*, and highlighted the *intensification of intolerance, xenophobia and racism*.

Particularly affected by these phenomena are immigrants from Portugal's ex-colonies. They tend to be young coloured people with little formal education. As they do not hold the necessary professional qualifications to equip them for lives in urban industrial societies, these immigrants are tied down to badly-paid jobs which will deter their social integration. Thus, many of them face serious problems in such areas as employment, housing, education, health care, social security and also in the area of social relations.

As they are not entitled to council housing or reduced mortgages to help them buy their own homes, the majority of these immigrants live in illegal, squalid shanty towns on the outskirts of big cities, especially around Lisbon. Here, poverty, racial problems and social ostracism can be easily seen. The density of these immigrant communities highlights the social and economical differences between them and the developed society around them, widening the *understanding gap* and increasing the risk of *social instability.*

Increased awareness on the part of both the state and citizens that these situations of social inequality may disturb the peace and social balance, and that societies now and in the future will become more and more multicultural in character are a condition *sine qua non* for the justification and implementation of intercultural education.

The new school reality

As school is society in microcosm, such things as the diversification of culture, social inequality, and intolerance are reflected in the school setting, and this has underlined the urgent need to take measures to implement intercultural policies. The school is becoming a multicultural place and this is due mainly to two factors: the establishment of education as a social right available to all citizens, compulsory and free at the basic level, and the arrival of students, of Portuguese nationality or not, of different cultures, languages and religions, factors that influence their behaviour, and their pace and style of learning.

Some of these are young or adolescent children of ex-emigrants or ex-residents of the former colonies that returned with their parents to Portugal. As they were born and raised outside continental Portugal, or lived abroad part of their lives, they have a different way of thinking and different cultural attitudes which were conditioned by the societies where they received their formative influences.

Others are also young or adolescent children of immigrants, refugees of asylum seekers who either came with their parents to Portugal, or joined them later on, or were already born here.

The cultural specificity of these students is often linked to learning difficulties which has an adverse effect on their school performance. They are also often connected to discriminatory attitudes, intolerance, xenophobia and racism.

The political context of emergence

The *establishment* in April 1974 of a *democratic political régime* in Portugal and the legal enshrining of human rights were two of the basic political tenets to ensure intercultural education in Portugal. From this point onwards, the *Constitution of the Portuguese Republic* establishes *'Nobody could be*

171

privileged, beneficed, prejudiced, deprived of any right or exempt from any duty attending ancestry, sex, race, language, territory of origin, political and ideological beliefs, instruction, economic situation and social condition.' (article 13, n°2).

As far as rights and duties are concerned, the Constitution confers equal treatment to national and foreign citizens with the exception of the political rights, the exercise of non-technical public functions, and the rights and duties that by law are exclusively reserved to the Portuguese.

Nevertheless, the Constitution considers the possibility of giving foreigners from countries with Portuguese as the official language a special status through the signature of international conventions in a reciprocal arrangement (article 15, n°3).

The definition of the rights of foreigners and ethnic minorities in the supreme Portuguese law had very important repercussions at the sectorial legislation level. However, the basic principles of democracy, participation and equal opportunities were introduced in the area of education through the *Education System Basic Law (LBSE)* in 1986: 'Education must foster a spirit of democracy in which other people and their ideas are respected. There must be open dialogue and free exchange of opinions (...)' (article 2, n°5.)

LBSE is the base of the general reform of the education system and it stipulates 'An education system is organised to ensure the right to be different, in which respect for individual people and projects is enshrined, and different ideas and cultures are given due consideration and value.'

The growing number of burgeoning social visibility of the immigrant phenomenon as well as the ripening of democratic culture has caused the involvement of immigrant associations, political parties, government and non-government associations in questions related to immigrants and ethnic minorities. These groups have served to put pressure on the State to use its official power and take measures to solve - directly or indirectly - the problems these minorities were facing, among which, education is especially important.

In addition to national factors, international ones have also influenced the carrying out of action in the field of intercultural education. One of the more important of the latter factors was Portugal's joining the European Community in 1986. In her capacity as a member state of the *European Union*, Portugal has had to adopt recommendations and directives concerning intercultural education and connected issues.

Section II

Political measures and educational practices

Government initiatives

Both individually and collectively, teachers, educators and community agents have expressed to the governmental entities their concern over the implications that cultural diversity has in schools. They have pressed for answers which will be meaningful to today's educational environment.

Project "Schooling in the intercultural dimension"/PEDI It is in this context that in 1990 various departments of the Ministry of Education promoted PEDI, an innovative project in the field of the schooling of cultural minority groups in Portugal.

The PEDI project was aimed at a limited target group of primary schools that were attended predominantly by children of Gypsy and African origin and pursued the following objectives:

- to reverse the ethnocentrism in school culture and legitimate the presence of minority cultures in the school;
- to try new learning and teaching strategies that allow for cultural continuity between the school and the family;
- to develop speaking and writing skills in the pupils;
- to abolish prejudice and to develop positive discrimination strategies;
- to create the psycho-pedagogical conditions to permit equality of opportunity to both access and success at school.

As it is recognised that teachers have a determining role in attaining these objectives, this project is predominantly geared towards the in-service training of those teaching in these schools.

During the training programme that they receive, the teachers are asked to reflect on the difficulties that they face in educational practice, to discuss methodologies, to exchange experiences, to pilot alternative teaching methods and to adapt teaching materials and evaluate progress.

Prominent among innovative teaching strategies applied are:

- the regular use of testimonial references arising from the pupil's socio-cultural background;

- the valuing and positive discrimination of the pupil and his social experiences as a building block for the acquisition of new knowledge;
- the encouragement of consciousness-raising exercises in the area of reading and writing;
- the creating and adapting of teaching materials.

The systematic evaluation of this project points to the following results in relation to:

The pupils:
- better motivation and increased spontaneous participation in the lesson and school life;
- enhanced and more rapidly acquired knowledge in the areas of reading and writing and consequently a significant improvement in levels of oral and written communication;
- better integration into the school system and consequent higher levels of sociability;
- a reduction in absenteeism;
- more satisfactory school results.

The school:
- an improvement in the socio-affective atmosphere between members of the school community;
- an improvement in the performance of the institution.

The teachers
- an incentive to undertake research;
- the acquisition of new knowledge and techniques;
- active and direct participation in change;
- an increase in value of their roles as well as better professional performance;
- a change in attitudes and expectations towards academic success.

Several publications based on the teaching methodologies piloted in the project were issued. They portray the cultural practices of the various groups involved and also incorporate methods for the development of educational practices.

The creation of SCOPREM SCOPREM (The Secretariat for Co-ordination of Intercultural Educational Programmes) was created within the Ministry of Education in 1991, a short time after the launching of the project previously described. This project brought together experts and representatives from the various departments and associations in the education sector.

This is a body specifically dedicated to the handling of educational considerations resulting from multiculturalism in Portugal. In the light of this, it was given the following responsibilities: '(...) to coordinate, encourage, and promote - within the education system - programmes and measures which gear education towards the values of co-existance, tolerance, solidarity and dialogue between peoples, races and cultures.'

SCOPREM has carried out a wide range of measures, among them gathering statistics, launching and supporting various educational projects of an intercultural nature, organising seminars and conferences on intercultural education and associated matters and publishing various titles.

Description of the universe and schooling situation of cultural minority groups

Among the measures carried out by SCOPREM, the annual gathering of statistics from basic education schools (attended by children aged between 6 and 14), first started in the academic year of 1990/1991, is especially important. The aim is to account for and locate minority cultural groups and their pass, fail and truancy rates. This work is of great importance for the setting up of subsequent educational projects related to the school population and the choices which educational reform is facing.

With the goal of identifying children of cultural minority groups, several categories were created based on the ancestry of pupils' parents: Cape Verde, Guinea Bissau, São Tomé e Principe, Angola, Mozambique, India and Pakistan, Macao, East Timor, Gypsies, Ex-Emigrants, Brazil, European Community, 'Others'.

The details which are shown up by this report reveal an increasing number of the descendants of minority cultural groups, contrasting with the overall regular decrease of the school population. In the academic year of 1992/1993 the pupils that belonged to cultural minority groups represented 8% of school population, but the dimension of each group varied a lot.

Ex-emigrants were the most representative category directly linked to the importance of emigration in the Portuguese population movements. The Capeverdians also made up a sizeable element, mainly in the first years of this teaching level. The categories of Angola and Mozambique were less important in numerical terms and they were best represented in the last years of basic schooling.

In decreasing order appeared the European Community category followed by the Brazilians but with a great difference between the two. Timor and Macao had an insignificant percentage. The Gypsies had a very high numerical representation in the first years but their number gradually decreased towards the later years.

The same survey revealed the geographical distribution of this population is asymmetrical, denoting large areas of concentration, mainly in Lisbon and Setúbal, which allows measures to be taken in the specific schools requiring intervention.

The average pass rate of minority cultural groups is lower than those of the school population overall, although the gap is being closed year by year. On the other hand, the fail and truancy rates are higher. It should be pointed out that the success rate at school varies greatly from group to group.

Approval of an inter-ministerial programme　　In April 1993 the then government approved the implementation of a programme combining measures for employment, professional training, education and social action. These sought to '(...) avoid situations of social exclusion and go towards creating suitable conditions to ensure immigrants and ethnic minorities will be integrated in to the Portuguese community.'

Regarding education in specific terms, the government promised to:

- Improve the measures underway in schools coming under the umbrella of the project;
- Promote intercultural education;
- Promote integration in schools and into the community of young people belonging to ethnic minority groups, seeking to provide equal opportunities;
- Foster the creation of peaceful and constructive ties between the school and the community.

This Ministerial resolution was the basis for the project described below.

The intercultural education project　　The Intercultural Educational Project was set up in the 1993/1994 academic year. It sets out to promote equal access to education, to value different cultures and to enshrine the right to be different.

This project covers a limited number of basic education schools in the cities of Lisbon and Porto and in the Algarve region, at which the majority of the pupils are from ethnic minorities. These schools are situated in socially disadvantaged areas and were considered priorities as their students had low pass rates and serious problems as far as social relations were concerned. The aims of the project are as follows:

- to adapt pedagogical practices to best suit the students and raise their pass rates.
- to provide remedial help for repeatedly failing students;
- to create and develop joint strategies among the school/family/ community, with each party playing an active role in the educational process;
- to develop workable schemes in intercultural educational intervention which can be used again and again in similar situations.

The project centres around the in-service training of teachers and other education agents, trying to increase and specialise their respective academic and professional qualifications.

Above all, the project places emphasis on working with the family and the community, seeking to involve them more and more in the educational process and school life.

The first phase of this project ended in the 1994/1995 academic year, with very positive results. These were especially at the level of material support and emotional and psychological support offered by the schools to the most needy students. The second phase, covering a larger number of schools, is currently in progress.

The action of NGOs

Society as a whole has shown interest in the area of intercultural education. Various non-profit associations and institutions were especially created for the purpose. Some of those already existing were involved in the development of new activities related to intercultural education. Just as an example we will refer to a few.

Regarding professional associations, we must mention the Teacher's Association for Intercultural Education/APEI. Their aim is to '(...) promote programmes and schemes which see education as concerned with the co-existence, tolerance, dialogue and solidarity between different people, ethnic groups and cultures.'

The work of this Association is really to do with training teachers, perfecting their professional and educational competence in the area of intercultural education. APEI also seeks to produce didactic material to support the practice of intercultural education, and works in organising, managing and supporting intervention projects in this sphere.

The *SOS Racism Movement* (which seeks to support anti-racist and anti-xenophobic activities) is also interested in intercultural education, and has shown its support in an innovative way.

At the beginning of the 1993/94 academic year, they promoted the 'Multicoloured School' project in 50 primary and secondary schools around Lisbon and the suburbs. This project is aimed at:

- raising awareness in schools to adopt attitudes of respect and open-mindedness to different cultures;
- denouncing discriminatory attitudes and situations;
- fostering the adoption of an universal perspective of solidarity and international co-operation;
- ensuring the right to different experiences and cultures;
- stimulating multicultural relations and the wish to know other cultures.

The methodology used to reach these objectives includes the use of audio-visual materials and the production in a multicultural and anti-racist perspective of pedagogical cards linked to the various academic subjects.

OIKOS, an institution linked to the *Movement for International Solidarity Between Peoples* is very concerned with the area of education to develop its beliefs and is thus working within the field of intercultural education.

OIKOS, always with the aim of promoting acceptance, understanding and interaction between different cultures, has organised conferences, exhibitions, cultural programmes and the production of teaching material to back up the various school disciplines. These have frequently taken the form of multimedia blocks.

Conclusions

In Portugal the focus on intercultural education is directly connected to the awareness of society's multicultural structure, to the respect for the democratic principles of equal opportunities and pluralism, and to an official social policy aiming at the integration of minorities.

However, although the legal framework for implementation is in place, the practical state of development of the various strategies for putting it into practice is at a very incipient stage and drastically reduced in scope. The following facts will prove this statement:

- the debate about intercultural education is basically theoretical and takes place mainly at scientific meetings;
- the amount of written material on the subject is very limited;
- research in this field has little support;
- the intercultural education strategy is rarely put into practice as the few existing projects are still at an experimental stage;
- initial and in-service teacher training does not include intercultural education; only those directly involved in the existing projects receive some kind of intercultural training;
- there is no properly thought-out multicultural approach to apply to the various academic disciplines and for this reason the work done is fragmentary;
- the multicultural perspective does not run all the way through the various levels of the education system. As well as being small-scale and superficial, the measures so far carried out are almost all at the level of didactic material, school disciplines and teacher training. Such important questions as the school administration and management, together with assessment are not seen in an intercultural perspective.

References

Carlos, Leonor Palma (1993), Imigração e Integração, in *Emigração, Imigração em Portugal*. Actas do Colóquio Internacional sobre Emigração e Imigração em Portugal, Séculos XIX e XX, Lisboa, Fragmentos, pp. 415-421.

Castro, Paula; Freitas, Maria João (1991), *Contributos para o Estudo de Grupos Étnicos Residentes na Cidade de Lisboa*, Lisboa, LNEC.

Castro, Paula (1993); *Vale do Areeiro: Reflexões acerca de Uma Realidade Multiétnica*, in "Estruturas Sociais e Desenvolvimento". Actas do II Congresso Português de Sociologia, vol.1, Associação Portuguesa de Sociologia, Fragmentos, (Estudos).

Cortesão, Luisa; Pacheco, Natércia Alves, (1991). *O Conceito de Educasção Intercultural: Interculturalismo e Realidade Portuguesa,* "Inovação", vol.4 (2-3), Lisboa, IIE., pp.33-44.

Costa, A. Bruto da; et al (1991). *Minorias Étnicas Pobres em Lisboa,* Lisboa, CML.

Entreculturas Secretariado *"Diálogo Entreculturas"*, Lisboa, Secretariado Entreculturas, (nos 1-8).

Entreculturas (1993), *Base de Dados Entreculturas,* Lisboa, Entreculturas.

Esteves, Maria do Céu (org.), (1991) *Portugal, Pais de Imigração,* Lisboa, IED.

França, Luis de (coord) (1992, *A Comunidade Caboverdiana em Portugal,* Lisboa, IED.

Guerra, Isabel, (1993) *A Educação Multicultural: em Busca de Novos Caminhos,* "Diálogo Entreculturas", Lisboa, Secretariado Entreculturas (5), pp.2 e 4.

Guerra, Isabel, (1993) *Contexto e Engquadramento do Projecto de Educação Multicultural,* "Forma", Lisboa, Ministério da Educação, pp.10-13.

Ministério da Educação, Multiculturalismo (1993), "Forma", Lisboa, DGEBS.

Ministério da Educação, *Projecto "A Escola na Dimensão Intercultural"* Lisboa sn. (policopiado).

Ministério da Educação,(1992) *Insucesso e Abandono Escolar,* Lisboa, GEP, (Biblioteca de Apoio à Reforma do Sistema Educativo).

Perista, Heloisa, Pimenta, Manuel, (1993) *Trajectórias Profissionais e Inserção Global dos Imigrantes Residentes em Bairros Degradados de Lisboa,* in "Emigração, Imigração em Portugal". Actas do Colóquio Internacional sobre Emigração e Imigração em Portugal, Séculos XIX e XX, Lisboa, Fragmentos, pp.434-445.

Pires, Rui Pena; et al, (1987) *Os Retornados. Um estudo Sociográfico,* Lisboa, IED.

Rocha-Trindade, Maria Beatriz, (1991) *Educação Pluricultural no Sul da Europa. O Estudo do Caso Português,* Colóquio "La Scuola verso una Società Multiculturale:, Firenze, (policopiado).

Rocha-Trindade, Maria Beatriz, (1993) *Migraçãoes e Multiculturalismo,* in "Escola e Sociedade Multicultural", Lisboa, Secretariado Entreculturas, pp.65-73.

Saint-Maurice, Ana; Pires, Rui Pena, (1989) *Descolonização e Migraçãoes. Os Imigrantes dos PALOP em Portugal*, "Revista Internacional de Estudos Africanos" (10 e 11), Liboa, Instituto de Investigação Cientifica e Tropical. Centro de Estudos Africanos e Asiáticos, pp.203-226.

Simões, Cristina (org.), (1992) *Documentos do Encontro "A Comunidade Africana em Portugal"*, Lisboa, Colibri, (Actas and Colóquios; 2).

Souta, Luis, (1992) *Educação Multicultural: um imperativo dos nossos dias*, "Educação e Ensino" (4) Setúbal, Associação de Municipios do Distrito de Setúbal.

Souta, Luis, (1991) *Educação Multicultural*, "Inovação", vol 4 (2-3), Lisboa, IIE, pp.45-52.

13 Intercultural education and teacher training

Xavier Besalu Costa

Introduction

All school education depends totally upon the views and capabilities of teachers, and especially those aspects of intercultural education which depend upon permeated values and concerns. What perceptions do practising teachers have about the presence of immigrant pupils in their classrooms? What are their fundamental attitudes towards those pupils who are culturally different? What do they think about their training in cultural diversity and about the training they need to face the challenge of pluralism in their classrooms?

Recent research carried out by Jordan (1994) suggests that many teachers have a simplistic, romantic and humanistic vision of intercultural education. It is a vision of good will, of good people, that responds to the democratic ideal of reinforcing respect and tolerance toward other persons. It is also a limited vision, because it is only focussed in the affective and attitudinal aspects and in external factors such as folklore. A representative of the Catalan Educational Administration said: "The majority attitude is to respect the culture of origin. Such rejection situations which do exist are in the absolutely minority".

However, Alegret (1993) shows, in his excellent work, that teachers respond just like the majority of the society towards the democratic and humanist ideal of interculturalism, being not consciously racist but racialist, i.e. they tend to neutralise differences when considering the role of the racial perspective in explaining human diversity. So they are establishing, unwittingly, the basis for the transmission of racism (as ideology, as attitude and as action).

On the other hand, according to our research in Girona (Besalu et al., 1993) categories like 'immigrant' or 'pupils belonging to a cultural minority' are explicitly rejected by teachers, who tend to attribute factors external to the school for creating this category and the problem. As one of them says: "Each child is a child. It is not a Catalan, Andalusian, Arabic... child. Each child is a child. You make a separation between things which we envisage as integrated".

In formal interviews teachers deliberately deny the notion that the presence of immigrant pupils constitutes a problem, but what is certain is that the same teachers generate negative expectations in relation to the academic achievement of these pupils and, in informal conversations, often appear to provide negative stories and conflict situations. Unconsciously, they ignore diversity rather than give an equitable treatment to all their pupils. That is what Grant and Koskela (cited by Jordan, 1994) designate the 'exemption syndrome', the tendency to give less value to these aspects, and to avoid questioning the educational practices in the (monocultural) school.

Furthermore, an important subgroup of teachers perceive these pupils exclusively from the perspective of having a deficit, and especially a linguistic deficit. They consider the minority culture to be a negative factor which distorts the educational process, a deficit for which we have to compensate, a problem we must solve. They have in practice, whether consciously or unconsciously, an ideal-pupil model structured on a hierarchical categorisation based on hypothetical characteristics which refer more to behaviour and social issues than to rational or strictly academic issues. In this hierarchy both immigrant pupils and indigenous pupils belonging to the lower social class tend to occupy the lower positions.

Although teachers often initially deny that the presence of these pupils in school will be problematic, when they talk about their experiences then the problems and difficult situations appear. Even so, these problems are attributed to extra-scholastic causes that are always generated, according to the teachers' perceptions, outside of the school. School is presented as a pure and neutral area, and not related to or concerned with socio-cultural problems. Unconsciously, it is being implied that problems of this type can only be solved outside of school and that all scholastic effort to deal with them is perfectly useless; academic failure is a failure of pupils themselves or of the social-family context. This explanation is enormously attractive because it combines, in most teachers' minds, contributions from two opposite traditions: firstly, the most conservative and worthy assertion that the school offers equal opportunities to all its pupils and differences in results are exclusively dependent upon personal ability and/or effort; and secondly, as a consequence of the theory of social reproduction, that they have confirmed the reproduction of legitimate characteristics of socio-economic and cultural inequality deriving from capitalistic education.

In terms of training, teachers are conscious of their lack of preparation in intercultural education and, according to our research, this is not considered as one of their high-priorities. Thus although it is recognised that the training received is practically zero, this reflects the actual demands of the teachers themselves which are scant and limited. Curiously, at the same time that the Spanish State is giving great importance to dealing with the diversity of pupils in the learning processes, through both official texts and courses for teachers, the references to cultural diversity are practically non-existent; the diversity which is spoken about only makes reference to that of pupils' attainment and abilities, to their interests and motivation.

From these considerations, some points of reference can be deduced:

a)   It is necessary to approach teacher-training not only from moral and attitudinal positions, but to insist on the understanding of the implications of intercultural education from academic, methodological and political positions.

b)   The pedagogy of diversity, an issue we shall take up later, must include the cultural diversity of the pupils and must have as one of its objectives education for diversity.

Theoretical perspectives on teacher training

'Imagine a swimming school teaching the anatomy and physiology of swimming, the psychology of the swimmer, the chemistry of water and the formation of oceans, unit costs of pools per user, the sociology of swimming (swimming and the social sciences), the anthropology of swimming (man and water) and, indeed, world history of swimming, from the Egyptians to the present day. All this accomplished through lectures, books and blackboards, but without water. In a second period, swimming pupils would be taken to observe expert swimmers for several months; and, after this solid preparation, they would be thrown into the sea, in deep water, on a stormy day in January.' (Busquet, 1974)

The swimming curriculum is a metaphor that exposes the usual scheme of work followed by initial teacher training.

There are different ideological directions for teacher training. Pérez (1992) reduces them to four:

a) The *academic perspective*, that conceives teaching as a process of knowledge transmission and of acquisition of the public culture. The teacher would have to be a specialist in different disciplines, an intellectual who puts pupil in touch with the science and the culture. The training of these 'academic' teachers will have to guarantee that they have acquired a wide knowledge of the disciplines that they must transmit; to understand the logic and epistemological structure of such disciplines; in the best of the cases, to know the historical evolution of their speciality disciplines and the research processes they use; and to be skilled in techniques for effective and meaningful transmission.

b) The *technical perspective* assimilates teaching to a technological intervention and converts it into an industrious science that searches, above all, for efficacy and efficiency. The teacher is going to be a technician, who must apply scientific theories that establish actions and techniques correctly. The training of 'technical' teachers fundamentally consists of a training in operative techniques, procedures (of diagnosis, of solution of problems), competences and intervention abilities (communication, decision-making, etc.). This training tends to be accompanied by an exposition of general theories on learning, instruction, education, ... and by the assumption of the legal prescriptions (provided by the appropriate educational administration) and techniques (dictated by handbooks and text books).

c) The *practical perspective* considers that teaching is, to a large extent, a craft activity, mostly practical, complex and singular, ambiguous and conflicting. Then teachers would be craftspeople, artisans, artists whose fundamental qualities are their experience, their vocation and their creativity. The training of 'practical' teachers consists of learning of practice by reproducing practice. In this case, it is essential to be directly and extensively in touch with expert teachers in order to be professionally socialised, since there is no theory of organised and proper teaching, learning the routines and solutions developed in a traditional professional culture and the adjustment of standard procedures to the requirements of the context.

d) The *critical perspective* also considers that teaching is complex, conflicting and laden with social values; which tries to make the citizens conscious of thinking and participating critically in the construction of a fairer society. Teachers are conceived as professionals who reflect, diagnose, investigate and act in an autonomous way and criticise their own practice; as intellectual catalysts, politically and morally committed, who help to form the conscience of the citizens and promote their freedom, i.e., as active agents of the production and diffusion of culture, and who have to teach alternative views of life and the world. The training of 'critical' teachers would consist of three elements:

- The acquisition of a cultural portfolio with clear political direction, to allow them to analyse the context and the world critically and whose main subjects would be constituted by the humanities: history, politics, economics, sciences and language of the culture, …

- The development of a capacity for critical reflection on practice to unmask the underlying ideology in daily educational practice, in the curriculum, in school organisation, in the assessment systems … through an action research process.

- The development of attitudes that define the intellectual catalyst: with a political and ethical commitment to school and society, able to work cooperatively, with a critical attitude to investigation and experiment.

In practice, a combination of the different positions is provided, but the conceptions of teachers, teaching, culture, etc. assumed by each training programme are determined by its paradigmatic direction, and of course the meaning of intercultural education will be constructed within that paradigm. From our point of view, the perspective which best meets the requirements of Intercultural Education is the critical one.

187

Culture and teachers in the modern context

> 'If we want to establish a solid basis for teacher training in intercultural education we should reflect on the concept of culture and of the teacher's role in the context in which they now find themselves.'
> (Ouellet, 1991)

Culture, as Camilleri (1985) says, is a particular, symbolic way to appropriate the world, only made accessible to the initiates to that view of the world through a socialisation process where language, communication and identity play a central role. Cultural identity, as far as it is a product of this process, would be fulfilled in a set of symbols, that would serve to identify one group and to differentiate it from the others. This 'perceived identity' has no integral essential existence, but exists only in relation to 'the others'. In the words of the Catalan philosopher Terricabras (1993):

> 'The principle of identity only operates in the mathematics, but applied to the individuals does not operate, and even less applied to the human groups. We all know that the identity is a lie. Then I propose to replace the concept of identity by that of identification, since I can identify myself neither with multitudes of things and cultures, without essentialism, nor with dogmatisms of any type.'

In a modern context, relationships of individuals with their particular anthropologic culture have been profoundly modified, due to the fact that it is very difficult to find in traditional solutions any answers to modern problems of existence, or to the relevant moral and ideological standards that could give sense to modern life. The pluralism, the uncertainty, the relativism, the accelerated processes of urbanisation and of the increasing power of global mass media, all constitute essential components of modernity which make it very difficult to acquire religious and moral certainties and militate against the creation of identifiably different individual and cultural identities. Equally, scientific and technological rationality is also a major new element involved by modernity. In spite of the occidentalist and eurocentric connotations from which it could be thought to derive, it is proper to recognise that this reality is distinct from, and independent of, any particular anthropologic culture. Today it forms part of the substratum of an 'endemic' culture (Simard, 1988) belonging to modernity, and one which has expanded like an epidemic (in a cybernetic and auto-regulated manner)

188

all over the planet, through the pervasive mass media. It is not possible, therefore, to maintain a static vision of culture, conceived as something given and finished in the past and that it is necessary to preserve, as a set of determined and clear procedures that govern people's lives. Culture is, as Pérez (1991) wrote, a "living area of production and transformation where everybody can participate and be more or less implicated with their community"; an open and ambiguous collection of representations and behavioural procedures that determine the life-styles of members of a community, but one that needs to be constantly recreated by them.

On the other hand, to incorporate ethnic minority pupils in school raises questions about the traditional function of the school as transmitter of hegemonic cultural models, and as a vehicle which legitimates a particular determined culture to the detriment of other cultures. These other cultures become, as a consequence, illegitimate and considered inferior. It also questions the representation of the culture presented by the school through its explicit curriculum. Gimeno (1992) comments, "it shows there are social groups which do not see their particular culture reflected in schooling and also proves the existence of an internal multiculturalism within in each culture" evidencing that what is a culture of a country or a social group is no more than a social construction, simplified and partial.

In relation to teachers, the metaphor of the teacher as intellectual catalyst, introduced by Giroux (1990), seems to be an extraordinarily powerful argument in the context of intercultural education. Such teachers are defined by the following features:

a) A person who not only transmits culture, but also produces it; teachers not only required to act, but also to think. This concept of teachers as intellectuals unites 'theory' and 'practice' in emphasising the necessity to think about personal practices and to use theory to solve the problems of that practice; it is a way of working that relates thought and action.

b) A professional who accomplishes an intellectual task and not an exclusively instrumental or technical role. All human activity implies some form of thought, even if it is routine; in the case of teachers, to define them as intellectuals puts the accent on the boundaries of their autonomy and the responsibility they assume in relation to objectives and conditions of learning in schools.

c)   The teacher as an intellectual must work in within ideological and practical conditions which allow him/her to think and participate daily in the teaching and learning processes of pupils. This requires the elimination of excessive demands on teachers, adequate pay, greater power to configure curricula and educational objectives for the school and to have more time to work with the community as a whole.

d)   The teacher as an intellectual is not a preacher, but a person who offers alternative visions of everything, who can clarify the tension between 'what is' and 'what must be', who opens new ways for practices against the hegemony. Teachers as intellectuals also means that they play a social, economic and political function through the pedagogies they use or approve; making evident the political interest and norms implicit in education; engage in the politics of instruction and of the school (seen not as an objective and neutral institution removed from economic, political and social interests) and engage in their own politics as a commitment to their own society.

e)   Teachers as intellectuals are, finally, people with awareness. Aware of their own cultural investment, of how their social class, their gender and their ethnicity have established their way of thinking and acting. Aware of the myths, falsehoods and injustices of the dominant school culture, of how this culture acts as a vehicle to disqualify and penalise the experience of cultural minorities. Aware that the part they play in the society should be consistent with their practice at school level.

Teachers as intellectual catalysts are situated between the language of critique and the speech of possibilities. The language of critique, Marx's ideological critique, has demonstrated evidently enough that schools are active agents of social, economic and cultural reproduction. But this language does not help the commitment to begin to challenge the hegemony, quite the reverse, it paralyses the process.

So we see how necessary is the language of possibility, of the thrilling utopia, that refuses to yield to power. This language of possibility offers an alternative to a critical pedagogy and promotes the capacity to generate conflicts. Furthermore it is concrete, because it starts with a determined group of actors, in a determined historical framework and with particular problems. As Giroux (1990) writes, "hope is practical; but desperation is useless".

From this argument, we can also extract some considerations:

a) The mission of education in a modern context is not to promote particular cultures, whatever they are, but to prepare future citizens to live in a world where particular cultures will be unable to respond to all the problems of existence. Its mission will consist in helping pupils to take their place, and to participate, in actively elaborating a new cultural framework that will break the boundaries of their own particular culture, to build with other members of the community a new world where life makes sense and where it is possible to find solutions to existential problems.

b) Intercultural education does not consist in having teachers with an exhaustive knowledge of every individual existing culture in their school, as if they were a kind of 'mini'-specialists in many things. In a modern context, the school should not promote cultural relativism, but it must recognise the relativity and the de-sanctification of all cultures (Camilleri, 1988). This implies that it should not be centred in cultures of origin, nor in the relationships between cultures, because it would imply too great a danger of working with stereotypes and forgetting individual reality. We should start from the cultural context of each person, emphasising similar features between them and relativising differences.

c) Intercultural education should not be understood as a purpose in itself, it is a way to promote communication between people from different cultures and to enable open attitudes to be established. In order to reach such an ideal, some elements seem fundamental, such as keeping close contacts with foreign cultural traditions and making a deep study of cultural, political and social sociology.

d) School or academic culture must act as a mediator between the pupil's own real culture and the external public or scientific culture. It is essential for the school to respect and to legitimate the histories, experiences and languages that form the particular culture related to its own pupils. Further, however, it will be necessary to organise illuminative processes which lead to a critical rediscovery of these histories, to explain how power and social inequality have structured the practices and ideologies of many groups. This cannot be done simply through personal or collective self-reflection, it is necessary to appeal to public or official elaboration of these histories.

e)   Teachers as intellectual catalysts, using the concept introduced by Giroux, would be defined by initiatives which need to be present in their training:

- A teacher would have to be a professional concerned with 'culture', who knows all that occurs all over the world. His/her training would have to guarantee a sufficient knowledge of scientific and humanistic culture to be interested in knowing the culture of the present.

- A teacher would also have to be an autonomous professional able to participate in the processes of action research. (S)he must be able to plan educational intervention and to submit it to public consideration; able to reflect on both his/her own practice and on the educational aims of the school. To do this teachers require a solid theoretical and practical training in action research processes.
- Teachers must also be capable of working in groups and be trained and prepared to work co-operatively.

- Finally, teachers should be committed professionals, making policy inside and outside the school. That is to say, concerned and responsible for improving the quality of teaching and the quality of learning of their pupils, and active members of their community, conscious of the fact that education is an instrument of society and of the fact that the objective of their work can not be other than the production of a freer and fairer society.

Training teacher as agents of change

We start from the idea that intercultural education is no more than an 'education of quality for all'. As stated in an earlier paper (Besalu, 1993) "Intercultural education is not only directed towards ethnic or cultural minorities, but to all the pupils. Intercultural education is an education for cultural diversity and not an education for those who are culturally different. Intercultural education is not a new humanist ideology, because it is within the best pedagogic tradition, which thinks that it is necessary to know about the diversity between people to educate them". This notion of 'quality education for all' is critical because those who suffer the worst consequences of bad schooling and misdirected education are precisely those who are most different.

To assimilate intercultural education to 'education of quality for all' is problematic in that it can be interpreted as a banal statement. To avoid this, we will direct our attention to some concrete elements that will help to explain the training in intercultural education which is being espoused, considering it as a way not a purpose, a method not an aim in itself.

The discussion about the educational treatment of diversity in schools underwent an important qualitative change when the policy 'to integrate' disabled pupils into ordinary educational establishments was established. It demonstrated that those schools most capable of accepting all kinds of pupils, regardless of their personal characteristics, and which were capable of giving a different answer to the particular needs of each one of them were precisely those schools which were already the most effective in educating their existing pupils.

At the level of training teachers, this issue has had two outcomes: on the one hand, the introduction of a number of specific elements relating to Special Education so that teachers recognise Special Educational Needs and can respond to them and, secondly, the implications of these concepts for all teaching has changed the view of the whole curriculum. It can no longer be based upon the false assumption of the homogeneity of the pupils, rather it must relate to the reality of the heterogeneity of the classrooms and be responsive to that diversity.

We believe that this realignment is also helpful for intercultural education. It is now necessary to be specific about the basic knowledge of what cultural pluralism and interculturality mean: the underlying concepts, the theoretical models, the policies practised by countries with more tradition in this field; and to reflection about culture, identity and cultural relativism. A content that prepares future teachers to face the conflicts that, inevitably, appear in relations between different cultural groups; to analyse the construction, reality and effects of prejudice; the historical, economic, political and psycho-social causes. Rather than being centred in the explanation of ancestral cultures and the definition of present identities (which too easily leads to the acceptance of these identities and to stereotyping the cultures, contributing as a result to isolation, to differentiation and racism) it would be better to try to understand the reality of immigration, "breaking the

193

idea of homogeneity of existing cultures" (Ouellet, 1991). The main objective of intercultural education is not to promote diversity, and even less, differences, but to remove the obstacles which obstruct intercultural communication, i.e. to maintain social cohesion whilst recognising individual identities.

On the other hand, as Marcello (1992) wrote, students starting their teacher training at University, already have established concepts and beliefs in relation to many professional and cultural problems. Because of this, initial teacher training has a responsibility to re-socialise them in the sense that they come to see themselves in a culturally diverse society. Ask them to write their personal histories - bearing in mind the resultant selectivity, and what making ideas clear and rational means - their life at school or the origins of their actual value-structures, can contribute to that re-socialization. The heterogeneity of these histories can be related later with the systematised knowledge of educational systems of foreign countries, to disclose the essential values of a community and the primary objectives of the formalised socialisation processes of schooling.

Finally, it is necessary that the intercultural dimension constitutes a thread running through the formative curriculum for future teachers, presenting different cultural and historical perspectives. It is the essence of education to develop concepts in their complexity, to incorporate the interpretations and visions of different historical moments and of different schools.

Training for commitment to the present not the past

'The school must explain reality or it is not a school'. (Corzo, 1989)

The first task teachers have to do is to help pupils to understand the world and, for this, they must know the world in which we live, its actual events, the reality of what is happening here and now, in order to dismantle the false arguments that Western culture, the culture of the 'North', hegemonic and capitalistic, uses to justify the 'status quo'. To be a teacher it is necessary to have clear ideas on social and political problems.

This would be a good practical description of the concept of teachers as intellectual catalysts: the commitment with the present time through the reading, utilisation and study of the mass media, especially newspapers, as an important tool of discussion, reflection and action. It is a simple idea: let newspapers enter the university classrooms to guarantee this commitment with the present, this minimal capacity to read the real world: "The level of knowledge acquired during their university training is insufficient for the complete reading of newspapers and, consequently, insufficient for the complete reading of reality, so teachers will be unable to prepare pupils with the cultural basis of citizenship" (AA.VV., 1985).

To study newspapers in the classrooms where future teachers are formed presupposes a human contribution and a real approximation to the world that has not previously been guaranteed in training programmes. Newspapers allow access to more and more current information, to unmask the self interests which justify information and opinions, to be closer to real social, political and cultural life; to fight for the freedom of the poor from a position of knowledge. This image of the world would not be complete without a basic knowledge of the economy (the manufacture of power) and of the information and cultural industry (the manufacture of knowledge), in short, without a realisation of which are the main sources of power in our contemporary world: "How can we give a degree to someone who does not know what the GATT is?" (Corzo, 1993)

If the school wants to be an agency, neither the only one nor the most important, which helps to change society, it will need teachers aware of the fact that their profession is not a simple workplace, but that they are exercising a political profession, and that they make a class-related choice.

Teachers must also be erudite people in the purest and less élitist sense of the word. They will be interested in everything, open to all perspectives, attentive to all the news, curious and vigorous, because their's is a cultural profession. Their scientific and technological culture will have to be sufficient for them to understand and to follow the ongoing events that are produced in a world rooted in the 'cultural illiteracy' of increasingly large numbers of 'alphabetised' citizens, to know the alphabet but not the words, able to read but not comprehend, unable to use what they learn at school to interrogate and understand reality.

Training to counter the concept of failure

Intercultural education must find educational strategies which allow pupils belonging to minorities to access real equality of opportunities, because these are the pupils with the highest index of 'scholastic failure'. This implies, primarily, that the problem of 'scholastic failure' is also a problem of the school and of the teachers and not only of the pupils and of their family environment. It requires, amongst other things, an in- depth review of the intentions, functions and methods of assessing students utilised by schools. Assessment has great strategic importance: teaching is done in a climate of assessing and that in turn determines the dynamics of the classroom and the teaching-learning processes: "Assessment becomes a formal structure for life in the classroom. Everything happens because of the expectations and the consequences of evaluation" (Santos Guerra, 1993).

To interrogate the problem of assessment is to start to analyse the main problems of academic education; pupils-teacher relations and inter-pupil relations, the transmission of knowledge, discipline, and relations with parents. The existence of assessment as unquestionable academic and judgmental practice not only has a pedagogic (formative) function but is also implicit in selection processes in social, hierarchical and certification situations. As the pupils of Barbiana (a school in Italy) wrote in 1967 in their famous 'letter': "So that the dream of the equality won't be only a dream we propose you... DO NOT FAIL... Because the school is a hospital that takes care of healthy people and refuses the sick" (AA.VV., 1969).

Public schooling, compulsory for all, cannot fail its pupils if it does not want to be seen as a major undemocratic sham. It is therefore one of the fundamental tasks of teacher training to change the idea that the assessment, selection and grading of pupils which are carried out by teachers are academically pure and objective and devoid of social stigmas.

As Stenhouse (1984) said, "to evaluate is to understand, and the conventional evaluations do not try to understand the educational process, they still work in terms of success or failure". Evaluation must first require that teachers themselves employ a systematical reflection process designed to improve their own practice: "Evaluation is based on evidence which teachers extract from reality; evidence which helps them to formulate value judgments about the task they are doing with their pupils; evidence that allows them to manage their actions, to modify their position in relation to the classroom in general, or to some pupil in particular" (Santos Guerra, 1993).

Training into commitment to practice

Teaching is basically a practical activity, and because of its commitment to action it morally commits those who undertake it. Teachers cannot be indifferent to what they teach or how their pupils learn, and much less to the fundamental relationship between teachers and pupils implicit in the interactive nature of teaching. This ethical aspect of education is a dimension that should not be lacking in the training plan of teachers, involving a moral commitment through the adoption of an attitude to the world by which to understand the school. It demands the active involvement of the teacher in ensuring a coherence between teacher actions and teacher intentions, reflecting the views of Freinet in assuming that the teacher cannot be confined within his/her school, in a narrow minded pedagogy, but will always bring to the task his/her own personal and professional commitments.

More specifically, the social dimension of teaching demands the participation of all of those who are involved, pupils, parents and teachers, in the planning, management and evaluation of the schools. Teachers, however, have a special responsibility in pursuing this participation. As Levin (1993) convincingly demonstrated through the 'Accelerated Schools' project in California, the fact that the scholastic community assumes responsibility for ensuring participation is an indispensable requirement to the improvement of 'quality education for all' and for the fight against 'scholastic failure'. Firstly, because it avoids blame being transferred between parents, teachers and students; secondly, because it generates a climate of confidence in the notion of quality education for all; and finally, because it creates a shared vision of the school situation and of the high-priority objectives which are required. The idea that it is very difficult to achieve an education of quality for all without the active participation of parents and pupils must also be developed in the initial training of teachers.

At another level, the training of critical teachers must find in 'practice' the main ingredient which will give sense and value to the theoretical and technical aspects of the course. Practice during the period of training is essentially a 'virtual space', in an unstable balance between reality and simulation, where students can plan, act, observe and reflect, yet without having the full responsibility for the effects of their actions. Teaching, understood as a social practice, can not be derived from the assimilation of academic knowledge, but presupposes a different acquisition process through a permanent dialogue with the real situation. The training of teachers, conceived as 'reflective practice' cannot be established by experts or through reading books, because it requires practice. Practice is conceived as the source of real and practical problems, problems which will be illuminated and explained by reflection and scientific knowledge which simultaneously provide viable alternatives and solutions. It needs to be made clear that 'practice' is not orchestrated and directed towards the application of academic knowledge, of some supposed fundamental science that outlines and solves the problems far from the context and the reality in which they are produced. It is to be regarded as a real action research process, through which the teacher is affectively, cognitively and morally implicated with the reality, questioning his/her own beliefs and participating in the reconstruction of that reality. As Stenhouse (1984) wrote: "The characteristics of professional teachers are the capacity to develop their own professional ideas and to systematically self-analyse, to study how other teachers work and to test new ideas through investigational procedures in the classroom."

Finally, in this complex commitment to practice, could be considered the procedure presented by Ouellet (1991) of the University of Sherbrooke (Canada). He 'invited' the participants to explore a foreign cultural tradition. The participants who accepted the 'invitation' were required to befriend immigrants from the Third World and begin to consider their country of origin. The programme stimulated visits to these countries and the learning of their language, and encouraged efforts to understand their cultural inheritance and their political and social evolution. In words of Ouellet, "To explore a totally different cultural universe, though not exempt of dangers, has an indisputable formative value".

Conclusions

In this chapter I have tried to develop a number of ideas which I will summarise:

a) Teachers have a humanist, limited and racialist vision of cultural diversity and intercultural education. Teacher training in intercultural education is rare, but yet it is still not perceived as a high-priority.

b) Teachers also have a 'Rousseaunian' vision of schools, as an arena located outside political and socioeconomic reality, autonomous and neutral.

c) There are different ideological intentions in teacher training, in relation to the conception of teaching and the images of teaching as a profession. The approach most supportive of intercultural education is the critical perspective, which is sustained on three fundamental pillars: cultural knowledge within a clear policy orientation, development of the capacity for critical reflection and an ethical commitment to schools and society.

d)   In the context of modern life, the relationships of individuals with their particular culture are profoundly modified, making it very difficult to acquire categorical certainties and to differentiate pure cultural identities. The mission of the education in this modern context is to explore the relativity of all cultures and to build a new cultural framework, not to promote any particular culture.

e)   Some elements which promote intercultural education in teacher training are: to introduce a specific subject element 'intercultural education' into the curriculum; to have clear ideas about the social and political problems in the world in which we are living; to have a solid scientific and humanistic culture; to change approaches to the function and practices of evaluation so that it is not used as a defeating mechanism; and to be actively involved with the world, the educational community and the profession.

f)   Intercultural education is a means to promote communication between people from different cultures, not a purpose in itself. Intercultural education is a new name for an education of quality for all.

These are only some elements of a discussion about intercultural education that in some countries, including Spain, has only just started. I want to be sure that teacher training is one of the strategic factors that can humbly contribute in the construction of a new society in a more erudite, open and fair world.

References

AA.VV. (i.e. multiple authors) (1969) *Carta a una mestra*. (Barcelona, Spain: Nova Terra).

AA.VV. (i.e. multiple authors) (1985) 'V Encuentro de Educadores Milanianos', *Boletín del Movimiento de Educadores Milanianos* 13 Salamanca, Spain.

Alegret, J.L. (1993) 'Cómo se enseñan los otros. Análisis de la presentación racialista de la diversidad étnica en los libros de texto de EGB, BUP y FP utilizados en Cataluña en la década de los 80?.' *Dissertation*. Universidad Autónoma de Barcelona, Spain.

Besalu, X. (1993) 'Per una educación intercultural' *Estudi General 12*. (Universitat de Girona, Spain).

Besalu, X., Alegret, J.L. et al. (1993) 'El discurso de la Adminisración educativa catalana sobre la escolarización de algunos alumnos inmigrantes extranjeros'. Paper presented in *Jornadas sobre Inmigración y Educación*. (Murcia, Spain).

Busquet, J. (1974) *La problemática de las reformas educativas*. (Madrid, Spain: INCIE).

Camilleri, C. (1985) *Antropología cultural y educación*. (Paris, France: UNESCO).

Camilleri, C. (1988) 'Pertinence d'une approche scientifique de la culture pour une formation par l'éducation interculturelle'. In Ouellet, F. *Pluralisme et école: Jalons pour une approche critique de la formation interculturelle des éducateurs*. (Quebec, Canada: Institut Québécois de Recherche sur la culture).

Corzo, J.L. (1989) *Leer periódicos en clase. Una programación para EGB, Medias, Adultos y Compensatoria*. (Madrid, Spain: Popular).

Corzo, J.L. (1993) 'Los ejes básicos de la pedagogia barbiana'. paper. Girona, Spain.

Gimeno, J. (1992) 'Currículum y diversidad cultural'. Rev. *Educación y sociedad* vol. 11 pp.127-153.

Giroux, H.A. (1990) *Los profesores como intelectuales*. Hacia una pedagogía crítica del aprendizaje. (Barcelona, Spain: Paidós-MEC).

Jordán, J.A. (1994) *La escuela multicultural. Un reto para el profesorado*. (Barcelona, España: Paidós).

Levin, H.A. (1993) 'Accelerating' la educación de todos los niños y niñas?. Paper presented in Congreso Internacional de Didáctica. La Coruña, Spain.

Marcelo, C. (1992) 'Desarrollo de la comprensión intercultural en los programas de formación inicial del profesorado'. Actas del X Congreso Nacional de Pedagogía. Salamanca, Spain.

Ouellet, F. (1991) *L'éducation interculturelle. Essai sur le contenu de la formation des maîtres*. (Paris, France: L'Harmattan).

Pérez, A. (1991) 'Cultura escolar y aprendizaje relevante'. Rev. *Educación y sociedad*vol. 8 : 59-72.

Pérez, A. (1992) 'La función y formación del profesor/a en la enseñanza para la compresión. Diferentes perspectivas'. In Gimeno, J. y Pérez, A. *Comprender y transformar la enseñanza*. (Madrid, Spain: Morata).

Santos Guerra, M.A. (1993) *La evaluación: un proceso de diálogo, comprensión y mejora*. (Málaga, Spain: Aljibe).

Simard, J.J. (1988) 'La révolution pluraliste: une mutation du rapport de l'homme au monde'. In Ouellet, F. *Pluralisme et école: Jalons pour une approche critique de la formation interculturelle des éducateurs*. (Quebec, Canada: Institut Québécois de Recherche sur la culture).

Stenhouse, L. (1984) *Investigación y desarrollo del currículum*. (Madrid, Spain: Morata).

Terricabras, J.M. (1993) 'La trampa de la identitat' *Nou Diari*. 12 Nov.

14 Comparative issues in teacher training programmes, planning in developing countries: co-operation and intercultural perspectives

Lucie Carrilho Ribeiro

Introduction

Nowadays, the concept of intercultural education is becoming more and more meaningful. This increasing interest is undoubtedly related to the fact that countries and cultures are now much closer, due to the rapid circulation of information, goods and services, the increasing importance of the media, and the facility people have in going from one place to another. The need to learn about other cultures, for many years due mainly to migration phenomena, has now become commonplace for reasons of political interest and of collaborative projects. People live in different countries and try to understand different cultures not because they are emigrants or because they want better to understand the immigrants but because there now exist larger perspectives of dialogue and even larger geographical spaces considered to be a common inheritance of different nations. Such proximity does not erase cultural differences but rather points out the need for knowing better those who live in a different cultural setting.

Intercultural education can then be viewed in a migrational context or in a co-operative context, playing an important role in both. It may be viewed in the migrational context of people coming from different geographical regions and now living in a country which has a dominant language, culture and values different from their own. In this regard, intercultural education attempts to develop, among migrants and citizens, attitudes and values of multicultural conviviality, acceptance of social differences, tolerance and solidarity. These values and attitudes prepare people from different countries to establish closer relationships, to appreciate better each other's cultures and prevent conflict and rejection of patterns of living different from their own.

Intercultural education may also be seen in a collaborative context of people coming from a more developed country to help and contribute, in a given area or sector, to the growth of a less developed nation. Those who are working on intercultural co-operation need fully to understand the problem of intercultural relationships and to be aware of negative attitudes which might turn into incompatibilities. In a co-operational context, the capacity to contribute, bearing in mind the interests of those with whom we are working and the resources available, is also required. It demands a capacity to forget temporarily our own cultural environment and to think and feel as though we were part of and belonged to a different group of people.

In this chapter I will discuss the lessons learned from co-operation with developing African countries as an illustration of the importance of intercultural understanding. I will focus on the developing of teacher training programmes but most of what I say can also be applied to other types of co-operational projects.

Cultural prerequisites of a project for a foreign country

When designing a teacher training programme for a country other than one's own, there is always a tendency or temptation to start from a set of assumptions derived from the cultural context to which one belongs. These are concerned with:

-       the academic background and the professional training we assume teachers already have;
-       the type of content to be included in the programme, according to our own opinion;
-       the strategies and methods we have previously used and which were successful;
-       learning resources and materials we are acquainted with and which have proved to be appropriate.

All such assumptions, well justified in our own cultural context, may prove totally inadequate in a different environment. This would be the case, for example, of an educator from Europe trying to apply in developing African countries, assumptions and concepts valid in his or her own cultural setting.

I recall, in this regard, the professional experience I had when co-operating with one of these countries, some years ago. There were teachers teaching grades 1-4 whose academic preparation did not go beyond the 5th and 6th grade, as well as teachers of 5th and 6th grade who had stopped studying after their 7th or 8th grade. The majority of teachers did not have an adequate scientific background nor did they have any pedagogic preparation. Furthermore, they had not acquired study and reading habits since the conditions to develop these interests did not exist in the country at that time. Bookstores were practically non-existent and in schools there had been no text books for the past ten years. A few library resources were located in the capital and only a small number of teachers could reach them.

This state of affairs, relating to the teachers' preparation, had immediate repercussions on the different components of a teacher training programme and any previous assumptions I might have made had to be dismissed:

-       the contents of the training programme could not be very comprehensive and demanding but needed to be relevant and carefully chosen;
-       regarding strategies, the programme should avoid long lectures which would not hold the teachers' attention but focus rather on developing teaching skills and presenting problematic situations for which the teachers would try to find solutions;
-       the reading materials should use very simple language, be as brief as possible regarding conceptual knowledge, but should provide abundant illustrative examples and exercises to clarify the concepts being explained.

This would certainly be a different programme from the one I would develop for my own country.

The example just given is intended to emphasise how much is required from someone who switches from one culture to another, and has to forget what is appropriate and meaningful in the cultural environment in which he grew up and try to understand a new and different situation. I would say that this effort to start without prejudice and preconceived assumptions is a necessary first prerequisite before beginning to design any programme, whether for teachers or for other purposes, in a country that is not one's own. Once this first platform has been attained, the foreign educator and co-operator is likely to be ready to assimilate a new environment and a new culture and to collect all sorts of required information so that the teacher training programme can be relevant and adjusted to this new context.

It might seem that the information gathered should refer exclusively, or mainly, to the system of education of the country with which we are working and to the different sub-systems encompassed. Such assumptions would be incorrect. The way of living, the customs and traditions, the economic, social and cultural contexts of that country constitute indispensable background data for the planning and implementation of the teachers' programme. Without this type of information one might make terrible - sometimes ridiculous - mistakes in apparently very simple situations. Let me give you an example, that should be true in the Democratic Republic of S. Tome and Principe, in Equatorial Africa.

Imagine you are having a training session with mathematics teachers and you want to give them an example of problems requiring very simple multiplication skills from the students. You could say: "I go to a food store to buy 3 pounds of potatoes. If a pound costs 2 shillings, how much do I have to pay?" Assuming you would naturally refer to the county's currency, the problem seems so easy, so universal, that it appears nothing can be wrong. Nevertheless, it is wrong from the beginning to the end.

In the first place, nobody would think of going to the food stores, which are practically non-existent, but rather to the daily street market to buy fresh food. In the second place, in S. Tome, scales are not used in the market nor measures such as pounds or kilograms. Everything is sold in units or small piles. You say: "I want 3 fish" or "give me 3 piles of tomatoes and 2 piles of cabbage leaves". In the third place, people do not eat potatoes but rather a similar tuber called 'matabala'. The situation described in the Maths problem would seem very strange to teachers and certainly not appropriate to the students. Instead of clarifying what they were trying to explain, teachers would be confused with what had been thought a very simple problem.

This means that if you are speaking of everyday situations you need to know about them. This is, therefore, another aspect to be emphasised: it is not possible to study a particular sub-system of a different culture - whether it be the country's educational system or any other - whilst disregarding the cultural environment in which it operates. Therefore, a second prerequisite before commencing to design an appropriate teacher training programme involves the effort to absorb this new environment and to adjust to it, in other words, to build a bridge between our culture and the new one in which we are living.

Designing a teacher training programme for a specific cultural environment

No teacher training programme is perfect or complete. Each tries to contemplate specific priorities previously identified whilst remaining aware that much remains to be done. In a developing country, the selection of components to be included in a programme is a crucial decision, because resources are scarce, the implementation conditions usually adverse, and what can be accomplished is only a small part of what is desirable. To determine the strongest priorities becomes something of extreme relevance and affects the development of the entire project.

The conventional Teacher Training Programme: choosing between opposite options: The problem to overcome here is that the general principles or guidelines of any teacher training programme in countries with few resources, still struggling to solve basic needs, usually conflict. Thus, a reasonable request for a sound and comprehensive programme can hardly be satisfied under the circumstances. Such a programme takes too much time and, whether it is a pre-service or in-service training programme, the education system probably cannot wait so long for new or more qualified teachers; it would also require, if it is a conventional teacher training programme, a larger number of qualified instructors the country most certainly does not have; finally, it would imply heavy costs, far beyond the usually small budget or the loans that international financing provides. Given these constraints, the training programme will have to be shorter and focus on essential, carefully selected, training requirements.

A second conflict usually arises between the scientific and pedagogical or professional training of in-service teachers. On the one hand, the lack of scientific preparation requires a programme covering at least, fundamental subjects that are usually part of the background of a high school graduate. On the other hand, teachers do not have any professional training and this cannot be neglected. Once again, these two basic components cannot be fully developed in a feasible training programme and a decision has to be made regarding the weighting of each one in the programme.

These concerns about scientific preparation and professional training lead to another: the balance between acquisition of knowledge and training of skills - and this is a third conflict I would like to point out. The training of teaching skills, important in any programme for teachers, becomes crucial in a cultural environment where training needs should have been satisfied much earlier. The teaching skills that are already a synthesis of scientific and pedagogic knowledge, using strategies such as demonstration and role playing, save time and have more impact than lectures or readings of written materials. To help teachers master a core of essential teaching skills that they can use successfully in their everyday classes becomes more important here than imparting to them a substantial body of knowledge, some of which will soon be forgotten while another part will soon be out of date. Pragmatic and immediate solutions which do not lower the quality of the training programme must be found.

The acceptance of all these constraints by someone coming from a country with more favourable economic and social conditions and where alternative and equally sound teacher training models can be implemented with success is not an easy thing to accomplish. It requires a great effort of cultural understanding, an honest assessment of what is better for the country we are working for and a strong discipline in decision making. In short, it asks for intercultural perspectives and the capacity of temporarily departing from our own culture to become part of a different one that we must make our own.

The Distance Education Teacher Training Programme: The possibility of an alternative of using distance education as a strategy for training teachers is not yet well known and until recently has not been thought of as an alternative in developing countries. The fact that is usually a multimedia system, calling for the existence of national television and video resources, makes it appear an expensive solution that is automatically put aside. The non-existence in those countries of the expertise necessary for the preparation of videotapes and audiotapes: the need to recruit this type of expertise from abroad: the initial heavy investment required: give the illusion that distance education is a very expensive strategy.

Nevertheless, whenever there are a large number of teachers needing in-service training, and foreign consultants are needed to design and deliver a conventional teacher programme, there is no doubt that distance education is by far less expensive as experience has already shown. Developing countries are presently becoming aware of the advantages of this alternative solution although it also presents some risks and limitations. The advantages can be briefly listed:

-    the pressure on teachers to complete the training programme in a period of time as short as possible, is much lower than in conventional programmes, since teachers are not out of their classrooms and students are not without classes;

- there are no problems of attendance, which is very important in countries where teachers are geographically dispersed (mainly in countries with several islands) and where means of transportation are scarce;
- there are no accommodation problems, sometimes a difficult problem to solve, nor the related expenditure;
- students can revise the different subjects included in the training programme as many times as they feel necessary;
- as a multimedia system, the training programme represents a powerful strategy, which has a great impact on teachers who do not have reading habits;
- different combinations of training components can answer specific needs of groups of teachers with different levels of preparation;
- finally, costs per trained teacher are low and less than those of a conventional training programme asking for a large group of consultants to stay in the country for long periods of time.

In listing all these advantages, it is assumed that the training programme has been carefully designed, taking into consideration the cultural context of the country, as already indicated earlier. In other words, reading materials cannot be long but must be easy to understand and must provide opportunities to practise skills and self evaluation of learning. Audiotapes cannot be boring, lecturing for long times but must rather be interactive, referring to specific questions raised by the teachers. Videotaping must not try to introduce many concepts in a single videotape but must rather explain, very clearly, relevant selected topics. Most of these concerns apply to distance education in any cultural environment, but they become naturally more pertinent in developing countries.

If a distance teacher training programme is developed on the basis of a set of inappropriate assumptions, given the specific cultural context of the country for which it is prepared, the damage may be severe and will lead to failure from the outset.

A final disadvantage of training programmes at distance must be mentioned: they do not include guided practice which is indispensable in pre-service teacher education. Therefore, in pre-service teacher training programmes, distance teaching must be supplemented by classroom observation, supervisor guidance and teaching practice.

The choice between a conventional and a distance education teacher training programme; the adoption of a specific structure for the different materials or training sessions; the preference given to some components over others, - all these decisions cannot be made outside the cultural context for which the programme is intended. Intercultural education helps prevent such great misunderstandings and develops a greater awareness of cultural differences that need to be taken into account.

Implementation of a Teacher Training Programme: It is vital to gain feedback on the design of the programme. It is not advisable to design a teacher training programme without checking, step by step, whether or not it is possible to implement it, given the difficulties existing in developing countries. Tasks that do not raise any implementation problems under normal conditions cannot be performed in some contexts with unexpected characteristics.

Suppose you have a teacher training programme in which systematic guidance and supervision of teachers is essential in the first phase of the programme. What do you do during the design and planning stage of the programme?

- you try to locate well prepared teachers who may become supervisors later on, when the programme begins;
- you estimate how many supervisors will be needed and the topics in which they should be specialists;
- you organise different teams, each one taking care of a given number of teachers according to the geographical areas to be covered;
- you verify if transportation is available.

At this point you probably feel confident that the supervision plan is feasible and can be successful, and you integrate it in the training programme as a required component. But it may fail, badly, because you do not know enough about economic and social environments quite different from those of your own country and you have not taken them into account.

What constraints exist to ruin your careful planning? I list several real ones I had to deal with in Africa:

- The country I was working in had, quite often, shortages of petrol and sometimes there was no petrol at all because the ship bringing the supplies did not arrive on the expected date; most cars could not be used during the entire shortage period and supervisors' visits to teachers automatically stopped;

- Sometimes, there were no tyres to be had in the entire country; therefore, when a tyre was completely worn out and needed to be replaced, since there was no new ones available, the car was immobilised until a new supply of tyres arrived in the country;
- A substantial number of cars, still running, had tyres already torn or even cut open and although they were still driven on roads in fair condition could not be used in areas of the country where roads were in bad shape.

All these transportation problems, hard for an outsider to foresee, were enough to prevent the planned systematic supervisor visits to classrooms.

There were other constraints. Each team of supervisors of different subject areas had to try to visit all the schools of a specific area on the same day. Consequently, the students' schedule had to be organised so that the different subjects were being taught at the time each supervisor arrived at the school he was going to supervise. If this was not taken into consideration at the time when the student schedules were being established the entire supervision plan would be ruined. There are many other constraints which might be enumerated. However, these examples aim only to illustrate the need to take implementation aspects into consideration while designing and evolving a teacher training programme for a developing country with a different cultural environment.

Project sustainability

A final word must be said about project sustainability because there is growing evidence that projects considered to be successful upon completion soon begin to deteriorate and their results may be regarded as unsatisfactory. This is because during the design and the implementation phase of the project, attention is not given to institutional development, and after its completion, government policy support and funding are not provided.

Institutional development is concerned with the training in managerial capabilities of groups or departments responsible for the implementation of the project, enabling them to assess progress and to adjust strategies in order to attain the project goals and objectives. Often even when such training takes place, those in charge are still not ready to assume full responsibility or do not have the necessary financial resources to continue monitoring the project and to ensure a strong performance after project completion. The lack of these two components in project designs may gradually weaken project benefits and investment returns. International funding agencies are becoming more aware of these circumstances and are recommending different types of action which might increase project sustainability.

Intercultural education and co-operation

What has been said could give the impression to someone unaware of intercultural problems that a developing country is a lesser participant, that a co-operator is someone who always gives something, and local people are the ones who receive what is given. This comprises a very poor notion of co-operation and would certainly ruin the possibilities of any intercultural bridge being established among people from different cultures. To co-operate is to work together on equal terms; it is a continuous exchange of views and perspectives; it is a common effort to find better ways of solving existing problems. Intercultural education helps us to understand the human similarities behind the cultural differences and helps us to see that the closer we are to other cultures, the more we become aware of their enriching differences.

The amount of learning provided by people of developing countries to those of more developed ones, the richness of their cultures, the amazing and imaginative solutions they can offer, the experience of a friendship that goes beyond cultural differences and makes it possible to work together within a larger perspective of world citizenship, is something that can be lived but hardly described and is certainly priceless.

15 Cultural diversity, curriculum development and support: challenges and promising practices

Peter D. Pumfrey

Introduction

> 'I believe deeply that all men and women should be able to go as far as talent, ambition and effort can take them. There should be no barriers of background, no barriers of religion, no barriers of race. I want.... a society that encourages each and every one to fulfil his or her potential to the utmost.... let me say here and now that I regard any barrier built on race to be pernicious.' (Prime Minister of the United Kingdom of Great Britain and Northern Ireland, September, 1991)

The set of values on which the above statement is founded are reflected in differing ways in the social policies and legislation of many countries. The gaps between political rhetoric and reality, between social theory and educational practice are considerable in all countries.

Cultural diversity and immigration

Consider the following six predictions. Do you think that they apply to the country in which you work?

Prediction 1.:   Immigration by families to countries where life-chances are perceived as being better than in their country of birth, is likely to continue and increase.

Prediction 2.:	The number of children of those immigrant parents who have already arrived in such favourably viewed countries will increase as a proportion of the school population.
Prediction 3.:	The development of an educational system and curriculum that utilises the benefits of cultural diversity will develop only slowly.
Prediction 4.:	In areas where virtually no immigrant families from minority ethnic groups reside, communities, schools and teachers will tend to see the education of such pupils as a problem to be addressed by others.
Prediction 5.:	Unless national policies are adopted that require all schools and teachers to acknowledge and adjust to the realities of a culturally diverse population, curriculum development is likely to take place only slowly, and in a piecemeal manner.
Prediction 6.:	The social consequences of *not* developing equal opportunities policies and curricula in a multicultural society are likely to be both painful and costly to a country.

These predictions have held, and still hold, for the United Kingdom. We have learned some important lessons. We still have much to do, but many promising starts have been made at national, local and school level.

Do you think that any of the above six predictions are valid in other European countries? If so, it is possible that messages, suitably adapted to fit the reader's particular social, cultural and educational contexts, may be derived from our experiences in the UK. and those of other countries with significant numbers of pupils drawn from a wide range of minority ethnic groups.

This chapter outlines the context, indicates some of the challenges that an influx of minority ethnic groups has presented, and describes some constructive responses. Challenges represents a two-sided coin: problems and opportunities. The former must be recognised and addressed and the latter identified and capitalised upon to the benefit of *all* children and their families. This is easily said but difficult to achieve. Despite this, the vision still has great merits. Consider the alternatives!

Turning to education, the following four questions concern both teachers undertaking their initial professional training and the much larger number of their qualified colleagues who have been working in schools for anything from one to forty years.

214

Q.1. Can primary and secondary school teachers in other European countries learn anything of value concerning the development of education in a multicultural society from colleagues in England in particular?

Q.2. What challenges does the increasing numbers of pupils from various minority ethnic groups present to an educational system?

Q.3. What responses to the challenges presented by cultural diversity identified hold promise?

Q.4. What are we doing to address such issues in our own schools and our respective communities?

The contemporary context

Historically, migration and immigration are longstanding international phenomena. In the 1990s, and for the foreseeable future, they represent highly complex, sensitive and emotive issues. The level and sources of immigration into the UK. have varied over time. In the first half of the 20th. century, immigration to the UK. was predominantly European in origin although longstanding groupings of non-European and 'coloured' minority ethnic groups have lived in cities such as London, Liverpool and Cardiff for hundreds of years. Most of the migration from the Caribbean and the Indian sub-continent to the UK. occurred after the 1950s. It was largely prompted by economic rather than political motives. The then British government invited immigrants. The only sizeable immigration of a political nature into the UK. since the 1950s was that of Asians from East Africa, following their expulsion from Uganda by Idi Amin. At present, the future of Hong Kong is likely to result in a significant influx of immigrants. The numbers eligible for entry have already been specified.

Emigration from the country in which one is born is a tremendous step, not lightly undertaken. Understandably, the vast majority of individuals and families wish to emigrate to countries in which their life chances, and those of their children, are perceived as being greater than if they remain in the country of their birth. The appeal of materialism is manifest in stable, prosperous and technologically advanced countries. This appeal is regularly reinforced by the visual and verbal messages about the lifestyles in these countries transmitted so rapidly across the world by the mass media. Increased mobility, symbolised by the aeroplane, and the availability of credit to pay the expense of moving, helps convert aspiration into actuality. Getting away from civil wars and the associated threats to life and limb, from the destruction, disease, starvation and anguish that such conflicts represent in many countries, are also important causes of migration.

215

The history of the USA has demonstrated that its 'melting pot' philosophy has signally failed to lead to the social cohesion its progenitors expected. This is not to assert that social cohesion is impossible between ethnic, religious and cultural groups living in the same country: merely to indicate that it is unusual, rarely spontaneous and not rapidly achieved. Fears of uncontrolled immigration into the USA from, for example, Mexico, the Caribbean, Latin America and many other less materially advantaged countries, have increased markedly over the last decade. Related concerns also exist in many European community countries: Austria, Germany, Italy France, Spain and the UK are but examples.

The issue of asylum is one aspect of the challenge of immigration. The distinction between political refugees (currently sympathetically viewed by many host countries) and economic refugees (not as sympathetically perceived) makes the point.

With the exception of Hong Kong mentioned above, the days of large-scale primary immigration into Britain appear to be over. Secondary immigration continues at about 80,000 per year. Declining flows of primary immigrants from the former colonies of the British Empire have been replaced by an increase in numbers claiming asylum from other countries. The same is true across all the countries in Europe. The projected birth rates in the UK. for the first twenty years of the 21st century show that an increasingly aged population will exist compared with 1997.

In 1995, it was reported that the number of foreigners registered as living in the then 12 member states of the European Union in 1992 totalled 15 million. The Migration Research Unit at University College London is reported as saying that '... less than 9 million fall into the category of people originating from outside the EU who are living in another EU country, but do not yet have EU citizenship'. These EU figures cover only *legal* immigrants who have registered as residents in one of the member states. The International Centre for Migration Policy Development in Vienna estimates that there is a further 3.5 to 5.5 million *illegal* immigrants in the EU population.

In 1993, 22,400 applications for asylum in Britain were made. This was five times the number seen five years earlier. 1,600 were recognised as refugees and granted asylum. A further 11,100 were given exceptional leave to enter Britain and 10,700 were refused entry. Between 1984 and 1993 the annual cost of detaining suspected illegal immigrants increased from £1.2 million sterling to £7.8 million sterling. The British Home Secretary is reported as saying 'We turn away people who might otherwise come in excessive numbers, imposing a burden on our public services when in reality they have no legal or other basis for so doing.'

216

In the UK, as in other countries, understandable, but often unwarranted, conscious and unconscious prejudices and suspicions exist mutually between ethnic groups, whether host or immigrant, large or small. It is important to acknowledge the existence of such tensions if they are to be constructively resolved. Politicians are sensitive to the possibility of racist reactions from the dominantly white British public (i.e. the majority of the electorate) if policies perceived as unduly advantaging ethnic minority groups are introduced. Suspicions that many ethnic minorities are not a part of British national identity are fostered by some right-wing politicians and writers and also by some extremist members of minority ethnic groups themselves. Similar concerns are manifest in countries across Europe.

Many misconceptions exist concerning the size, growth and composition of minority ethnic groups living in Great Britain. Both teachers in training and qualified teachers here have been shown to lack accurate information in this field, despite the facts being available through the reports of the Office of Population Censuses and Surveys. Very few of our citizens could rank by size the minority ethnic groups resident in the UK.

In a total population of 54,055,693, approximately 2,969,549 people from minority ethnic groups live in Britain. They comprise approximately 6.0% of the population (Ballard and Kalra, 1994). Over the past forty years, this percentage has increased as follows: 0.4% in 1951; 1.00% in 1961; 2.3% in 1971 and 3.9% in 1981. These minority ethnic groups are predominantly resident in the large centres of population. Immigrants, and their children who may well have been born in this country, are not evenly distributed geographically. This means that many schools have no pupils on their rolls who are members of minority ethnic groups. To such schools and their communities, multicultural education is often (and very mistakenly) seen as, at worst, an irrelevance and, at best, a low priority in relation to curriculum revision and development. In Britain, Indians currently comprise the largest group (N = 834,574), followed by Afro-Caribbean (N = 667,964), Pakistanis (N = 474,400), Other Asians (N = 191,162), Bangladeshis (N = 161,271) and Chinese (N = 151,889).

In terms of membership of the major religious beliefs, approximately 1,200,000 citizens are Muslim, 600,000 Sikh, 300,000 Hindu and 300,000 Jews. There are many other smaller religious groups. Christianity remains the official religion of the UK. Whilst certain ethnic groups can be broadly linked to particular religions, to assume a one-to-one link would be extremely misleading. Numbers of individual members of the majority group comprising the host population are adherents of virtually every available religion, or none.

Significant numbers of British citizens profess atheism, agnosticism and/or humanism.

Is the demography of ethnic membership and religious affiliation well-known to educationalists in your country and to teachers in your schools? Are the educational implications of immigration and of cultural diversity being considered? Are policies being developed, promising practices being identified and resources being made available nationally, locally, and in individual schools to address the challenges?

In a world of increasing economic, social and political interdependence, the formal educational system of a country has an increasingly important role to play. As a consequence of growing immigration, European countries are increasingly pluralist. Inexorably the cultural, ethnic, religious and social compositions of a country's population will continue to evolve. Resources and power will be redistributed. Tensions will arise between dominant and minority groups as this process occurs. As has happened throughout history, the 'Have-nots' in society will challenge the 'Haves'. How this situation is addressed through the school and the community of which it is a part, is of the essence. The only aspect of any society that is constant, is change. In an increasingly culturally diverse society, schools play a central role in educating pupils for life now and in the future.

What will that future be? In what type of society do we wish our children and their children to live? Is there a common core of values that hold the promise of a cohesive and tolerant pluralist society, or will sectional interests subvert this aspiration? Underpinning such matters lie the nebulous, but extremely potent, concepts of 'fairness' and 'equality of opportunity'.

> 'One of the major problems facing societies in almost all parts of the world is the inadequate accommodation of social equity with cultural diversity. The lack of discourse between the two systems, cultural and social, means that there are fewer common ideologies on the basis of which accommodations can be negotiated, for ideologies themselves are not static; the very process of discourse for accommodation can generate a greater overlap between the two systems'. (Lynch, Modgil and Modgil, 1992)

The crises arising from the neglect or denial of this issue can be seen in virtually all societies. Consider a *few* of the very many candidate countries where ethnic, cultural and religious rivalries cause conflicts and chaos. These include many of the republics that have replaced the Soviet Union plus Afghanistan, Angola, Australia, Brazil, Cambodia, Canada, Ceylon, Cyprus, Egypt, Eritrea, Fiji, Iran,

Kashmire, Latvia, Malaysia, Morocco, Nicaragua, India, Israel, New Zealand, Lebanon, Nigeria, Pakistan, Saudi-Arabia, South Africa, Sri Lanka, Sudan, the United Kingdom of Great Britain, the other eleven member states comprising the European Community, and the United States of America. Is *any* country exempt? Probably not.

Pessimists will argue that discourse on any matter can all too easily lead to polarised and intransigent positions. Nationalism and religious fundamentalism are powerful forces individually. In combination, their social power is amplified. Typically, both nationalism and religious fundamentalism demand a conformity that all too frequently marginalises minority groups. 'Those who are not for us are against us'. Such slogans simplify and distort complex concerns and are extensively used as emotionally-laden and powerful techniques of mass persuasion. Realists normally suspect the appeal of such superficial 'soundbites' and accept that, whereas detailed analysis and discussion are more difficult, they can lead to longer-lasting and more mutually beneficial resolutions. In contrast, many fundamentalists consider compromise to be weakness and, as such, unacceptable. Tolerance is one of the first victims of such intransigence. Ethnic cleansing is one extreme consequence.

In any society, characterised by cultural, ethnic and religious diversities (amongst others), the deeply held moral and political value systems of individuals and groups are continuing sources of tensions and disagreements. Some customs and behaviours of *any* ethnic group can anger members of other cultural groups. Indeed, this tendency to be intolerant of the unfamiliar is characteristic of the human condition. What is collectively of even greater importance are the means adopted within a society to address and resolve the often mutually exclusive demands presented by particular pressure groups at given times in particular social contexts.

The recent wars and continuing tensions in the Balkans underline the destructive mayhem to which extreme nationalist, ideological and religious beliefs can rapidly lead. The Balkanisation of Britain, or of any other European country, is not a scenario many citizens would advocate or anticipate with enthusiasm.

If a country is not to move towards increasing intolerance, it is essential that divergent opinions held by various ethnic groups are, at the very least, respected. Respecting the opinions and values of others, even if one disagrees strongly with the views expressed, is one of the key attributes of a democratic society. Changes are achieved by the ballot box and not by semtex: evolution, not revolution, is the preferred process.

The models that teachers and other adults present to children are potent determinants of both the current and future attitudes and behaviours of the younger generation. Example is more effective than exhortation. If we provide models of intolerance in our classes, schools and communities, we encourage it. If we sow the wind, we will reap the whirlwind. The attitudes and values that teachers demonstrate daily in their work in both the classroom and the community, coupled with the values that underpin agreed and explicit policies and practices that determine the curriculum, are of the essence in education for life in a pluralist society.

Provided that the six predictions given in the Introduction are all likely to be false, action on the school curriculum can be deferred - for a while only. In a Europe (and world) in which virtually all countries are becoming increasingly multicultural, it cannot be delayed indefinitely.

On the other hand, if the predictions appear valid, a review of curriculum policy and practices by both government and schools is imperative.

Challenges

Limitations of space mean that only three major challenges have been selected for consideration. These are interdependent. All derive from the prime objectives of ensuring equality of opportunity in the context of multicultural education in a democratic society. In this context, equality of opportunity implies the elimination of underachievement.

Challenge 1: providing a curriculum for all pupils in a multicultural society

'When in Rome, do as the Romans do'. Supporters of this position nowadays assert 'If migrants choose to come to this country, it is their responsibility to adapt to our ways and not ours to adapt to theirs'. Is this an adequate basis for a multicultural educational policy and practices? If migrants choose to move to a country, are admitted and accepted as full citizens of the country, is it reasonable to expect the established citizens and institutions (including schools) of the host country reciprocally to become aware, tolerant of, and adapt to, the cultures of minority ethnic groups, the value systems underpinning them and the cultural customs being introduced?

Provided that readers can accept the anachronism of gender bias within it, the following quotation contains an important truth concerning the varied ethnocentricisms to which we are all prey. It comes from an influential book concerning the nature of prejudice. 'No person knows his own culture who only his own culture knows'.(Allport, 1954)

All citizens living in a democracy are equal under the law. All have equal rights (often vocally asserted and claimed); all have reciprocal responsibilities (less frequently recognised). Rights and responsibilities are but two sides of a coin. A concomitant responsibility of all cultural groups is the development of an increased awareness and tolerance of the nature of cultural diversity in their society.

An ancient proverb asserts that 'Coming events cast their shadows before'. As has always been the case, the 'seeds' of the nation, society and its component cultures that will develop in the UK, or in any other European country, have long been sown. Metaphorically, these seeds are already sprouting. Will the social fruits of future harvests be bitter or sweet? What social legacies are we leaving our children and their children's children? Can the tensions between, on the one hand, communality, co-operation and co-existence and, on the other, those of competition, conflict and confusion, be constructively addressed? In their turn, what 'seeds' will our children inherit, propagate and harvest?

With reference to often economically relatively powerless immigrants, can the rank weeds of institutional and individual racism be acknowledged, identified, rooted out and replaced with tolerance in our schools, communities and country? Can amity arise from the ashes of acrimony and animosity between ethnic, religious and cultural groups?

The UK has a history of racial and religious intolerance. We are not alone. Even in recent years, our cities have seen serious riots having racial overtones. Minority ethnic groups continue to be on the receiving end of racial harassment including arson and murder. Inter-ethnic minority groups exist and are also manifest. At a more mundane level the incidence of racist name-calling continues to be a cause of concern in many schools (Pumfrey and Verma, 1990). Pupils from certain ethnic minorities are, as groups, perceived to be underachieving in their studies. Their underachievement is antithetical to equality of opportunity.

'In education, there is evidence of significant underachievement among some ethnic-minority groups. It is more difficult in this area to identify and measure the nature and extent of discrimination, but the Commission's investigation in Birmingham showed different levels of suspensions which could not be explained by factors other than race; research published in the Swann Report revealed discriminatory patterns of behaviour in the classroom; and the Eggleston Report in 1986 pointed to discrimination of pupils to sets, streams, etc. It is also disturbing that ethnic minorities are under represented amongst those who hold power in the education system whether as governors, administrators, inspectors or teachers.' (Commission for Racial Equality, 1991)

Despite such events, our experience in the UK. is that, given the considerable goodwill existing between ethnic and cultural groups, social cohesion is possible, but requires *considerable and continuing* efforts by all levels of society. The government has its responsibilities for educational (and other) policies and resources. So too does the community, the school, its staff and the parents and children that the educational system exists to serve. 'Laissez-faire' is a totally inadequate approach to ensuring that equality of opportunity is achieved within a democratic multicultural society.

Challenge 2: competence in the language of the host community

A second challenge relates to the first. It specifically concerns the variety of languages spoken as their mother-tongue by minority ethnic groups. It has been estimated that in state schools in the Greater London area, over 160 different languages are spoken. If children are to benefit from what is provided in an educational system based on competence in all aspects of the English language, the challenge becomes 'How can schools best ensure such learning takes place?'

The government document on English and the National Curriculum summarises the challenge:

> 'Bilingual children should be considered an advantage in the classroom rather than a problem. The evidence shows that such children will make greater progress in English if they know that their knowledge of their mother tongue is valued, if it is recognised that their experience of language is likely to be greater than that of their monoglot peers and, indeed, if their knowledge and experience can be put to good use in the classroom to the benefit of all pupils, to provide examples of the structure and syntax of different languages, provide a focus for discussion about language form and for contrasts and comparisons with the structure of the English Language.' (Department of Education and Science and the Welsh Office, 1988)

Whilst one might justifiably cavil at such an unnecessarily lengthy and labyrinthine sentence, it makes important points.

In the light of the vast range of languages spoken in the schools in Britain, mother-tongue teaching with pupils who know very little English presents considerable difficulties in some localities. The establishment of teams of specialist teachers to assist pupils and teachers in schools with children whose mother-tongue is not English has been a most constructive and effective response.

Challenge 3: social cohesion in a multicultural society

The third challenge focuses on how the development of education for citizenship in a multicultural society can be achieved within schools as part of the school curriculum.

In 1987, Margaret Thatcher, the then British Prime Minister, was stressing the importance of the individual. She asserted that 'There is no such thing as society...'. Not all citizens and politicians (including many of her colleagues) agreed with her views, even though the importance of individuals and families was also acknowledged by Thatcher. Much earlier in the 19th. century the importance of 'Education for Citizenship' had received recognition. Ways in which Citizenship could be encouraged through the school curriculum had been developed. The roots of the idea probably lie with the Reform Bill 1886 which created a mass male electorate. The earliest known text was *The Citizenship Reader*. This was published in 1886 and between then and 1904 was reprinted twenty-four times (Abrams, 1993).

Consider the prescient words of a former head of the State Educational Services in England and Wales concerning the work of secondary schools: 'If those democratic institutions, which we in this country agree are essential for the full development of the individual, are to be preserved, some systematic training in the duties of citizenship is necessary. The conditions in which we live today and the problems that confront us call for a fresh emphasis in the work of education on the social and civic responsibilities which inevitably await the citizen'. In this same book in which these words appear, the methods that can be used in eleven secondary schools subjects are described. Interestingly, *this took place over 60 years ago* (Association for Education in Citizenship, 1936).

After the murder in 1995 of Philip Lawrence, Headteacher, at his secondary school by an adolescent, the call by the widow for a constructive educational approach to develop a more ethically based society has received support from all political parties. In this movement, the renewal of civic values among Britain's young is central (October, 1996).

This educational challenge is perennial! At the end of the 20th century, and into the 21st century, it will become even more pressing. It is a concern for all countries.

Responses

Response to challenge 1

Equality of opportunity is, in large measure, based on educational attainments and examination results. An equal opportunities policy seeks to ensure that avoidable underachievement is alleviated. In Britain, the attainments of pupils from minority ethnic groups have been a matter of concern for a number of years (Verma and Pumfrey, 1988). Because of what appeared to be the relative underachievement of certain minority ethnic groups in their basic skills, a Committee of Inquiry into the Education of Children from Minority Ethnic Groups was established under the Chairmanship of Lord Swann. Its published report was entitled *Education for All* (Committee of Inquiry, 1985). This set out a series of measures whereby schools, in co-operation with their communities, could help raise attainments and reduce the underachievement of pupils from certain minority ethnic groups.

Teachers are faced with heavy teaching and assessment loads. These are their major concerns in the interests of the pupils in their care. How can time be made for the reading, reflection and reorganisation required if they are to adapt the curriculum for a culturally pluralist society? Can this be left to individual schools or is a collective national response required? In England and Wales, a national strategy, relevant to all pupils was adopted.

In 1988 in England and Wales a National Curriculum was legally established under the provisions of the Education Reform Act 1988. The National Curriculum is intended for *all* pupils. Its principle objectives are ones that colleagues in democratic countries will almost certainly have little difficulty in accepting.

- To promote the spiritual, moral, cultural, mental and physical development of pupils at the school and of society; and
- to prepare such pupils for the opportunities, responsibilities and experiences of adult life.

The inclusion of the word 'cultural' in the above list of five key aspects of development merits comment. It denotes an explicit political acknowledgement of the importance of cultural diversity in our society, and of the complex interactions between all five, in education. The objectives apply to all pupils, irrespective of religious, ethnic, cultural or social group. For each aspect of the curriculum a syllabus (Programme of Study) is specified. All schools are to be formally inspected every four years to ensure that they are 'delivering' the National Curriculum.

Table 1
The components of the National Curriculum in England and Wales for the age range 5:00 to 16:00 years

Subjects

Religious Education;	Geography;
Mathematics;	Modern Language;
English;	Art;
Science;	Music;
Technology;	Physical Education.
History;	

Cross-curricular elements

Cross-curricular Dimensions (central educational orientation):

Equal opportunity;	Multiculturalism.

Cross-curricular Themes (cross-curricular strands permeating the curriculum):

Economic and industrial understanding;	Health education;
Careers education and guidance;	Education for citizenship;
	Environmental education.

Cross-curricular Skills (transferable skills capable of being applied and developed in different curricular contexts):

Communication;
Numeracy;
Study skills;
Problem-solving;
Personal and social skills;
Information technology skills.

The organisation and teaching techniques characteristic of Primary schools differ from those of Secondary schools. The former tend to be less formal than the latter. Despite this, the above elements can probably be recognised by most teachers, whether in initial training or already qualified and experienced.

In the context of a multicultural society such as the UK, is it possible to modify a curriculum so as to educate for cultural pluralism?

It was precisely this aspiration that led to the production of a four volume series of books entitled *Cultural Diversity and the Curriculum*. Two were for secondary school teachers and two for Primary school teachers. At each level, Religious Education and other Subjects were considered. A further two volumes address the Cross-curricular elements (Pumfrey and Verma, 1993a, 1993b; Verma and Pumfrey, 1993, 1994).

These four volumes provide a cornucopia of suggestions concerning how cultural diversity can be integrated into the methods and materials that comprise a curriculum. These ideas are drawn from the UK. perspective. They capitalise on the experience of teachers and other professionals who have been engaged in multicultural education for many years, both in the UK. and elsewhere. despite the limitation of these ideas having been developed within a UK. perspective, the principles, practices, initiatives and resources described, discussed and listed will provide important sources of ideas. These can be adapted and developed to suit any educational system in which cultural diversity is accepted as a key educational and social concern having implications for the social cohesion of the entire state.

Cross-curricular themes additional to those listed in Table 1 were also addressed in volumes 2 and 4 as follows:

Volume 2 (Secondary schools) (Verma and Pumfrey, 1993).
Countering racism in British education;
Personal and social education: a Black perspective;
Gender issues in education for citizenship;
European Community understanding;
Cultural differences and staff development; and
Accountability and the local management of schools.

Volume 4 (Primary schools) (Verma and Pumfrey, 1994).
Personal and social education;
Gender issues;
The multicultural dimension in the Primary National Curriculum;
Children with Special Educational Needs;
The European dimension;
Information technology (IT): Using computers as a tool; and
Initial teacher education and ethnic diversity.

As further evidence of the extensive network of organisations concerned with developing and providing materials for use in schools, a selected number of those currently operating in England are listed in Table 2. Addresses are also provided.

Table 2
Some key sources of information on multi-cultural education in England

Access to information on multi-cultural education resources (AIMER),

Faculty of Education and Community Studies, The University of Reading, Bulmershe Court, Earley, Reading, RG6 1HV.

Acorn (Percussion) Ltd., Unit 34, Abbey Business Centre, Ingate Place, London, SW8 3NS.

African Video Centre, 7 Balls Pond Road, London, N1 4AX.

Afro-Caribbean Education Resource, (ACER), Wyvil School, Wyvil Road, London, SW8 2TJ.

Avon Section 11 Education Team, Education Development Service, Horfield, Bristol, BS7 OPU.

Bilingual Support Service, Crosby Primary School, Frodingham Road, Scunthorpe, Humberside, DN15 7NL.

BBC Educational Development, P.O. Box 50, Wetherby, West Yorkshire, LS23 7EZ.

Board of Deputies of British Jews, Woburn House,Tavistock Square, London WC1H OEP.

Centre for Ethnic Studies in Education, School of Education, University of Manchester, Manchester M13 9PL.

Centre for Multicultural Education, Rushey Mead Centre, Harrison Road, Leicester, LE4 6BR.

Centre for Multicultural Education, University of London Institute of Education, 20 Bedford Way, London, WC1 OAL.

Centre for Research in Ethnic Relations, Resources Centre Librarian, University of Warwick, Coventry, CV4 7AL.

Centre for World Development Education, 1 Catton Street, London, WC1R 4AB.

Childsplay, 112 Tooting High Street, London, SW17 ORR.

Christian Education Movement, Royal Buildings, Victoria Street, Derby, DE1 1GW.

Close Links, c/o Grimwade Street, Ipswich, IP4 1LS.

Commonwealth Institute Resource Centre, Kensington High Street, London, W8 6NQ.

Council for Education in World Citizenship, Seymour Mews House, London, W1H 9PE.

Development Education Centre, Selly Oak Colleges, Bristol Road, Birmingham, B29 6LE.

Early Years Trainers Anti-Racist Network, The Lyndens, 51 Granville Road, London, N12 OJH.

Education Development Centre (EMSS/MPU), Popes Lane, Oldbury, Warley, Sandwell, B69 4PJ.

Education Development Centre EO Unit, Room 14, Field Road, Bloxwich, Walsall, West Midlands, W53 3JF.

Education Materials, OXFAM, 274 Banbury Road, Oxford, OX2 7DZ.

Elm Bank Teachers Centre, Mile Lane, Coventry, CV1 2LQ.

Ethnic Minority Project, 103 Preston New Road, Blackburn, BB2 6BJ.

Faculty of Multicultural Education, Martineau Education Centre, Balden Road, Harbourne, Birmingham, B32 2EH.

Folens Publishers, Albert House, Apex Business Centre, Boscombe Road, Dunstable, LU5 4RN.

Heights Culture Shop, 13 Middle Row, Stevenage Old Town, Herts.

Hounslow Primary Language Service, Civic centre, Lampton Road, Hounslow, Middlesex, TW3 4DN.

Humming Bird Book and Toy Service, 136 Grosvenor Road, St. Pauls, Bristol, BS28 1YA.

Institute of Race Relations, 2-6 Leeke Street, King's Cross Road, London, WC1X 9HS.

Islamic Cultural Centre, 146 Park Road, London, NW8 7RG.

Joint Council for Welfare of Immigrants, 115 Old Street, London, EC1V 9JR.

Kemet Educational Materials, Consultancy, 111 Lakeheath, London, N14 4RY.

Kirklees Supplementary Schools Project, Multicultural Education Unit, Huddersfield Technical College, New North Road, Huddersfield, HD1 5NN.

Leeds Development Education Centre, 153 Cardigan Road, Leeds, LS6 1LJ.

Letterbox Library, Leroy House, 436 Essex Road, London, N1 3BR.

Manchester City Council Education Committee, Peace Education Project, North Manchester Resources Centre, Harpurhey, Manchester, M10 7NS.

Marigold Bentley and Tom Leimdorfer, Education Advisory Programme, Friends House, Euston Road, London, NW1 2BJ.

Minority Group Support Service, Southfields Old School, South Street, Coventry, CV1 5EJ.

Minority Rights Group, 379 Brixton Road, London, SW9 7DE.

Multicultural Education Centre, Stirling School, Prospect Place, Doncaster, DN1 3QP.

Multicultural Education Service, Spencer Centre, Lewis Road, Northampton, NN5 7BJ.

Multicultural Resource Centre, Holne Chase Centre, Bletchley, Milton Keynes, MK3 5HP.

Multicultural Support Team, Jennie Lee Community and Professional Centre, Lichfield Road, Wednesfield, Wolverhampton, Staffordshire, WV1 1PC.

Multicultural Education and Language Service, Broadbent Road, Oldham, OL1 4HU.

National Association of Racial Equality Councils, 8-16 Coronet Street, London, N1 6HD.

National Educational resources Information Service, Maryland College, Leighton Street, Woburn, Milton Keynes, MK17 9JD.

National Union of Teachers, Education and Equal Opportunities Dept, Hamilton House, Mabledon Place, London, WC1H 9BD.

Peace Education Project, North Manchester Resources Centre, Harpurhey, Manchester, M10 7NS.

Peterborough Centre for Multicultural Education, 165a Cromwell Road, Peterborough, PE1 2EL.

Publications Unit, Jordanhill College of Education, Southbrae Drive, Glasgow, G13 1PP.

Refugee Council, Bondway House, 3-9 Bondway, London, SW8 1SJ.

Resources for Learning Development Unit, Sheridan Road, Horfield, Bristol, BS7 0PU.

Runnymede Trust, 11 Princelet Street, London, E1 6QH.

Standing Conference on Racial Equality in Europe, Unit 303, Brixton Enterprise Centre, 444 Brixton Road, London, SW1 8EJ.

Star Apple Blossom, 13 Inman Road, London, SW18 3BB.

Zuma Art Services, Kings Place, 16 Stony Street, Nottingham, NG1 1LH.

Response to challenge 2

For understandable financial and cultural reasons, minority ethnic groups tend to form in geographical locations where socio-economic deprivation is relatively high. The local authorities in these areas are already under considerable financial pressures. A system of discretionary grants was developed in 1966 to help local authorities provide services designed to alleviate the difficulties of 'Commonwealth immigrants' in fields such as housing, health and education. A 'Commonwealth immigrant' was interpreted as a person, adult or child, born in another country of the Commonwealth, who has been ordinarily resident in the United Kingdom for less than ten years, or the child of such a person. More recently eligibility has been extended to certain immigrants from non-Commonwealth countries. Initially the grants were authorised under the provisions of the Local Government Act 1966. In England and Wales, this source of discretionary funds is colloquially referred to as 'Section 11 funds'. The grants originally covered 75% of certain of the costs. As the result of a review, this was subsequently reduced to 50% (Home Office, 1990).

In 1992, the principle that Section 11 funding was designed to assist in supporting was stated as:

'The reduction of racial disadvantage which inhibits members of ethnic minorities from playing a full part in the social and economic life of this country.... by helping local authorities meet the costs of employment of additional staff required to overcome linguistic or cultural difficulties and thus gain full access to mainstream services and facilities.' (Home Office, 1992)

Education has always been a major recipient of Section 11 grants. The reason for this is that many of the more recent immigrant families to the UK. did not speak English. The government used this special discretionary funding to encourage education authorities to establish services providing children with additional help in becoming competent in English. The government's aims for these grants are:

- to remove barriers to true equality of educational opportunity for ethnic minority pupils;
- to give school-aged children whose mother tongue is not English a command of English which, as far as possible, is equal to that of their peers; and
- to help such children achieve at the same level as their peers in all areas of the curriculum.

According to Home Office estimates, the 1992/3 allocation was expected to fund 800 projects with 10,600 posts. This represented an increase in posts. There are usually more applicants for grants than monies available to fund them. According to a survey carried out by a registered charity known as the Local Authorities Race Relations Information Exchange (LARRIE), some 32% of youth projects and 81% of projects supporting the teaching of English in schools were supported (Local Authorities Race Relations Exchange (LARRIE), (1993).

Considerable fears were subsequently expressed that the reduction in the percentage of grants for specific projects would reduce the work that could be done. In February, 1995 it was anticipated that one in eight language support staff would lose their jobs by the end of the financial year in April, 1995. One authority, Tower Hamlets, was reported as having lost 150 section 11 jobs in 1994. In another London authority, Lewisham, a report dated 17th. March, 1995, states that 138 Section 11 teachers had been issued with redundancy notices. The situation was serious.

Albeit somewhat belatedly, the government did respond to the evidence and argument presented to them asking that they review their policy and provision. The Minister listened. Also on March 17th, 1995, it was reported that the Home Office was to make an additional £30 million pounds available to fund 300 new Section 11 ethnic minority support projects on top of the £53 million already promised for projects up to 1996-7. The government asserts that this new money will lead to jobs for 1,800 teachers, 300 classroom assistants and 900 project workers primarily in the field of language support.

The most recent evidence on the basic skills and examination results of minority ethnic groups is encouraging. Despite this, for certain minority ethnic groups, the extent of underachievement remains a matter of serious concern. Fortunately, it is well-established that the longer minority ethnic group children have been educated within the English educational system, the higher their standards of basic literacy and, subsequently, their school-leaving examination grades.

With reference to reading standards at the ages of 8:00 to 9:00 years, it has also recently been shown in an inner-city area that the reading standards of white monolingual and Asian bilingual pupils are equivalent in terms of both reading accuracy and reading comprehension. Although the evidence is somewhat tangential, it has been argued that Section 11 staff have made an important contribution to reducing underachievement (Pumfrey and Chughti, 1995).

Would a Section 11 legal and financial arrangement be of any value within the educational context of other countries where one is not already in existence?

Response to challenge 3

Whether in Britain, or in virtually any country, national identity is likely to remain a potent concept. The 'whole' of that identity is likely to be greater than the sum of its ethnic, religious or culturally distinctive parts. In the UK., the dynamic equilibrium between the values, beliefs and behaviours of a wide range of interest groups are addressed through democratic processes. The nationalisms of Scotland and Wales are examples. That within Northern Ireland has been less well dealt with as yet. At times, and in particular circumstances, marked tensions occur between ethnic, cultural and religious groups. They also occur between myriad other groups: political parties and football teams make the point. Longstanding regional rivalries, based on history and geography, also exist in the UK.

231

Whilst democratic processes are far from perfect, they appear to have considerable advantages to all involved in comparison with currently available alternatives based on bombs, bullets and totalitarianism. The case for education for citizenship as part of the National Curriculum has been developed in the UK (National Curriculum Council, 1990).

The value of values

In any society, the existence within its population of shared values encourages social cohesion: the absence of a set of commonly held values represents a condition under which social disintegration is more likely to occur. This issue is of central relevance to social policies including equality of opportunity and anti-racism in any democratic society. It has profound implications for education. In a multicultural society such as the UK., characterised by marked cultural, ethnic and religious diversities, is there a consensus of values that can be used to strengthen social cohesion?

The officially appointed School Curriculum and Assessment Authority (SCAA) addressed this issue in 1996. A forum of 150 individuals drawn from varying cultures, ethnic groups and faiths (together with agnostics and atheists), was convened. Membership of the forum was drawn largely from individuals working with young people. Their task was to consider whether it was possible to identify a statement of values that 'all men and women of good-will' would support. In essence, the wider community was being asked 'What are the values on which schools can rely on public support?' The identification of such a consensus would provide teachers with a secure basis on which to strengthen the provision of spiritual, moral, social and cultural education within the National Curriculum both in specific lessons or through the medium of other subjects. A set of explicit shared values would also be important in both earlier and later stages of education, and to society as a whole.

In the event, the forum was able to identify a consensus and to produce a statement of values. It was first published on October 30th, 1996. The set of values is divided into four areas: Society; Relationships; Self; and Environment. In each instance, there is an accompanying set of 'principles for action'. A copy of this statement of values can be found at the end of this chapter in Appendix 1.

On seeing the statement of values, the Secretary of State for Education and Employment expressed concern that the forum had failed to give clear support to 'traditional family values'. She commended the process of seeking consensus, but had reservations concerning the statement of values in its first published form. 'Schools do a great deal of excellent in this area but teachers need clear, practical advice to help them in delivering their responsibility to provide pupils' spiritual and moral education.'

A widespread consultation on the statement of values is to take place. The Chairperson of SCAA. is reported as saying that this will include a public opinion poll, together with views obtained through a representative sample of 3,200 schools. The forum was scheduled to reconvene in January, 1997 and to consider whether any revisions are required to the statement of values in the light of the feedback received. The forum's advice to government was presented in February, 1997.

The strategy adopted by SCAA has a number of strengths. These include the active involvement of various individuals and groups in our society whose cultures and beliefs encompass many varied and complex sets of values. Despite this diversity, an important initial consensus has emerged. Another strength is the sets of explicit principles for action that have been agreed.

Amongst the weaknesses of the approach, is the level of generality of what has been agreed. Typically, agreement concerning principle is relatively easy compared with translating these principles into acceptable and effective practices in schools. As always, 'The devil is in the detail'. That is probably where important disagreements could emerge. Time will tell. In the interests of enhancing a social cohesion that benefits all members of our society and simultaneously reducing the alienation caused by conscious and unconscious prejudices, building bridges is a more promising strategy than building barriers. Recognition of the importance of education in preparing youngsters to play a responsible part in a democratic society led to the establishment in 1989 of the House of Commons Speaker's Commission on Citizenship. Guidance on the principles was published in November, 1990 and the topic was identified as one of the five cross-curricular themes within the National Curriculum (see Table 1.). A survey carried out in the same year showed that 43% of schools had agreed policies on citizenship. The Centre for Citizenship Studies in Education was established in 1991 in response to the Speaker's Commission. It has produced an information pack whereby schools are shown how to carry out an audit of existing citizenship activities that are *already* being carried out within the National Curriculum. A further two complementary organisations were established. Their names and addresses are as follows:

Centre for Citizenship Studies in Education,
Queens Building,
University of Leicester,
Barrack Road,
Northampton,
Leicester.

The Institute for Citizenship Studies,
20, St. James's Square,
London, SW1.

The Citizenship Foundation,
63, Charterhouse Street,
London, EC1.

All teachers will know that the establishment of such national organisations is but a first step. It is how and what is done within the schools and their communities that, *to a significant extent*, determines whether tolerance and responsibility between all ethnic, religious and cultural groups will flourish. It is not easy for schools to model the democracy and tolerance that they are charged with fostering in their pupils. It is possible.

A major danger for schools is that politicians readily attribute to them responsibilities for matters that are equally the concern of parents, local communities, governments and countries. Despite this caveat, when we consider how education for citizenship in a multicultural society might be encouraged, schools and teachers matter.

Conclusion

In the UK, it is a legally-required condition of official approval of a course of initial teacher training that the issues of equality of education and multicultural education be formally and systematically covered in the context of the National Curriculum (see Table 1.).

Student teachers undertaking initial training could, to advantage, consider how adequately their training and experiences both in the university and their practical placements, has equipped them to meet the challenges of educating pupils in a multicultural society.

In this respect, being able to distinguish between the nature of prejudice (to which all individuals and social groups are prey) and racism (in which prejudice is linked with power), represents a worthwhile first step.

A further way of evaluating their preparation is to consider what is likely happening in the schools in which they will shortly be employed. Reconsider Question 4 posed earlier in the Introduction to this chapter:

Introduction: Q.4.   What are we doing to address such issues in our own schools and our respective communities?

This leads to the following suggestion. At an initial stage in deciding what organisational and curricular developments may be needed, the staff of *every* school should discuss, in open session, the following twelve questions.

Has our school implemented the following actions?

1.   Ensured that all staff members, including the headteacher and senior staff, have taken or will take courses on the philosophical, moral, educational, economic and legal bases for the construction and development of a multicultural curriculum?

2.   Ensured that all staff, starting with the headteacher and senior staff, have taken or will take courses on anti-racism?

3.   Distinguished between the individual and institutional aspects of racism in society in general and in education in particular?

4.   Established contact with representatives of the various minority ethnic groups whose children attend the school?

5.   Consulted colleagues in adjacent schools to consider how they are addressing the challenges of developing an educational programme for pupils growing up in a multicultural society?

6.   Checked on the availability of curriculum resources at international (e.g. UNESCO.) and national levels?

7.   Visited schools having a considerable number of pupils from minority ethnic groups in order to observe and discuss colleagues' curriculum policies, practices and resources?

8.   Considered collaborating with colleagues in other schools in undertaking any staff development work that may be required?

9.   Developed a democratically agreed and publicly available policy document specifying a school commitment to equality of opportunity and multicultural education?

10.   Contacted and involved representatives of the various minority ethnic groups whose children attend the school in considering the objectives of the curriculum and its implication?

11.   Revised recently each aspect of the school curriculum (both subjects and cross-curricular elements) in terms of the objectives, syllabus and pedagogy appropriate to *education for all* in a multicultural society?

12.   Planned how the efficacy of the curriculum can be assessed in relation to the school's equal opportunity and multicultural policy?

References

Abrams, F. (1993) 'Rights, duties and the greater scheme', *Times Educational Supplement*, No.4020, 16th. July.

Allport, G.W. (1954) *The Nature of Prejudice*, Reading, Mass., Addison-Wesley.

Association for Education in Citizenship in Secondary Schools (1936) *Education for Citizenship in Secondary Schools*, London, Oxford University Press.

Ballard, R. and Kalra, V.S. (1994) *The Ethnic Dimensions of the 1991 Census: A Preliminary Report*, Manchester Census Group, University of Manchester.

Commission for Racial Equality (1991) *Second Review of the Race Relations Act 1976*, London, Commission for Racial Equality.

Committee of Inquiry into the Education of Children from Minority Ethnic Groups (1985) *Education for All*, (The Swann Report), Cmnd. 9453, London, HMSO.

Department of Education and Science and the Welsh Office (1988) *National Curriculum: English for ages 5-11*, London, HMSO.

Home Office (1990) *A Scrutiny of Grants under Section 11 of the Local Government Act, Final Report December 1988*, London, Her Majesty's Stationery Office (HMSO).

Local Authorities Race Relations Information Exchange (1993) *Guide to Section 11 Funding: Research Report: Part 1*, London, LARRIE.

Lynch, J., Modgil, C. and Modgil, S. (1992) *Cultural Diversity and the Schools, Vol.1, Education for Cultural Diversity: Convergence and Divergence*, London, The Falmer Press.

National Curriculum Council (1990) *Curriculum Guidance No.8. Education for Citizenship*, York, National Curriculum Council.

National Curriculum Council (1992) *Starting out with the National Curriculum - An Introduction to the National Curriculum and Religious Education*, York, National Curriculum Council.

Pumfrey, P.D. and Chughti, I. (1996) Bilingualism and the reading attainments of 8:00-9:00 year-old pupils: evidence and interpretation. In B. Neate (Ed.) *Literacy Saves Lives*. United Kingdom Reading Association, pp.155-167.

Pumfrey, P.D. and Verma, G.K. (Eds.) (1990) *Race Relations and Urban Education: Contexts and Promising Practices*, London, The Falmer Press.

Pumfrey, P.D. and Verma, G.K. (Eds.) (1993a) *Cultural Diversity and the Curriculum, Volume 1, The Foundation Subjects and Religious Education in Secondary Schools*, London, The Falmer Press.

Pumfrey, P.D. and Verma, G.K. (Eds.) (1993b) *Cultural Diversity and the Curriculum, Volume 3, The Foundation Subjects and Religious Education in Primary Schools*, London, The Falmer Press.

Stone, S. and Pumfrey, P.D. (1990) 'The Child using English as a Second Language (ESL) and the National Curriculum 5-11', in Pumfrey, P.D. and Verma, G.K. (Eds.) (1990) *Race Relations and Urban Education: Contexts and Promising Practices*, London, The Falmer Press, pp.259-275.

Verma, G.K. and Pumfrey, P.D. (Eds.) (1988) *Educational Attainments: Issues and Outcomes in Multicultural Education*, London, The Falmer Press.

Verma, G.K. and Pumfrey, P.D. (Eds.) (1993) *Cultural Diversity and the Curriculum, Volume 2, Cross Curricular Contexts, Themes and Dimensions in Secondary Schools*, London, The Falmer Press.

Verma, G.K. and Pumfrey, P.D. (Eds.) (1994) *Cultural Diversity and the Curriculum, Volume 4, Cross Curricular Contexts, Themes and Dimensions in Primary Schools*, London, The Falmer Press.

Appendix 1: The statement

The forum divides the subject into four areas: society, relationships, self and environment. In each case, a statement of values is accompanied by a number of 'principles for action'.

Society

We value truth, human rights, the law, justice and collective endeavour for the common good of society. In particular, we value families as sources of love and support for all their members and as the basis of society in which people care for others.

On the basis of these values we as a society should:

- understand our responsibilities as citizens;

- be ready to challenge values or actions which may be harmful to individuals or communities;

- support families in raising children and caring for dependants;

- help people to know about the law and legal processes;

- obey the law and encourage others to do so;

- accept diversity and respect people's right to religious and cultural differences;

- provide opportunities to all;

- support people who cannot sustain a dignified life-style by themselves;

- promote participation in our democracy;

- contribute to, as well as benefit fairly from, economic and cultural resources;
- make truth and integrity priorities in public life.

Relationships

We value others for themselves, not for what they have or what they can do for us, and we value these relationships as fundamental to our development and the good of the community.

On the basis of these values, within our relationships we should:

- respect the dignity of all people;

- tell others they are valued;

- earn loyalty, trust and confidence;

- work co-operatively with others;

- be mutually supportive;

- respect the beliefs, life, privacy and property of others;

- try to resolve disputes peacefully.

Self

We value each person as a unique being of intrinsic worth, with potential for spiritual, moral, intellectual and physical development and change.

On the basis of these values, we as individuals should:

- try to understand our own character, strengths and weaknesses;

- develop a sense of self-worth;

- try to discover meaning and purpose in life and how life ought to be lived;

- try to live up to a shared moral code;

- make responsible use of our rights and privileges;

- strive for knowledge and wisdom throughout life;

- take responsibility for our own lives within our capacities;

Environment

We value the natural world as a source of wonder and inspiration, and accept our duty to maintain a sustainable environment for the future.
On the basis of these values we should:

- preserve a balance and diversity in nature wherever possible;

- justify development in terms of a sustainable environment;

- repair habitats devastated by human development wherever possible;

- preserve areas of beauty wherever possible;

- understand the place of human beings within the world.

16 Citizenship, national identity and the Europeanisation of the curriculum

Dean Garratt and John Robinson

Introduction

When the Education Reform Act (1988) (ERA) became statute in England and Wales the structure and organisation of the curriculum was, for the first time, enshrined in a prescribed manner. Despite earlier protestations and later evidence the nature of that prescription was heavily subject oriented with core subjects (English, Mathematics and Science) and foundation subjects (Technology, Geography, History, Music, Art, Physical Education and Modern Foreign Languages (in the Secondary phase only) together with Welsh in Welsh schools). The core and foundation subjects, together, constituted what was the National Curriculum and each subject had statutory content in terms of Programmes of Study and required goals in terms of Attainment Targets. In addition to the National Curriculum schools also had a requirement to deliver Religious Education which, when combined with the National Curriculum, made up the Basic Curriculum. In announcing these arrangements the body which at that time was responsible for the organisation of the curriculum, the National Curriculum Council (NCC), recognised that, on its own, the Basic Curriculum was an inadequate preparation for young people on the threshold of adulthood. As a consequence the NCC provided guidance relating to the 'Whole Curriculum'.

The Whole Curriculum was to embrace the Basic Curriculum together with cross-curricular themes, skills and dimensions which were collectively known as the cross-curricular elements. Specific guidance was published relating to five named cross-curricular themes namely Education for Economic and Industrial Understanding (EIU) (NCC, 1990a), Health Education (NCC, 1990b), Careers Education (NCC, 1990c), Environmental Education (NCC,

1990d) and Education for Citizenship (NCC, 1990e). These five cross-curricular themes were contextualised by an earlier guidance document on the Whole Curriculum (NCC, 1990f). Despite these publications, however, as we have identified elsewhere (Garratt and Robinson, 1994a) the cross-curricular themes tended to remain marginal to teachers' interests and a subsequent review of the National Curriculum under the Chairmanship of Sir Ron Dearing (1993) has further undermined the status of such themes (see Garratt and Robinson, 1994a), despite the contribution which the themes can, or should, make to learning. Consequently, it would be interesting to be able to go back to a time before the Education Reform Act (ERA) (1988) in England with a blank sheet of paper and try to construct an holistic curriculum which would have as its central pillars cross-curricular understandings.

We say this for two main reasons. Learning is a messy, high risk business and the construction of highly compartmentalised, discrete subject vehicles for learning is a contradiction of the ways in which people learn. Secondly, cross-curricular understandings are much more likely to contribute to learning which promotes concerns like solidarity and social justice. Although to make such a time traveller's dream come true is completely out of the question, what is certain is that if such a journey were undertaken the resulting curriculum would bear little resemblance to that which teachers in England are working with today. Does this mean, then, that the National Curriculum and the associated cross-curricular themes can contribute little to the higher concerns of democratic learning we have identified? In this chapter we want to argue that the answer to this question is 'No'. However, to turn the cross-curricular themes into something worthwhile will require the adoption of a pragmatic approach to the Guidance offered by the National Curriculum Council documents referred to above, in order that the curriculum can be constructed and reconstructed into an holistic experience for young people.

There have been a number of critiques of the cross-curricular themes which have identified several shortcomings. For example, the manageability, coherence and teachers' understandings of the cross-curricular themes have been questioned, as has the extent to which the themes have been implemented in schools (see, for example, Carr, 1991; Hargreaves, 1991; Jamieson, 1991; Maw, 1993; Webster and Adelman, 1993; and Whitty, Rowe and Aggleton, 1994). In total, it would appear that these shortcomings add up to a charge that the cross-curricular themes constitute in reality an unprincipled collection of incoherent offerings rather than themes. We would argue, however, that this is an inaccurate analysis. One underlying current which runs throughout the themes, and which provides coherence, is the concept of citizenship. But therein lies a problem in that the citizenship referred to is in relation to a particular Nation rather than any reference to European or even Global citizenship.

The concept of citizenship can be a very useful one, however, for reasons which we will elaborate on in what follows, the propositional status of the knowledge concerning citizenship and the market orientation of the curriculum which the Guidance documents construct combine to militate against the English National Curriculum acting in a way which positively supports inter-cultural understandings and the achievement of higher democratic concerns. We would propose that a reconceptualisation of the curriculum which builds on the foundations offered by the cross-curricular themes supplemented by the missing, sixth theme, namely the European Dimension, would allow young people to construct a model of themselves as citizens within a European community. This would be achieved by offering alternative models of citizenship which challenge the narrow, market dominated notion of citizenship and thereby promoting inter-cultural understanding. However, before we identify how the Europeanisation of the curriculum might achieve such goals we will interrogate the cross-curriculum thematic Guidance to identify the propositional and narrow nature of the advice offered by the National Curriculum Council.

The cross-curricular thematic guidance

At first sight the cross-curricular themes, published by the National Curriculum Council (NCC), might appear to be unprincipled. Despite claims that the themes "are inter-related and share common features" (NCC, 1990a, p.1), their appearance in separate guidance documentation and the identification of separate subject knowledge, understanding, skills and attitudes within individual documents have been seen by Mackenzie (1990) to suggest that incoherence is the founding principle upon which the themes are based. We would challenge such a conclusion by suggesting that the themes, far from being a collection of disparate and unrelated concepts, are in fact principled. They are principled, however, in a way which works counter to an holistic notion of education and against a curriculum which propagates a cohering European and cross-cultural identity. We want to suggest that a number of unresolved issues concerning the themes, and citizenship particularly, need to be thought through before European and National identities might be made compatible (if not wholly consistent), and before objectives of an holistic education can be met and a culture of isolationism can be bridged.

In earlier analyses of the cross-curricular themes several issues which characterised the cross-curricular themes and which contributed to the incoherence in the school curriculum were identified (Garratt and Robinson, 1994b). The issues were Modernity, Marginalisation, Balkanisation, Propositional Knowledge and the contradictions which they incite. They clearly have a bearing upon coherence and cross-cultural identity since conceptually they can be seen to foil contestability and openness and cooperation and collaboration. These values, we feel, are prerequisites for a coherent and holistic cross-cultural model of citizenship where definitions are challenged (Carr, 1991) and openness and collaboration can work to combat isolationist fears. One pair of issues, Morality and Modernity, are particularly striking in the sense in which they interfere with an holistic model of citizenship education and we think it appropriate to revisit and discuss these issues in more detail here.

Recent literature monitoring educational developments has supported a view about the increasing prominence of market forces within the system. This pervasiveness has been recognised not only in terms of ideologically influenced curriculum guidance documentation (Robinson and Garratt, 1994; and Maw, 1993) but also in how the system is managed in terms of teacher pay structures, local management of schools and the imposition and implementation of examination league tables (Chitty, 1992; IPPR, 1993 and Wallace, 1993).

It has been suggested by Poole (1991) that the modern world calls into existence a conception of morality which is consistent with a 'commercial' or 'market' society. Poole considers that commercial society has created three major conditions; a social division of labour, a legal framework of private property and an individual propensity for self-interested behaviour. The latter is particularly telling since in order for the market to operate effectively choices are made which involve the individual treating 'others solely in terms of their contribution to his/(her) own goals' (1991, p.7). In so being, individuals can be seen to operate in ways which overlook an altruistic or ethical approach to decision making and actions and instead behave in ways which make use of a utilitarian concept, as the basis for decision making, where the role of reason is to minimise individual costs and maximise individual benefits.

Although utilitarianism is generally seen as embracing the general happiness, its meaning here is concerned with a narrower view endorsed by Bentham (1970). The corollary is that utilitarianism can engender a morality which is consistent with the impersonality of the market; the end being given and the means being justified on the basis that the end is realised. The implications for citizenship are such that individuals might not be given the opportunity to feel for the situation of others in society in an holistic way which views them as sensitive, emotionally complex beings who feel, love and care. An alternative scenario is that the morality of the market enjoins individuals to perceive others in ways which preclude a humane aspect, focusing instead upon a belief which reduces people to unfeeling, cold and impersonal obstacles blocking the path to economic freedom and capital gain. In this context, love and friendship are treated only equally with other forms of happiness and pain and, therefore, may only be valued instrumentally (Poole, 1991). In Weberian terms (see, for example, Gerth and Mills, 1946) this can be seen as a necessary condition for the efficiency of capitalism, since instrumentalism requires the negation of love, hatred and the like so as to allow calculations to be made more effectively.

This ideological position can be exposed by referencing the technically rational (Grundy, 1987) structure of curriculum product. Underpinning the rhetoric of cross-curricular themes guidance is, arguably, a technical rationality whose orientation is about controlling and managing the environment. Such a line of thought is consistent with Tarrant's (1991) interpretation of Bentham's (1970) Legislator. In a way that the Legislator 'decided what the subjects' happiness was to be and directed them towards it by various manipulative means...(he) was in fact an extension of the educational system, destined to keep the populace in perpetual tutelage' (Tarrant, 1991, p.60).

It can be argued, therefore, that statements of a propositional nature made in cross-curricular guidance literature support a similar argument. For example, in Curriculum Guidance Four; Education for Economic and Industrial Understanding (EIU), it is asserted that pupils 'need to know and understand certain basic economic concepts, for example, the idea that making economic decisions should involve an analysis of costs and benefits'; and that they should know about 'key economic concepts such as production, distribution and supply and demand'; 'how business enterprise creates wealth for individuals and community'; 'what it means to be a consumer'; and to 'cooperate as part of a team in enterprise activities' (NCC, 1990a, pp.3-5). Clearly some of these statements make strong assumptions about the benefits of entrepreneurship and the needs of pupils. The controversy lies not in the advocacy of enterprise (although its usefulness has been questioned - see Jamieson, 1991) but in the skewed private-sector approach to learning (see for example, Chambers and Squires, 1990), whose tendency is to promote an unbalanced citizenship model. If juxtaposed with a propositional code of behaviour, endorsed in Curriculum Guidance Eight: Education for Citizenship, which supports a 'concern for others, industry and effort, self-respect and self-discipline, as well as moral qualities, such as honesty and truthfulness' (NCC, 1990e, p.4), then as Webster and Adelman argue, there is an implicit assumption of a 'well-behaved citizen' and the implanting of 'a moral imperative ... which could raise difficult questions for a multicultural school' (1993, p.88). Speculation of this nature does raise serious questions about the manipulative tendencies of both documents by implicitly marrying a private sector, neo-liberal approach to EIU and a morally passive code of behaviour described within the citizenship document. These linkages do little, if anything, for the development of a 'positive participative citizenship' model since they reinforce a model which, to misquote Carr, is 'synonymous with its own institutional embodiment' (1991, p.380).

Another example is borne out in the questionable notion that costs and benefits should be used as a basis for economic decision making. Questionable, that is, in terms of the prevailing morality, since a neo-liberal economics perspective and private morality are not easily separated. Moral decision making can then become blurred and confused as society experiences a convergence of public and private moralities, possibly culminating in the over spill of a utilitarian dogma in the private lives of citizens.

This dilemma is contextualised within Curriculum Guidance Seven; Environmental Education, which states that 'economic and industrial understanding is of particular importance in making decisions about environmental issues' (NCC, 1990d, p.4). If this is so then are we to believe that the purpose and function of Environmental Education is to protect the economic sensibilities of EIU whilst concurrently adding legitimacy to its mandate? It is conceivable that if EIU is of importance in making decisions about environmental issues and if economic decisions should necessarily involve an analysis of costs and benefits, then clearly environmental decisions might not be reflected upon holistically and in a way which considers social costs in absolute terms; irrevocable damage to the environment has no price. A welfare economics approach to environmental education effectively makes it the servant of its economic master, as is exemplified by issues like the dismantling of the Brent Spar oil platform. Within this ideological atmosphere citizens are, arguably, more inclined to overlook the complexity of the environment which their actions affect and instead reduce decision making to the facile nature of self-interested instrumentalism. Furthermore, one essential contradiction within Environmental Education is the notion that pupils ought to have a 'concern for human rights' (NCC, 1990d, p.5). This claim is surely incompatible with a moral perspective which is likely to be the outcome of the full implementation and embedding of EIU. Interestingly this threat was recognised by O'Riordan (1981), Huckle (1983) and Pepper (1984) in the early 1980s when they discussed the implications of Environmental Education being tackled in a technocentric way - by advocating Education about the Environment - which manages and accommodates the environment by protecting the political and economic status quo.

In addition, Curriculum Guidance Five: Health Education, can also be seen to follow a similar path through the support and reification of the idealised family. For example, certain propositional statements reveal that pupils should 'recognise the factors involved in setting up and maintaining a home, planning and having a family; know about the role of the father and mother and their relationships before and after the arrival of children' (NCC, 1990b, p.16) and also 'be aware of the part that family life can play in happy and fulfilling relationships' (NCC, 1990b, p.19). Such statements are telling if contextualised within the political, economic and moral environment during the construction of the cross-curricular discourse. To quote the then Prime Minister 'family break down ... leads to poor results in school. It is serious not only for these children but also for the health of society' (Margaret Thatcher quoted in the Times, 36/05/1988, p.12). More recently Virginia Bottomley has expressed concern about a good strong family upbringing stating that 'without them, individuals are like a frantic whirl of atoms, attached to no one, responsible to nothing, creating a vaporous society, not a solid one' (quoted in Brindle, 1993, p.2). Are we to understand that alternative notions of the family are to be sidelined? The imposition of clause 28 of the 1986 Local Government Act is one institutional constraint which prohibits the promotion of homosexuality and in so doing denies the opportunity for an alternative debate of family composition. Can we not suggest, therefore, that taken in context, the centrality of motivation for the reification of the idealised family is instrumental (Gerth and Mills, 1946) and functional (Parsons, 1959) rather than philanthropic?

Citizenship and national identity

Clearly the arguments above have far reaching consequences for citizenship and more so if, conceptually, citizenship is expected to embrace a European identity. It has, for example, been noticed by several authors (see, for example, Webster and Adelman, 1993; and Carr, 1991) that Curriculum Guidance Eight: Education for Citizenship (NCC, 1990e), is a vague document failing to offer strict definitions of rights and duties or indeed of how they are constituted. Perhaps in some other context, this might be viewed positively, since a lack of prescriptiveness would seem to provide an opportunity for debate and potentially for a model of citizenship predicated on positive participation (Carr, 1991; Quicke 1992; and Vincent, 1993). Unfortunately, however, we would argue that the NCC's notion of good citizenship is narrowly defined within the accompanying cross-curricular themes literature.

If this is so, then are we to believe that good citizenship is about individuals pursuing their own goals and behaving in ways which promote selfishness? Believing so would imply that notions of 'wealth' and 'health' discussed in those propositions above have become inextricably linked with the pursuit of money, performance and material gain. Under this pretence, individuals are, arguably, influenced by a type of one-dimensional thought where false consciousness is realised and decision making becomes 'immune against its falsehood' (Marcuse, 1964, p.12). A market oriented model of citizenship, in this context, is arguably the antithesis of an approach which embraces the common good or a community model of citizenship which permits active participation, openness and challenge. As Carr notes, 'positive participative citizenship presupposes a critical understanding of, and a desire to transcend, the limitations of its own contemporary institutional expression' (1991, p.381).

The community model is one model which makes strides to do this. It sees the term 'community' as the embodiment of a plurality of interests, needs and aspirations of its citizens. For this to occur, education must necessarily be viewed as a process which articulates and reconciles people's experiences and expectations. As such the common good or community model of citizenship must hinge upon 'active citizenship' (Allen, 1992), which entails individuals leading autonomous lives of their own choosing as morally responsible individuals. This moral responsibility is learnt through attempting to achieve considered reflective choices on the type of life to live. Such reflection is predicated upon informed decision making. This informed position requires knowledge not only of what the individuals are going to do but also what consequences are likely to follow from the action(s) (Crick and Lister, 1974). It is what White (1983) describes as 'education in power' or, as Crick (1975) suggests, it is founded on the procedural values of freedom, toleration, fairness, respect for truth and respect for reasoning. 'Community', then, becomes obligation. Mead, (1986), describes the nature of this obligation towards oneself and one's fellow citizens as being the distinguishing feature between actions as 'full citizens' and not doing so. Citizenship, that is community membership, is then, the embodiment of individual responsibility, self-respect and achievement orientation (Morris, 1994) which allows, as Fullinwider (1988) notes, the achievement of instrumental goals like social peace and human capital investment and non-instrumental goals like solidarity and social justice.

The problem which arises from the above argument is that which questions whether individuals, supposedly acting in a morally responsible way, can pursue their own interests whilst concurrently contributing to the common good. One author who would answer positively to this question is G.E. Moore

(1903). In rejecting the notion that individual and common goods are in direct opposition, he argues in no conceivable way can my own good be divorced from the universal good. The term 'good' by this understanding is an absolute. If, therefore, something is good for me it is not my possession of it which makes it good but simply that it is good. In so being, the goodness of a thing cannot exist privately, since if an individual pursues something because it is good for him/her, it must also be the target of pursuit by others; its goodness is, therefore, universal. In this sense if everyone pursues those fruits which contribute to their own individual happiness they will at the same time be acting in ways which enhance, rather than impair, the common good.

We would, however, wish to challenge the notion that egoism is reasonable on two grounds. First, if one considers, as Haydon does, that the modern world is experiencing a substantial increase in the 'co-existence of differing values within one society' (1993, p.2), then it would stand to reason that notions of 'good' and 'bad' are a matter of subjective determination and not the simplistic absolute which Moore (1903) assumes. This presupposes that notions of 'good' and 'bad' are not necessarily consistent with notions of 'right' and 'wrong', respectively. It may be considered, for example, that in having a good life an individual has been industrious, enterprising and has achieved a reasonable level of wealth. If in doing so, however, this involved behaving disingenuously or in ways which caused damage to others or the environment, then it is questionable whether he/she actually has led a good life. To be distinguished here are differences between having and leading a good life. While the former pertains to self-interest, the latter encompasses a moral connotation, a notion of 'rightness' and embraces the spirit of morally responsible decision making. In this way, the terms 'good' and 'bad' mean different things to different people; institutional self-interest can only work to exacerbate this tendency.

Our second objection to egoism is based upon the paradoxical truism of self-interest. The self-evidence of self-interest is open to question since on one level individuals are, arguably, incapable of transcending existing social structures and therefore have not been exposed to alternative models of citizenship. Interests which appear to be self-evident might therefore be fallacious. Alternatively, one might argue that for self-interest to be self-evident, it must be beneficial and advantageous to the individual. If, as Habermas suggests, the fundamental interest in 'the preservation of life is rooted in life organised through knowledge and action' (1972, p.211), then it is more than questionable whether actions based upon knowledge rooted in technical interests are effective in preserving the species. The arguments detailed previously would appear to suggest not and in so doing reject any idea that self-interested behaviour predicated on an all-pervasive market model of citizenship is beneficial or even desirable for the individual.

If there is any truth in our argument, it can be seen that cross-curricular theme guidance - rooted in technically rational thought - can be harmful not only for the private interests of individuals but also for the common good. The current education system arguably falls through the fault line in terms of achieving a coherent and holistic platform for citizenship. A passive model of citizenship preoccupied with the morality of the market fails to consider alternative perspectives and moreover ones which consider active participation on the part of citizens. One-dimensional thought in this sense quashes the idea of citizenship involving a European identity - since the market philosophy selfishly denies alternative approaches. Consequently cross-cultural identities are viewed negatively and in ways which undermine those already established by the sovereignty of the market.

The Europeanisation of the curriculum

Some spectators might view the Europeanisation of the curriculum as a novel but subversive idea which would struggle to achieve any sort of credibility. In thinking so, they would of course be partly correct. Whilst this vision is certainly not new, the inclusion of a European Dimension in the curriculum would inevitably offer a serious challenge to the current economic and political stances held by the New Right. As Whitty and Menter explain, the New Right orthodoxy on one hand rests 'on the economic libertarianism of thinkers such as Friedman and Hayek but on the other it is based on social and moral authoritarianism' (1989, p.52). It can be seen, therefore, that the philosophical position of cross-curricular thematic guidance is, based on those arguments above, one which is consistent with this New Right ideology. In this light, any anticipation of European involvement or a cross-cultural approach to citizenship within cross-curricular guidance, would seem threatening, since its intentions are to promote identities other than narrowly defined and Nationalistic ones. As Hogan reminds us 'the new (educational) virtuousness recognises key interests associated with schooling, but its first concern is to redefine those in terms of its own orthodoxies and to tailor them to the current priorities of government' (1992, pp.143-144). We would argue, therefore, that the omission of a European Dimension within cross-curricular guidance was not accidental, but instead the protection of an 'ideology of public interest' (McAuslin, 1980 cited in Vincent, 1993). The fact that such a dimension is missing need not necessarily have been the case.

On 24 May 1988, The Council of Ministers of The European Community issued a resolution (88/C 177/02) on the European Dimension in Education. The stated objectives of the resolution included strengthening young people's sense of European identity, preparing young people to take part in the economic and social development of the Community, making young people aware of the advantage and challenges of the Community and improving their community. Member states were also required to set out their policies on the European Dimension. This the (then) DES did in February 1991 (DFE 1991). This document states that 'the European Dimension is one of several cross-curricular themes' (DFE, 1991, p.4). In June 1990, an officer of the NCC spoke at a conference at St. Martin's College, Lancaster at which she set out the terms of NCC's definition of the European Dimension and strongly indicated that NCC would be publishing Guidance (to become CG9) on the European Dimension in early 1991.

The NCC's definition of the European Dimension followed almost word for word a synopsis of Resolution 88/C 177/02 (Pagliacci 1990), and the aims of the cross-curricular theme on the European Dimension further developed this resonance by stating that for pupils the aims would be to:

'- inform the whole curriculum and act as a focus point for pupils' acquisition of knowledge and skills acquired in the various curriculum areas:

- promote a sense of European identity, including the provision of first hand experience where appropriate:

- help pupils to acquire a view of Europe as a multicultural, multilingual community which includes the UK:

- enable pupils to acquire knowledge, skills and experiences which enable them to live and work in Europe comfortably but not uncritically:

- prepare young people to take part in the economic and social development of the community and make them aware of opportunities and challenges:

- develop knowledge of economic and social aspects: - encourage awareness of the variety of histories, geographies and circumstances:

- further an awareness of European development past and present with 1992 only a stage:

- promote an understanding of common European ideals while developing an awareness of Europe's interdependence with the rest of the world' (Pagliacci, 1990)

Since February 1991, there has been a largely deafening silence from the DFE on the European Dimension. This is clearly a missed educational opportunity, but also, we feel, a purposeful sidelining on the government's part. It has been noted, for example, by Maw (1992) that the selection of favoured cross-curricular elements was spuriously decided upon in Circular No.6. This enabled the NCC to use its framework unproblematically, allowing a definition of cross-curricularity to be 'rooted in the common sense of wide acceptance' (1992, p.68).

Despite such political undercurrents, it may be viewed that this absence is not really a problem. Convey, Grisly and Winter suggest that a 'European Dimension to most of the cross-curricular themes is fairly evident' (1993, p.31). We feel, however, that although it might be self-evident to some, given the context in which the themes are placed more explicit guidance is required in order to redress the current emphasis.

In this respect, we feel, that the English curriculum could learn some valuable lessons from their European counterparts. An examination of practice throughout Europe reveals a very different picture with regard to the cross-curricular themes, their emphases and their implementation. For example, in the (then) Federal Republic of Germany, Mindham (1991), and in the Netherlands, Robinson (1991) found very different degrees of emphasis concerning cross-curricular themes. As we have tried to show elsewhere in England there is a heavy emphasis on issues like EIU as a cross-curricular theme reflecting the New Right ideology identified above (Robinson and Garratt, 1994). However, in the Netherlands, for example, there are about sixty cross-curricular themes some of which are embedded in the curriculum through legislation. Some of these themes reflect EIU in England, but they are placed alongside a much wider perspective. Recently in the Netherlands, a policy document has been published which places International Understanding centrally within the school curriculum (Oonk, 1993, p.55).

Clearly based upon the evidence of practice in Europe, the European Dimension could have provided the forum within which the other themes could have been contextually placed. As Wiegand (1992) has shown pupils' sense of place locates their understanding of the other cross-curricular themes, especially

252

Citizenship, Environmental Education and EIU. For example, the Resolution of 24 May 1988 notes that the objectives of Environmental Education will be enhanced if action at Member State level is supported by action at Commission level. This might typically include incorporating Environmental Education issues into current commission activities such as promoting meetings between young people from different member states.

What the Commission regards as appropriate for Environmental Education, we feel, could be equally appropriate for the other themes. In other words, the European Dimension, ought to be the cohering cross-curricular theme. We would propose that like Environmental Education, thematic guidance for a European Dimension can be constructed and implemented in three different ways: education in and through Europe, education about Europe and education for Europe. Education in and through Europe would involve face to face and telematic communication between school pupils and teachers in differing member states. Education about Europe would involve, amongst other things, extending pupils' knowledge of the languages, environments and cultural heritages of other member states. Education for Europe (which in this context we consider to be the most important element) would involve raising awareness about the shared interests which pupils have with pupils in other countries about the social and cultural fabric of the European Union. The role which the European Dimension can play in promoting such inter-cultural understandings is encapsulated in the arguments contained in the Commission of the European Communities Green Paper - Green Paper on the European Dimension of Education (Com (93) 457, 1993), which promotes the idea that the European Dimension supports the development of a notion of citizenship which is European rather than National. We would argue that, if lessons were learned from cross-cultural experiences, then coherence of the cross-curricular themes would also be enhanced and some of the contradictions would be lessened. For example, an appreciation of economic and social development on a global scale which would be a possible learning outcome of Environmental Education sits unhappily with the implicit goals of EIU within a market led economy (Robinson and Garratt, 1994). This paradox is exacerbated by the previously mentioned claim that one of the attitudinal goals of EIU is a 'concern for human rights' (NCC, 1990a, p.5). Some would argue that such a concern runs counter to a globalisation of capitalism as a mode of production.

For us, guidance which makes explicit the role of the European Dimension would go a considerable way to answering some of the questions we have posed about cross-curricular coherence, the notion of an holistic curriculum and inter-cultural understandings. As Shennan notes, three themes are coming together which raise the importance of the European Dimension.

These are social and economic integration, developments in new technologies and the expanding vision of 'Europeanness' as a consequence of political change in Eastern Europe (1991, p.20). As the Northern Ireland Curriculum Council (NICC) note in their Introduction to Thinking European (guidance materials for schools on the European Dimension):

> 'the development of greater European awareness among pupils and teachers...can be accommodated within current work by schools, as a means both of implementing the statutory requirements of aspects of programmes of study as well as many objectives of the educational (cross-curricular) themes.' (NICC, 1992, p. iii).

Adding the European Dimension to the English curriculum would, we feel, solve many of the problems we have identified concerning the current incoherent cross-curricular provision and open up many new and worthwhile educational opportunities. The ideological atmosphere within which teaching and learning has been taking place over the last fifteen or so years in England has predominantly been a backward looking questioning atmosphere. This questioning has mainly focused on the initial decision to join the 'Common Market'. In this chapter, what we have tried to argue is that rather than looking back teaching and learning should be taking place in an atmosphere of looking forward. Looking forward, that is, to what membership of the European Union (and the obvious Europeanisation of the curriculum which follows from that membership) would contribute positively to young people in this country, through enhancing their inter-cultural understandings and lessening their xenophobia.

References

Allen, G. (1992) 'Active Citizenship: A Rationale for the Education of Citizens?' in Allen, G. and Martin,I.S.(eds) *Education and Community: The Politics of Practice* (London, Cassell).

Bentham, J. (1970) *An Introduction to the Principles of Morals and Legislation* (London, Athlone Press).

Brindle, D. (1993) 'Lone parents rear one in 5 children', in *The Guardian* 18/03/93.

Carr, W. (1991) 'Education for Citizenship', *British Journal of Educational Studies*. vol. XXXIX no.4 pp.373-385.

Chambers, I. and Squires, S. (1990) 'Business Education and Economic

Awareness - Friend or Trojan Horse?' *Economic Awareness* vol.2 no. 2, pp.21-25.

Chitty, C. (1992) *The Education System Transformed* (Manchester, England, Baseline Books).

Convey, A., Grisley, B. and Winter, C. (1993) 'Geography and the European Dimension in the National Curriculum' in Speak, C. and Wiegand, P. (eds) *International Understanding Through Geography* (Sheffield, England, Geographical Association).

Crick, B . (1975) *Basic Concepts: Document 3 of the Programme for Political Education* (London, The Politics Association).

Crick, B. and Lister, I. (1974) 'Political Literacy: the centrality of the concept', in Crick, B. and Porter, A. (eds) *Political Education and Political Literacy* (London, Longman).

Dearing, R. (1993) *The National Curriculum and its Assessment: Final Report* (London, School Curriculum and Assessment Authority).

DFE (1991) *The European Dimension in Education : A Statement of the UK Government's Policy and Report of Activities Undertaken to Implement the EC Resolution of 24 May 1988 on the European Dimension in Education* (9 London, DFE).

Fullinwinder, R.K. (1988) 'Citizenship and Welfare' in Gutman, A. (ed.) *Democracy and the Welfare State* (Princeton, NJ, USA, Princeton University Press).

Garratt, D. and Robinson, J. (1994a) 'Opportunities missed or deliberately avoided: The invisibility of the cross-curricular themes in Dearing', *British Journal of Curriculum and Assessment* vol.4 no.3 pp.13-17.

Garratt, D. and Robinson, J. (1994b) 'Coherent Cross-Curricularity (part one): some philosophical issues to be resolved', *Journal of Educational Change and Development,* vol.14 no. 2, pp. 27-39.

Gerth, H.H. and Mills, C.W. (1946) *From Max Weber: Essays in Sociology* (New York, Oxford University Press).

Grundy, S. (1987) *Curriculum: Product or Praxis?* (Lewes, Sussex, England, Falmer Press).

Habermas, J. (1972) *Knowledge and Human Interests, 2nd Edition,* (London, Heinemann).

Hargreaves, D. (1991) 'Coherence and manageability: reflection on the National Curriculum and cross-curricular provision', *The Curriculum Journal* vol.2 no.2, pp.33-41.

Haydon, G. (1993) *Education and the Crisis in Values: should we be philosophical about it?* (London,Tufnell Press).

Hogan, P. (1992) 'The Sovereignty of Learning, The Fortunes of Schooling and the New Educational Virtuousness', *British Journal of Educational Studies*.vol. XXXX no. 2, pp.134-148.

Huckle, J. (Ed.) (1983) *Geographical Education: Reflection and Action* (Oxford, England,Oxford University Press).

Institute for Public Policy Research (1993) *Education a Different Version - An Alternative White Paper* (London, IPPR).

Jamieson, I. (1991) 'School work and real work: Economic and industrial understanding in the curriculum', *The Curriculum Journal* vol.2 no.1, pp.55-67.

Mackenzie, C. (1990) 'Cross-curricular dissensions', *Education* 2 November.

Marcuse, H. (1964) *One Dimensional Man* (Boston, USA, Beacon Press).

Maw, J. (1993) 'The National Curriculum Council and the Whole Curriculum: reconstruction of a discourse?' *Curriculum Studies* vol.1 no.1 pp.55-74.

McAuslin, P. (1980) *The Ideologies of Planning Law* (Oxford, England, Pergammon Press).

Mead, L.M. (1986) *Beyond Entitlement* (New York, Free Press) .

Mindham, C. (1991) *E.I.U. in German Primary Schools mimeo*, Crewe and Alsager College of HE, Crewe, England.

Moore, G.E. (1903) *Principia Ethica* (Cambridge, England, Cambridge University Press).

Morris, L . (1994) *The Underclass and Social Citizenship* (London, Routledge).

NCC (1990a) *Curriculum Guidance 4: Education for Economic and Industrial Understanding* (York, England, NCC).

NCC (1990b) *Curriculum Guidance 5: Health Education* (York, England, NCC).

NCC (1990c) *Curriculum Guidance 6: Careers Education* (York, England, NCC).

NCC (1990d) *Curriculum Guidance 7: Environmental Education* (York, England, NCC).

NCC (1990e) *Curriculum Guidance 8: Education for Citizenship* (York, England, NCC).

NCC (1990f) *Curriculum Guidance 3: The Whole Curriculum* (York, England, NCC).

NICC (1992) *Thinking European: Ideas for integrating a European Dimension into the Curriculum* (Belfast, Northern Ireland, NICC).

Oonk, H . (1993) 'Netherlands policy to promote the internationalisation of education', *EDIT,* vol. 3, Spring, pp. 55-56.

O'Riordan, T. (1981) 'Environmentalism and Education', *Journal of Geography in Higher Education* vol.5 no.1, pp.3-18.

Pagliacci, E. (1990) *The European Dimension in Education: The NCC's Perspective*, paper given at the European Dimension in Education Conference, S. Martin's College, Lancaster, England.

Parsons, T. (1959) 'The Social Structure of the Family' in Anshen, R.N. *The Family: Its Functions and Destiny* (New York, Harper and Row).

Pepper, D. (1984) *The Roots of Modern Environmentalism* (London, Routledge).

Poole, R. (1991) *Morality and Modernity* (London, Routledge).

Quicke, J. (1992) 'Individualism and Citizenship: some problems and possibilities', *International Studies in Sociology of Education* vol.2 no.2, pp.147-163.

Robinson, J. (1991) *Vocational Education in the Netherlands*, mimeo, Crewe and Alsager College of HE, Crewe, England.

Robinson, J. and Garratt, D. (1994) 'Inter-dependence and Controversial Issues: Environmental Education and Economic and Industrial Understanding as Cross-Curricular Themes', *The International Journal of Environmental Education and Information* vol.13 no.4, pp.415-428.

Shennan, M . (1991) *Teaching about Europe* (London, Cassell/Council of Europe).

Tarrant, J. (1991) 'Utilitarianism, Education and the Philosophy of Moral Insignificance', *Journal of Philosophy of Education* vol.25 no.1, pp.59-67.

Vincent, C. (1993) 'Education for the Community', *British Journal of Educational Studies*. vol.XXXXI no.4, pp.366-380.

Wallace, G. (1993) 'Managing Economic and Industrial Understanding and other cross-curricular themes through whole curriculum planning', *Economic Awareness* vol.5. no.2.

Webster, A. and Adelman, C (1993) 'Education for Citizenship' in Verma, G.K. and Pumfrey, P.D. (Eds.) *Cross-Curricular Contexts: Themes and Dimensions in Secondary Schools The* (Lewes, England, Falmer Press)

White, P. (1983) *Beyond Domination* (London, Routledge and Kegan Paul).

Whitty, G. and Menter, I. (1989) 'Lessons of Thatcherism: Education Policy in England and Wales 1979-88', *Journal of Law and Society* vol.16 no.1, pp.42-64.

Whitty, G., Rowe, G. and Aggleton, P. (1994) 'Subjects and Themes in the Secondary School', *Curriculum Research Papers in Education* vol.9 no.2, pp.159-181.

Wiegand, P. (1992) *Places in the Primary School: Knowledge and Understanding of Places at Key Stage 2* (Lewes, England, Falmer Press).

17 Intercultural issues in health education: towards a conceptualisation of interculturality in health education and promotion

Gaye Heathcote

Introduction

The paper explores the contradictions which emerge between the interests of individuals and those of communities in the context of the currently fashionable 'empowerment' approach to health education/promotion. These contradictions are rendered ideologically transparent by reference to definitions, classifications and methodologies suggested by contemporary commentators on the subject of enabling individuals and communities to define and take initiatives in relation to their own health needs. The discussion necessarily provides a critique of health education predicated on individualism in its various expressions, but equally casts doubt on health promotion activity that embodies principles of community development. Here the issues surrounding health promotion in pluralistic societies and specifically those comprising multicultural groupings, remain problematic. Nevertheless, a more recent strategy that attempts to shift emphasis from problem-based approaches to health education/promotion, towards setting-based approaches may be capable of creating an acceptable intercultural basis for increased empowerment and political literacy.

Historical overview

The concept of 'empowerment' has enjoyed considerable vogue in Western health education/promotion for at least two decades although its origins as a distinctive strategy were clouded by an absence of genuine theoretical analysis and by the existence of other, sometimes complementary, but often quite disparate approaches or emphases. Empowerment is a key concept in exploring apparent contradictions between the health needs of individuals and those of groups, particularly in a multicultural society. It is also highly pertinent to the examination of so-called 'settings-based' approaches to health education/promotion which promise to provide a basis for a new inter-cultural conceptualisation of community action for health. Before proceeding with such an analysis, however, it will be helpful to comment briefly on two notions - health education and health promotion - and their relationship to 'empowerment'.

The history of efforts to enhance health, whether through education, medical intervention, environmental control, or any other measure, extends back in time as far as that of health care itself. Since the mid-nineteenth century it has emerged in Britain as a discipline and a profession in which some of the major landmarks have been the sanitary reforms, a series of Education Acts, the emergence of health visiting and the institutionalisation of health promotion practices into the National Health Service. During the 1970s 'health education', as it was generally known, was seen as a potentially exciting and burgeoning field of activity that successfully drew together medical knowledge and social science methodology to identify suitable targets for medical intervention and behavioural change. However, its political agenda had already been recognised. As Tuckett observed in 1979:

'Views concerning health and illness in society are always related to the distribution of power and authority within it ... Health education is, and must be a political and ethical activity. The choice of a health education strategy will both reflect and influence social and political organisations'. (Tuckett, quoted in Beattie, p.164)

By 1981, Tones (1981) was already identifying 'four different philosophical approaches to the practice of health education', viz., an 'educational' approach based on the principle of 'informed health choices', a 'preventive' approach involving the modification of behaviour responsible for disease, a so-called 'radical' approach which linked health problems to social economic and political factors and a 'self-empowerment' approach which focused on personal growth through enhancing self- esteem and self-assertiveness.

During the early 1980s, commentators were preoccupied with the distinction between 'health education' and 'health promotion'. This was triggered by the WHO's Alma Ata Declaration (1978) and its emphasis on 'health promotion' (alongside the other major themes of equity in health, the role of community participation, the use of a multisectoral approach, the importance of the primary health and system and the strengthening of international co-operation). Governments, through public policy, had a special responsibility to ensure the basic conditions for a healthy life and for making healthier choices easier to make. This was to be matched by both planned and spontaneous action for health on the part of individuals and groups, and by increasing emphasis on self-reliance and self-initiative. Health promotion came to be seen as 'both health education and all attempts to produce environmental and legislative change conducive to good public health' (Dennis et al., 1982) or, put another way, health promotion comprises 'efforts to enhance positive health and prevent ill-health through the overlapping spheres of health education, prevention and health protection' (Downie, Fife and Tannahill, 1990). By 1995 however, following the Ottawa Charter's 'Health for All by the Year 2000' (1986), the Acheson Report (1986) that clarified the concept of public health, the 'Health of the Nation' (1991) which stressed the centrality of health promotion in achieving health targets and The Patient's Charter which set out the rights of individuals and the standards of a responsive NHS, the dual importance of health education and health promotion was being re-emphasised (Baric, 1995). Significantly, too, empowerment was being hailed as a 'cardinal principle' in these areas of activity (Downie, Fife and Tannahill, ibid).

Within this brief introduction to the historical development of ideas about health enhancement, one can begin to pick up some of the threads which have been woven into the currently fashionable orthodoxy of 'empowerment' and its reflexive form, 'self-empowerment', and to examine whether, and to what extent, the practical realisation of this concept can serve the best interests of both individuals and communities, particularly when these interests are positioned in a multicultural society. Notions of informed choice, behaviour modification and the development of self-esteem as a foundation for health choice-making have, in the past, variously informed strategies for health education/promotion. Whilst some commentators have struggled to achieve conceptual clarity by developing explanatory frameworks for the content and processes involved, others (eg. Naidoo, 1986) have offered a critique of such approaches for having embraced ideologies of individualism (which are overtly or covertly 'victim-blaming') and which have resulted in problem-oriented interventions (Rodmell and Watt, 1986). 'Self-empowerment' too has, arguably, the ring of aggressive individualism which may relate uncomfortably to the communitarian values of groups. On the other hand, health promotion, as envisaged in the Ottawa Charter and subsequent policy documents, claims to enhance the health status of both groups and individuals by facilitating choices relating to life-style and health issues, whilst commensurately increasing individual autonomy. Re-assessment, therefore, of the concept of empowerment would seem essential in order to understand its relationship to both individual and community health experience, and to evaluate its possible role in the development of intercultural health promotion where groups and individual health needs may be sharply differentiated in the pluralistic setting.

Perspectives on 'empowerment'

'Empowerment' is widely used in the health and social welfare services and clearly involves power and its distribution.   However, it is currently commandeered by widely differentiated interest groups and has become a politically contested term.   Indeed, as Ward and Mullender (1993) wryly observe:

> '... empowerment has become the current bandwagon ...... and is being used to justify what are, in fact, varying ideological and political positions. Because it creates a vogue image and an aura of moral superiority, it affords protection against criticism. Yet the term lacks specificity and glosses over significant differences. It act as a 'social aerosol,' covering up the disturbing smell of conflict and conceptual division.' (p.147)

This appears, at first sight, to be an uncharitable perspective. Empowerment enables individuals to raise questions of control, to challenge oppression such as paternalism or racism or to secure citizens' charters, whilst self-empowerment fosters understanding of processes such as consciousness-raising, autonomy, demystification, challenge and positive self-image. Other skills associated with these terms are those of effective interpersonal communication, self-advocacy, assertiveness and facilitation, whilst other qualities can be listed as respect for others, sensitivity towards social and cultural difference and self-confidence. In short, empowerment holds out the promise of a liberating relationship with ourselves and others in which power, now equalised, is harnessed in the achievement of a good and beneficent society, a society in which individuals can develop their own potential for a healthy life and in which previously powerless groups can secure improved health chances.

These apparently compelling attributes may well have been bestowed on the basis of mere cosmetic attractiveness. A classificatory scheme, devised by Beattie (1992), offers an instrument for gaining a greater insight into the appeal of 'empowerment' and the extent to which its tenets have penetrated current thinking in health promotion. Beattie's scheme establishes 'the repertoire of health promotion' in terms of two bi-polar dimensions, viz., mode of intervention (authoritative or negotiated) and focus of intervention (individual or collective). Two strategies along the 'negotiated' axis are of particular interest here - 'personal counselling for health' (individually framed) and 'community development for health' (collectively framed).

Personal counselling for health

Personal counselling for health (PCH) involves individuals, alone or in groups, engaging in 'active reflection and review of their own personal lifestyle and their individual scope for change'. Skills seen as central in bringing about the required shift in values and behaviour are confidence-building, self-assertion, decision-making, action-planning and the use of contracts (Kanfer and Goldstein, 1975, quoted in Beattie, ibid). The client is assisted in these processes by a facilitator acting on a one-to-one basis or in concert with a supportive peer group using non-directive techniques. Beattie comments that PCH is often claimed to be 'apolitical' though 'multi political' seems more appropriate as, by his own admission, the term is sometimes appropriated by the New Right (which perceives its possibilities of privatisation and individual self-help) and sometimes by factions of other political colours - 'moderates, liberals, democrats and some of the New Left who approve of its anti-authoritarian and humanistic style.' Nevertheless, the criticism that whilst giving individuals a more active, reflective and reflexive role which can be personally invigorating, the emphasis of PCH is on coping with the status quo of structural inequality and not with political action to bring about changes at a macro level.

This version of individualism which manifests itself through a focus on habits, attitudes and values, known often as 'lifestylism', remains a problematised area of analysis. The identification of 'unhealthy' lifestyles is necessarily rooted in notions of individual inadequacy and patterned according to stereotypical views of certain social and cultural groupings in society (1986), notwithstanding the conclusions of the Black Report that 'it is difficult to begin to explain the pattern of inequalities except by invoking material deprivation as a key concept' (Townsend and Davidson, 1982, p.21). As Mitchell (1984) states:

'Illness is socially constructed and ... working class people experience more ill-health than middle class people, not through choice but because

... they are exposed to a health-damaging environment over which they have little control.' (p.98)

In this context, choice is not a relevant concept. Even individual behaviours (cigarette-smoking, sedentary leisure, dietary habits) are not a matter of choice but are shaped by structural imperatives and by commercial promotions.

Pearson (1986) provides further comment on 'lifestylism' by demonstrating the way in which medical ideologies have influenced the development of health promotion initiatives aimed at black and ethnic minorities in Britain. Campaigns, policies, research studies and health education materials, she argues, are racist because they focus exclusively on the culture of people from black and ethnic minority communities and reconstruct these cultures as deficient, alien, pathological and essentially resistant to the changes identified by white experts as necessary for health. This results in:

'..... an approach to health education which is depoliticised, diverting attention away from the social causes of black people's ill-health and stressing instead their deficient culture, 'ignorance' and unwillingness to change.' (Pearson, ibid, p.40)

In locating both the cause and solution to black people's health problems outside the political arena and advocating the deceptively cosy and self-styled neutrality of integration and assimilation, the cult of individualism masks the structurally determined phenomena of individual and institutionalised racism, of material disadvantage and unfavourable social evaluation which shape the health experiences of many in minority groups in Britain.

Two further contemporary versions of 'lifestylism' have been recently identified by Skrabanek (1994) as 'healthism' and 'coercive medicine'. Healthism is defined as a movement which marks a change of emphasis from individual attempts to stay healthy to a state ideology. Skrabanek states:

'Human activities are divided into approved and disapproved, healthy and unhealthy, prescribed and proscribed, responsible and irresponsible. Irresponsible behaviour includes activities dubbed by moralists as 'vices' such as 'immoral sex' and the use of drugs, both legal (alcohol and tobacco) and illegal, but it can be extended to not going to regular medical check-ups, eating 'unhealthy' food, or not participating in sport. The proclaimed aim of healthism is the 'health of the nation' with an implicit promise of a greater happiness for all.' (pp 15-16)

Skrabanek is also critical of the New Public Health and of medical practitioners such as GP's 'who are willing to become agents of the state and take on 'health promotionment' (p.146). He states:

'Today's epidemiology has become the bottomless spring of such dubious truths converted by statistical sleight-of-hand to required certainties ... The ways of implementing healthist politics include the substitution of health education by health promotion propaganda; the introduction of regular 'health' screening for all citizens; the coercion of general practitioners, through financial incentives, to act as agents of the state; the presentation of the politically corrupt science of healthism as objective knowledge; the taxation of goods deemed to be 'unhealthy'.' (p.138)

The most vociferous accusations against individualistic health promotion - such as 'lifestylism', 'healthism', the practice of 'coercive medicine' and the medicalisation of race and culture - have been formulated as contraventions of general human rights and roundly condemned as an elaborate and malicious deception known as 'empowerment'. Pearson (1986), however, in seeking a pragmatic solution, concludes that the antidote to racist health promotion is the de-professionalisation of health care and health education/promotion and the employment of multiracial staff at all levels. This, however, arguably revisits a situation in which individuals, although possibly empowered in the PCH sense, are destined to work within socio-economic and political parameters which inevitably support those very arrangements which serve to disempower whole collectivities and particularly cultural and ethnic groupings.

Empowerment, therefore, only provides an adequate foundation for practice when matched to a potential to challenge inequality, oppression and the exploitation of one individual by another or one group by another. At the heart of this issue are the real politics of health promotion which revolve around the contentious issue of whether health promoters should be working to maintain the status quo or to tackle the structural causes of health inequalities; whether 'empowerment' boils down to enabling people to develop coping strategies that promote acceptance of their biography or offer political skills to become involved in struggle for radical, social change. In response to 'antihealthists', Baric and Baric (1995) suggests that 'rights and duties' can be represented as a continuum, the polarities of which are 'total state control' and 'total individual freedom' and that it is possible to locate 'all the countries in the world' somewhere on the continuum between these two points, according to the political system and values of each country. They further state:

'One of the expressions of each political system will be the health care available to the citizens. The reform of the NHS has tried to move the UK health care system some way towards the 'individual freedom' end of the spectrum. This fact has not been taken into account by the 'antihealthists' who still believe that the system promotes 'coercive medicine' which would place it considerably nearer to the 'state control' end of the spectrum. In view of the existing situation, this criticism is out-dated and does not fit present-day attempts to introduce greater individual responsibility and choice into health care. It also does not reflect the fact that mechanisms of social support still exist for those who cannot benefit from the market economy and still depend on state support.' (Baric and Baric, pp.52-53)

Many will be saddened by this expression of opinion: it reflects much of the old paternalism and 'pathologising' of the previous two decades and recycles the time-weary rhetoric of individual responsibility and choice. In the light of continuing re-affirmation of the findings of the Black Report and of the challenge of health promotion in a multicultural society, progress can legitimately be questioned.

Community development for health

Beattie (ibid.) describes community development for health (CDH) as interventions in which groups of people who have similar concerns or are in similar circumstances, come together to take joint action to improve health prospects. It has a similar pedigree to PCH in that it appears in different forms under different labels such as 'self-help health', 'community-oriented health education', 'health outreach' and 'community health action'. It is essentially concerned with mobilising groups (which may include 'direct voluntary action by embattled groups') and may include those such as local residents' groups, black and minority ethnic groups, gay and lesbian groups, women's groups, community-oriented social work or adult and community education (examples cited by Beattie). It represents ...

'... a way of helping groups of people who are otherwise alienated or depowered in matters of health - the most deprived or oppressed groups - to 'find a voice' for themselves.' (Rosenthal, 1980, cited in Beattie, p.176)

The role of the health promotion worker in CDH work has attracted comment as being unfamiliar and open to criticism. It will involve facilitation (rather than direction), securing access to resource-holders and policy-makers and undertaking advocacy. The hazards are those of being perceived as exploiting the trust of the community, of using it as a sop to deliver the all-too-familiar and largely irrelevant official rhetoric of professional-led health needs. Community members may, under such circumstances, be duped into another, this time collective, version of self-deluding self-empowerment which does little more than raise unreal expectations and increased awareness of social and material disadvantage. As an antidote, Ward and Mullender (ibid) urge that 'the vacuum of empowering activity in the mainstream of professional practice' needs to be filled by self-directed group work rooted in 'anti-oppressive values in which practitioners' are challenged to combine their own 'efforts with those of oppressed groups without colonising them'. They state:

> '... This is achieved by placing the reins in the hands of service users organised together in groups, and by offering them help in achieving their own goals, in place of the customary 'we know best' of traditional practice. Both user-led analysis and user-led action work better in such groups, grounded as they are in collective strength.' (Ward and Mullender, p.153)

Individualism versus communitarianism

PCH and CDH are two strategies, both of which could claim to be based on 'empowerment': the political and ideological assumptions which they respectively embody are, however, substantially different. PCH which promotes skills and values for the self-empowerment of individuals, has to be dismissed in its current form as tame, probably dishonest and certainly not capable of throwing light on, let alone challenging the uneven distribution of health choices which lie at the least of much ill-health. When located in the context of a multicultural society, health promotion appears to reconstruct culture in a way which negatively differentiates it from some perceived norm.

CDH appears, at least initially, to present a more promising strategy for health promotion in a multicultural society. There are certainly successful case-studies to support this view (developed under the aegis of, for example, the London Community Health Resource, the Community Health Initiatives Resource Unit, the National Community Health Resource and the Health Education Authority's Professional and Community Development Division). In examining health promotion as a frontier of contemporary cultural change, Beattie (ibid.) uses the concepts 'grid' and 'group' (see Douglas, 1970; 1978) to examine the extent to which a culture imposes rules and constraints on its people and coerces individuals through being members of a 'bounded face-to-face unit'. He further uses ideas from Bernstein (1971; 1975) and from Foucault (1972) to identify the particular rhetoric of CDH. His conclusions (cautiously summarised here as this part of his paper is the least detailed and developed), are worth considering in the context of multicultural health promotion. These are:

(i)   Within the paradigm of CDH, individuals in groups experience a free and open order. Its members relate on the basis of 'likeness', described as a 'religion of co-operation and a purity of collaborative subcultures'.

(ii)   The boundaries of knowledge are 'open' in that the process of 'coming to know' (through 'fluid, negotiable and diffuse' means) is given prominence over the known (which is 'fixed, stable and closed').

(iii)   Groups come into existence and maintain themselves by reference to multiple networks. Communities, now sensitised to notions of inequality and injustice, confront, challenge and attempt to change policies and services. Despite networking and sometimes establishing a national profile, such groups are perceived by society's majority groups as essentially marginal, possibly a nuisance and sometimes dangerous. Generally, they are not deemed to be sufficiently vocal or powerful to overturn tradition and the taken-for-grantedness of social arrangements.

Theorising of this kind is not always matched by practice. Empirical and anecdotal evidence abounds of the tensions that may arise in a pluralistic (multiethnic, multicultural, multifaith) society between individuals and the groups to which they belong. Accounts of cult membership (in which fanatical leaders incite mass suicide and human sacrifice on a massive scale, arranged marriages, sexual practices against children, organised prostitution, female circumcision, self-mutilation) chart the imposition of religious, social, cultural or political values on apparently reluctant individuals. Institutionalised and state-led infringement of human rights is also empirically supported. In criticising the Alma Ata Declaration, Skrabanek (ibid.) mocks the statement 'health is a basic human right' because it was delivered in a repressive regime (the then Soviet Union) and was supported by Brezhnev, Baby Doc, Idi Amin and 'scores of representatives of other murderous régimes, totalitarian states and military dictatorships' (Skrabanek, p.43). He also cites the following as a further example from Singapore:

> 'The Senior Minister of State for Education announced a new government strategy to combat obesity amongst school children - they are to be given marks for their weight in their report books, so that their parents, when checking on their academic progress would also see their grade for health and fitness.' (Straits Times, 6.12.91, cited by Skrabanek, p.141)

The demands on 'empowerment' as a health promotion principle to (simultaneously) liberate individuals, develop respect for others and enable the articulation of group rights and needs, throw up curious paradoxes at a number of levels. Refusing a blood transfusion to a dying child or a pain-killing injection to a cancer victim, being asked to excuse an obese Asian girl from participation in physical exercise or not to refer to the absence of certain vitamins in a traditional diet, may compromise the health educator morally, socially and pedagogically. Moreover, in community settings, individuals may be oppressed by the very groups which are meant to be liberating them, where group values run counter to the ideals of personal growth and well-being and where communitarian arenas are transformed into hegemonies which oppress, rather than fight oppression. Finally, there are problems in the relationships between community groups and the State. There is, for example, a fundamental contradiction in a situation where an initiative designed to give expression to the needs of a minority group is paid for from state funds and contributed to by individuals who are opposed to the celebration of marginal groups. Also problematic are situations in which education highlights examples of social and cultural differentiation, of autonomous action, of inequality and disadvantage and, additionally, provides individuals and groups with the skills and qualities to act. However, without resorting to coercion, propaganda and punitive measures, how can it ensure that groups do not commandeer political, religious, ideological or any other set of values from a major reference system for self-justification and self- aggrandisement, at the expense of its group members or those of other groups in society? How can a parity of groups be harmoniously maintained in a society if autonomy is interpreted as freedom to perpetuate beliefs and practices which orthodoxy sees as positively harmful to health? The concept of empowerment, even in the ostensibly more promising context of CDH, has not yet solved these issues.

From 'problems' to 'settings': a possible basis for inter-cultural health promotion

The demands placed on 'empowerment' and the contradictions which result from attempts to reconcile the interests and rights of individuals with the needs of communities has been exacerbated by the emphasis in health promotion, prior to the Ottawa Charter (1986), on a problem-based approach, heavily influenced by the ease with which epidemiological and etiological data can be collected. Since Ottawa, however, the WHO has been changing the emphasis towards a 'settings - based' approach which plans interventions for a target population in the different settings relevant to that population. This change of emphasis is summarised by Baric (ibid.) thus:

'i)   It recognises that any population group will have a number of health problems, and, therefore, does not limit itself to one problem.

ii)   It also accepts that the health problems present in that population group are the consequences of the functional relationship between the environmental and personal factors associated with that population.

iii)   It considers the interaction between these two groups of factors as being reflected in the lifestyle of that population.

iv)   It takes into account the fact that different aspects of a person's lifestyle are associated with the different settings in which that person lives, reproduces, learns, works, utilises different services, enjoys leisure, etc.

v)   It treats each of these settings as a system which is characterised, for example, by a certain structure, norms, participants, interaction and values.

vi)   It recognises that each of these settings is a part of a wider system and is interdependent with other parts of the system in terms of providing services or mounting interventions.' (Baric, pp. 199-200)

Baric goes on to describe and evaluate in considerable detail a number of case studies illustrating this approach - the health promoting (HP) health care system, H-promoting general practice, H-promoting hospitals, H-promoting general dental practice, H-promoting schools, H-promoting community services, H-promoting charitable organisations, H-promoting communities and a healthy enterprise in a healthy environment (ibid., pp. 331 - 536).

   Caring, holism, ecology, the setting qua organisation and the active involvement of communities are key foci in this re-orientation; advocacy, mediation and enablement are the key measures for its implementation; the tasks identified for health promotion action are building healthy public policy, creating supportive environments, strengthening community action, developing personal skills, reorienting health services towards increased participation from all interest groups. The shift from communities articulating and tackling problems to conceptualising communities as 'settings' which proactively identify and develop, across the different interest groups, action for health promotion, may be able to give CDH a new meaning and resolve some of the contradictions around 'empowerment'. The CDH approach can be adapted to an organisational model which considers the key characteristics of that model, including its opinion leaders as well as its managers. Baric (ibid.) sees 'managers', in this model, as being appointed by the organisation and its stake-holders rather than 'brought in'. They would then:

> 'provide a healthy environment for the members of that community ..., integrate health promotion into the policy and strategies employed in running that 'community' and .... enable networking with similar 'communities' as well as creating 'healthy alliances' with other 'communities' (organisations) in that area. The members of that 'community', with the help of the external agents, are expected to gain competence in improving their life through change, in accordance with the organisation's accepted rate of change and the available system.' (Baric, p.202)

The New Health Education Promotion movement is recent in origin and has had little time to be evaluated. It is still the case that most health promotion is still only partially and opportunistically integrated into the various experimental settings. The best known examples are the European network of healthy cities, health-promoting hospitals and health-promoting schools. Nevertheless, against the context of reservation with previous problem-led approaches, particularly those associated with the needs of minority ethnic and cultural groups, the contradictions of empowerment in the individual-community tension, and the only-partial successes of CDH initiatives, the 'settings' approach may well offer advantages for intercultural health promotion.

Intercultural health promotion is defined here as health promotion in a multicultural society which does not differentiate, isolate and 'medicalise' according to culture (or any other dimension of structured inequality) pathology or create stereotypes of 'deficient', 'inadequate' or 'ignorant'; rather, it involves individuals and groups in a range of role-related settings which intersect, overlap and interact harmoniously. This has the effect of networking through and across individuals and groups so that, through membership of communities as organisations, they form part of 'open' subsystems which constitute a heterogeneous society. The possible advantages of the New Health Education/Promotion movement in this context are:

(i)   Each setting, treated as an organisation, will represent a social entity, recognisable by its structure, functions, roles, goals and defining targets. The principles of empowerment, respect for others and facilitation - and its attendant contradictions - can be better articulated and resolved than in a (single) problem - oriented context.

(ii)   The interconnectedness of 'mixed-membership' settings to the wider (multicultural) society may better ensure equity, equality and a more acceptable distribution of power between groups than was apparent in the previous CDH experience.

(iii)   The election of 'managers' rather than the identification of 'gatekeepers' as the 'natural' leaders of a community may ensure a mandate and a consensus to represent the views, interests and priorities of the group.

(iv)   The principles of the Ottawa Charter, if successfully implemented in the spirit in which they were conceived, may well achieve 'the empowerment of communities, their ownership and control of their own endeavours and destinies'. The role for community development is to draw on ... 'existing human and material resources in the community to enhance self-help and social support, and to develop flexible systems for strengthening public participation and direction of health matters. This requires full and continuous access to information, learning opportunities for health, as well as funding support.' (Ottawa Charter, 1986)

Concluding remarks

Health enhancement as praxis has been historically contested by two major protagonists - health education and health promotion. This has been more than a conceptual mapping exercise: rather it has been a complex range of perspectives, sometimes oppositional and sometimes complementary, that have sought to identify the appropriate scope, aims, contexts, principles and agencies of this field of activity. As such, health education/promotion has been, and remains, a political enterprise, always underpinned by ideological and power-related assumptions. The two major paradigms examined in this paper, individualism and collectivism/communitarianism, have been shown to have used the concept and associated methodologies of 'empowerment' to achieve contrasting objectives. Both have been shown to be problematic, particularly when individual and community interests are juxtaposed, although community development for health was seen to offer part-solutions to the problematised area of minority groups' health needs and their articulation. The conclusion of this paper is that the New Health Education/Promotion movement, with its emphasis on settings-based rather than problem-oriented activity, holds out the promise of a foundation for a genuinely intercultural health promotion in line with the definition of intercultural health promotion developed here.

References

Baric L. (1995) *Health Promotion and Health Education in Practice, Module 2: The Organisational Model*, (Hale Barns, Barns Publications).

Baric L. and Baric L.F. (1995) *Health Promotion and Health Education, Module 3: Evaluation, Quality, Audit*, (Hale Barns, Barns Publications).

Beattie A. (1991) 'Knowledge and control in health promotion: a test case for social policy and social theory', in J.Gabe, M. Calnan and M. Bury (eds) *The Sociology of Health Education*, (London, Routledge).

Dennis J. et al (1982) Health Promotion in the Reorganized National Health Service, *The Health Services*, November 26.

Downie R.S., Fyfe C. and Tannahill A. (1990) *Health Promotion: Models and Values*, (Oxford, Oxford University Press).

Mitchell J. (1984) *What is to be Done about Illness and Health?*, (Harmondsworth, Penguin).

Naidoo J. (1986) 'Limits to individualism', in S. Rodmell and A. Watt (eds) *The Politics of Health Education*, (London, Routledge).

Pearson M. (1986) 'Racist notions of ethnicity and culture in health education', in S. Rodmell and A. Watt (eds) *The Politics of Health Education*, (London, Routledge).

Rodmell S. and Watt A. (1996) 'Conventional Health Education: Problems and Possibilities' in S. Rodmell and A. Watt (eds) *The Politics of Health Education* (London, Routledge).

Skrabanek P. (1994) *The Death of Humane Medicine and The Rise of Coercive Healthism*, The Social Affairs Unit, (Bury St Edmunds, St Edmundsbury Press).

Tones B.K. (1981) 'Health education: prevention or subversion?', *Royal Society of Health Journal* 101.

Townsend P. and Davidson N. (1982) *Inequalities in Health: The Black Report*, (Harmondsworth, Penguin).

Part V

Interculturalism and intergroup relations

18 Classroom relationships in three cultures: comparative classroom ambiance in the UK, France and Lithuania

Michael C. Johnson

Classroom ambiance and the behaviours of the classroom participants is vested in the beliefs and personal constructs of those participants. If pupils and teachers share different perceptions then friction occurs. If classrooms within different dominant cultures are constructed on different priorities and intentions then misinterpretations occur and any intercultural comparisons become invalid. Education can only be discussed in a framework of interculturality if there is knowledge of the different inherent constructs. This chapter describes studies using Fraser's 'My Class Inventory' (MCI) on an 'opportunity' basis in France and Lithuania following initial use in the UK. The MCI enables social interaction in a classroom to be explored through the perceptions of the participants, the teachers and the pupils. The way in which the research is reinterpreted in the three different contexts relates to different priorities and approaches. Even though the basic exploratory instrument proves useful in illuminating the classroom in all three countries, its interpretation and development proves strikingly different.

The significance of the classroom

For some years now in the UK. there has been a strand of educational practice, 'therapy' and research relating to the pupil's view of the environment he believes he is a part of. This phenomenological approach stems mainly from the work of George Kelly and his fundamental postulate that, 'A person's processes are psychologically channelised by the ways in which he anticipates events' (Kelly, 1963, p.46) or, put simply, behaviour is a function of experience. Each of us constructs our own individual set of worlds on the basis of the experiences we have had in them. Those experiences are unique because they are set against a similarly individual aggregation of earlier experiences. We act in accordance with these constructs. Lewin (1951) describes a similar way of understanding the different behaviours of individuals in apparently similar situations in his 'field theory'. A field is, 'the totality of coexisting facts which are conceived of as mutually independent', (p.240). Where Kelly writes of 'constructs' and 'construct systems', Lewin postulates facts having 'psychological significance' for individuals. What both theorists are indicating is that whilst in normal, day to day interactions a generality of experience and expectation can allow social groupings to proceed with reasonable effectiveness if difficulties in interpersonal relationships or group dynamics arise then it may well be that a more detailed understanding of 'personal worlds' will be needed. It is also implicit that interventions to increase this effectiveness are likely to involve a detailed, overt understanding of what constitutes those experiences and expectations for the individuals involved. Kelly's 'Sociality Corollary' (op. cit., p. 95) gives particular weight to this with the statement: 'An individual may engage in social relationships with another insofar as s/he can construe that individual's construct system'. Clearly intercultural understanding is a central ingredient in any such construct.

The classroom is clearly a special case of such social relationships. It is, usually, a more or less forced grouping of people. There are short and medium and long term overt imposed goals for all of them and separate, more informal goals and intentions for individuals and groups. There is an imposed status hierarchy but within this a negotiated distribution of power varying over time. Warham (1993) has effectively discussed this negotiation of power in primary classrooms. Given that overt, external goals and pressures differ for different priorities in different cultures there is reason to assume that different classrooms will reflect different experiences. However, it is not clear when such differences exert their influence or just how the negotiation of individual perception and its determinants takes place. There will clearly be pressures within the classroom from the different constructs which derive from the pupils' differing cultural and home experiences. Equally the pressures from 'majority' cultures will impose different classroom constructs in different cultures. This chapter begins to look at how both of these intercultural distinctions can be explored.

There are cases when the normal interpersonal relationships in a classroom have broken down and in which the pupils' power should be subverted or overridden. Examples are the use of 'behaviour modification' or 'assertive discipline'. Such structures rely on either the ultimate attractiveness for the pupil of being at school or the school's determination only to have enrolled those pupils who conform to school norms. They also assume that teachers can agree a commonality of behaviour resulting in a whole-school approach. We would claim that, as in society, there are certain basic, common standards and courtesies that should be observed because they make for a pleasant environment and are generally neutral to the learning process. These should be captured in a clear, simple whole-school rule structure, articulated by a similar class rule structure and maintained by a fair, consistent reward and sanction system. However, we would also claim that within this, identification of and, if possible, negotiation about classroom interpersonal relationships is vital if learning is to have an appropriate place and importance for the pupils.

Three European contexts - the United Kingdom, France and Lithuania

Our interest in this chapter is cross-cultural issues. The three countries in which the schools mentioned are placed have very different concepts of education. UK primary schools have prided themselves for many years on the quality of their teacher-pupil relationships and the creation of learning environments. The accent has been on the creation of situations within which pupils can learn through experience as much as through teaching. The Bullock Report on 'Language Across the Curriculum' (DES, 1975), The Cockcroft Report (DES, 1982), and The Nuffield Project on Mathematics (Albany, 1986) are examples of official encouragement of this manner of working. Even the National Curriculum which grew out of a political critique of over-use of such methods emphasises the importance of experiential learning in history and geography and the use of concrete examples and materials in mathematics.

In France, teacher education, inspection and appraisal is much more centralised and schools more formal in their methods than in the UK. The physical layout of the room is appropriate for teacher exposition and questioning and more use is made of class-based lessons using illustrations and the chalk-board followed by individual pupil work. Text books are often in evidence and work is marked on a right/wrong basis.

In Lithuania the situation is, in general, even more formal. 'Recitation' is the main teaching mode. Teacher education courses are long (5 years) and contain much theory of didactics and pedagogy. Partly because of lack of books these subjects are taught by lecture exposition where students take detailed notes which they learn to recapitulate for formal examinations twice a year. Failure in an examination results in the loss of part of an already meagre grant. Using these same principles, a teacher will prepare lessons for the pupils on subjects covered in their text-books. S/he will 'recite' the lesson to the class who will answer questions on it and then perform text-book exercises. They will work on it again for homework and the following day will be asked, in turn, to recite what they have learned. Each week they are given a grade out of 10 for each subject to report to their parents. For both pupils and students, the emphasis is on individual effort and results and on sanctions rather than rewards.

The research instrument: the 'My Class Inventory'

We have indicated the three different national contexts within which the research was carried out. The intention was to explore how different contexts led to different research questions, but whether never-the-less common notions arise from the outcomes. In the research described below the common factor in each case is that the teachers were personally involved in the research in the sense that there was an intention to use the information derived from the questionnaires to yield insights into the dynamics within the school for discussion by the staff involved. Translations of the research instruments were performed by people with knowledge of the national primary schools and pupils and therefore the meaning of the questions was captured as far as possible. Test instruments were not 're-standardised': the aim was see if meaningful results could be obtained. We will present the results country by country and then offer a comparison and some implications.

The instrument used in the studies reported in this chapter is the 'My Class Inventory' (MCI) (Fraser, 1983, 1986, 1989). It is geared towards primary school aged pupils and consists of a two part 50 item questionnaire asking both pupils and teachers what they think and how they feel about the ways in which their classes operate. There are 5 sub-scales to each scale, each with a minimum score of 5 and a maximum of 15:

- **Satisfaction -** the degree to which the class is a happy place and the pupils enjoy being in it.

- **Friction -** the degree to which other pupils in the class are 'mean', think only of themselves and fight.

- **Competition -** how far pupils cooperate or compete in their work.

- **Cohesion -** how far pupils are friendly with and like each other.

- **Difficulty -** how 'hard' the work is felt to be and how 'smart' you have to be to do it successfully.

Twenty five questions enquire about either teacher or pupil perceptions of what actually takes place in their classroom (Actual scale) after which a further 25 invite them to consider how they would prefer things to be (Preferred scale).

Thus it becomes possible to reveal four useful 'match - mismatches':

- The pupils' actual and preferred perceptions of what happens in the classroom;
- The teacher's actual and preferred perceptions;
- The teacher's and pupils' actual perceptions;
- What the teacher and pupils would prefer to be happening.

Clearly, if such an instrument is to be used for fully valid and reliable comparisons in different cultural environments, well standardised norms are needed. So far, these are only available for Australia and are currently being developed in the UK. However, we are more concerned with a more qualitative form of comparison. We are interested in whether the MCI can enhance the dialogic quality of classroom interactions between teacher and pupils:

- Does introducing information based on a common set of parameters enable the actors to harmonise or at least mutually understand their perceptions?
- Can they agree on action that can be taken to gain a greater match on those variables they feel to be important in making the classroom a more effective place?
- Does the degree to which this can happen or the methods that the classes employ in undertaking it vary in different countries?

No claim is made that the results are representative of any national similarities or differences apart from the fairly obvious facts that the interpersonal structure within any school class is worthy of study, it differs between classes in a school and that the instrument used here is robust enough to describe it in very different situations.

Three opportunities - variations on a theme

United Kingdom

Our interest in the MCI began with the need to instrument a research project being mounted by the Drama Department at the Didsbury School of Education.

281

It was felt that there was a shared perception amongst teachers of drama that involvement in the process of educational drama had beneficial effects not just to individual pupils but also to classrooms in terms of ethos and interpersonal relationships. However, little research seemed to have been done attempting to validate these assumptions. The intention of the project was to work intensively over a period of one year with certain teachers in a group of inner-urban primary schools. Preliminary results of the project itself will be only briefly reported here, our main concern will not be just to 'measure' the five factors but for the teachers concerned to enquire within their own classroom context why it is perceived in this way and how a situation nearer to the 'Preferred' might be sought.

France

I was also the coordinator of a Trans European Mobility Project for University Staff (TEMPUS). This involved three years work to devise a new structure for teacher education at the Siauliai Pedagogical Institute, Lithuania, to facilitate the integration of pupils with SEN into mainstream schools. TEMPUS projects are structured round a minimum of two European Union (EU) partners and one from an 'Eligible' (i.e. ex-Soviet) country. Our EU partner was France represented by the IUFM (Teachers' Training College), Grenoble. One of the tutors concerned had a joint role as School Inspector and one of the schools for which he was responsible agreed to administer the MCI to its pupils. The school had 7 classes ranging in age from 6 to 11 years. The results were fed back to the school for comment on and discussion by both teachers and pupils.

Lithuania

As part of the work in Lithuania, a large mainstream school 'Sventupis Mokykla' having about 2,000 pupils aged 7-17 became a 'Centre of Excellence' to experiment with and disseminate by demonstration the results of the project. Lithuania had just emerged from 40 years of Soviet domination. During this time being 'different' in any way was seen as something either to be 'treated' or concealed. Consequently, attitudes towards pupils or people with special needs were somewhat negative and the concept of an 'affective curriculum' within which to explore the feelings of pupils towards themselves, others, education and society was absent. The process of integration and/or inclusion would require teachers, pupils and parents to come to terms with this concept and one of the vehicles by which teachers in the school were encouraged to consider the emotional atmosphere and inter-personal relationships within their classroom was the MCI. It was administered to the whole of the lower school, 4 year groups of pupils aged 7 to 11, yielding 895 usable inventories from pupils and 31 from teachers. (These latter must be treated with some caution because reliability is only acceptable at 'class' level.)

Results of studies

(Note: only a limited amount of the data available will be presented in the context of this chapter. A more detailed paper is under preparation.)

In reporting results, the following abbreviations will be used in all tables:

Factors:	Satisfaction - SAT;	Friction - FRI;	Competition - COM;
	Difficulty - DIF;	Cohesion - COH;	
Scales:	Actual - A;	Preferred - P.	

e.g. 'preferred level of satisfaction' is SATP. The minimum score on any scale is 5, the maximum 15.

United Kingdom - the effects of educational drama

In the UK study, test-retest data were obtained on 144 pupils in 6 classes in three schools where educational drama was being used with certain classes on the theme of 'cooperation'. The pupils were all aged 10 years and each of the schools was in a similar inner-urban area with quite high indicators of socio-economic difficulty.

Table 1
Main UK data by schools

School 1				
	October		June	
Variable	A	P	A	P
SAT	10.77	12.91	11.05	13.50
FRI	12.07	8.40	11.34	7.30
COM	12.77	8.94	12.51	8.59
DIF	7.66	7.35	6.88	6.81
COH	8.40	12.39	9.29	13.21

School 2				
	October		June	
Variable	A	P	A	P
SAT	13.74	13.74	13.36	14.28
FRI	7.04	7.22	8.84	6.12
COM	8.82	7.89	9.96	7.24
DIF	7.41	7.04	6.64	7.24
COH	11.59	12.33	10.60	12.44

School 3				
	October		June	
Variable	A	P	A	P
SAT	12.65	13.52	11.21	13.25
FRI	9.53	7.03	11.24	7.02
COM	11.06	9.15	11.06	7.97
DIF	6.70	6.67	7.43	6.55
COH	11.03	13.53	10.67	12.88

The scale scores for each school (Table 1) show a different pattern in all but Difficulty. In all three schools the work is seen as not difficult and this is how the pupils want it to be. There is also agreement on Satisfaction. All schools

284

score reasonably highly on Actual Satisfaction with the Preferred score being about 2 scale points higher in each case. There were major differences between the schools on the other variables of Friction, Competition and Cohesion. Cohesion is a particularly interesting measure in that 'Actual' levels are reasonably high in School 2 (low friction, low competition) and School 3 (moderate friction, high competition) but low in School 1 which has high friction and competition. Preferred levels are again similar across the schools - 12.3 to 13.5.

What is clear is that over all three schools the pupils have a common view of the sort of classroom they would like to be taught in. It has work they find easy and enjoy, where pupils do not fight each other, you don't have your work compared with that of other pupils with whom, therefore, you can be friends.

At the end of the year it is clear that the School 1 scores have remained stable apart from a slight drop in both Friction scales. There is less friction and the pupils seem to like it. In the other two schools the situation is different. In both there is an increase in Actual Friction. Preferred Friction in School 2 drops and remains stable in School 3. In School 2 there is also an increase in Actual Competition whilst in both schools Preferred Competition drops by about 1 scale point.

The work on Drama only occurred in one class in each of Schools 1 and 3 (the relevant teacher left School 2 in mid-year) and so to consider any effects from this we need to consider actual variations between classes in these schools.

In School 1, Class 1 had the Drama input. This class was basically stable over the year with high levels of Friction and Competition and also Satisfaction though with low Cohesion (friendliness), as might be expected from high friction and competition. Preferred Competition, strangely, went up and Actual Difficulty dropped. The drop in Actual Friction seen in the School One figures was all contained in Class 2 differences which did not have the drama input. Class 2 also had a drop in the Actual Competition and in the Preferred values, it seems that having experienced a drop in the amount of conflict in this classroom they want even less! Concurrently, and unsurprisingly, Actual and Preferred Cohesion (friendliness) increased 2 scale points.

In School 3, Class 1 had the Drama input and showed no change in any of the 'Actual' variables but wanted an increase in Satisfaction and a decrease in Friction and Competition. It was Class 2 which showed the most change. Actual Satisfaction had a marked drop of 3 points with an interesting concurrent drop of 2 points in Preferred Satisfaction. The pupils appear to have come to the conclusion that their classroom is unlikely to be a happy place and so the best thing to do is to stop wanting it to be so. This was reinforced by a rise in both Actual Friction and in Preferred Friction. Finally, Difficulty in this class went up by nearly 2 scale points. There is further evidence that all was not well in this class from the fact that Actual Cohesion remained at a moderately high level but Preferred Cohesion dropped. Perhaps in this class it is as well not to try to be too friendly.

Teachers views of their classes

In School 1, Class 1 the children were viewed by their teacher as being predominantly of low ability, expressing poor motivation, low self esteem and behavioural difficulties. They were aggressive, uncooperative and, consequently, a very difficult class. As time passed, however, her intensely hard work generated a semblance of team spirit and whole class feeling. Some children, though not all, became more co-operative with each other and the class teacher. Their self esteem increased and their approach to drama work became more positive which reflected on the children's achievements in other areas of the curriculum. A very difficult class that got through the year intact, feels that it is better able to do its work and may even be able to cope with a little more competition.

In School 3, Class 1, the children were viewed by their teacher as very able overall with one very gifted child and one of very low ability. As a class, they lacked cohesion. As the academic year developed, the low ability child did not make reading or social progress while the rest of the class grew in 'togetherness'.

It would seem that whilst not producing any major changes in the cooperativeness of the classes concerned in these two schools the drama teaching has been an 'insulating mechanism' against more deleterious changes that might have been expected to occur. In School 3, this 'insulation' is even clearer. The other two classes in the year were clearly breaking down in terms of interpersonal relationships yet Class 1, having the drama input not only retains its initial levels but also becomes confident enough to hope that there could be more Satisfaction and less Friction and Competition.

The French results

A one form entry primary school in the Grenoble area was visited in Autumn 1994 and it was agreed to seek the pupils' views of the psychosocial environment in their classroom. The results would be fed back to the school for the teachers to discuss with each other and to seek the pupils' views of their accuracy. The scales were translated into French in Grenoble and the vocabulary checked to make sure it was suitable. The discussions at the school were recorded by the teachers and facilitated by the Inspector without contact with the researcher.

In the French translation the following factor descriptions were used:

- **Satisfaction -** how enjoyable do you find the work and how comfortable do you feel in class?
- **Friction -** how much arguing is there amongst the pupils, are they kind to each other and do they always want to do what they feel like doing without thinking of the other's needs?
- **Rivalry -** how important is the other pupils' work? When there is a lot of rivalry the pupils feel that they must rush to finish first and be the best. They are disappointed when they do not succeed. (Competition)
- **Unity -** to what extent does each individual feel responsible for and want to be friendly with and help the others? Success for everyone in the class makes them feel happy. (Cohesion)
- **Difficulty -** how difficult the pupils felt it was to complete their work.

As will be seen below, the teachers followed up the MCI enquiry to clarify and investigate some of the apparent outcomes.

Table 2
Mean scores by classes, Grenoble (France)

Age/Class	Satisfaction Act.	Pref.	Friction Act.	Pref.	Competition Act.	Pref.	Difficulty Act.	Pref.	Cohesion Act.	Pref.
6 yr/1	11.8	11.7	8.5	8.5	10.5	10.1	9.9	9.9	10.9	11.0
6 yr/2	12.6	13.7	8.2	5.8	11.8	9.4	9.7	8.5	9.8	13.7
7 yr/3	13.4	13.8	9.5	7.6	11.7	10.0	8.1	8.0	12.0	13.8
8 yr/4	12.5	13.5	9.4	7.0	12.5	11.8	9.0	9.0	8.7	11.1
9 yr/5	13.5	13.8	7.3	6.1	14.2	12.9	6.9	7.2	10.8	12.7
10 yr/6	14.7	14.5	7.3	5.7	11.4	9.4	5.8	5.9	13.0	14.1
11 yr/7	13.4	13.4	8.5	7.2	13.4	11.2	6.0	6.3	9.8	11.4

Profile of the school

Table 2 shows that there are two scales which show high levels of agreement between the 'actual' and 'preferred' scores - Satisfaction and Difficulty. No class shows more than 1 scale point of difference in their mean scores. It would seem that these pupils like the work to get easier as they get older and believe that it does! One may speculate about the reasons for this finding. Perhaps the pupils develop increasingly sophisticated skills for learning as they move up the school or teachers develop more differentiated methods of teaching or the work actually does get easier. However, neither of these suggestions explains the very clear trend line, the only divergence from which is in Class 4. The teachers' discussions about this will be of interest. Particularly if they can find out what the pupils mean by 'work' and if this changes as they move up the school. Similarly, what do they mean by 'hard work'? Again are there changes with age? Are these definitions and changes the same as those of the teachers?

The next two variables to be considered are Competition and Cohesion. Cohesion shows a reasonably constant relationship between the Actual and Preferred values, the pupils would always prefer their class to be an even more friendly place than it already is. Interestingly the one divergent score is from Class 4 which has the lowest Actual score and the second highest difference between Actual and Preferred scores of 2.4. All the classes would marginally prefer the level of Competition to be lower. Class 4 has the lowest difference between Actual and Preferred scores. It seems that the pupils cope with the levels of Competition they feel exist preferring them to be always a little less. It will be interesting to see if the teachers can find out where the pupils believe the Competition comes from and how they feel it can be lessened. Is this a school, class or home phenomenon, for example?

Finally, Friction. Actual levels are moderate, being highest in classes 4 and 5. There is no discernible trend over the classes, maybe a slight drop over classes 3 to 6, but again the difference between the Actual level of Friction felt and that Preferred is constant at about 2 to 2.5 scale points. It would seem that the pupils can alter their coping strategies to relate them to the level of unpleasantness they feel from their peers.

Profiles of the French classes

Class 1 has such close associations between Actual and Preferred scores that either they are too young to understand the difference as stated in the questions or else to grasp that things might be different in class as they have no standard of comparison. This is partly validated by the fact that the one variable showing a difference is Cohesion - basically how friendly the other pupils are - this being well within the experience of all these young children from other friendship groups and interactions.

In Class 2, quite large differences appear on Friction (2.4), Competition (2.4) and Cohesion (3.9). The classroom is perceived as less friendly than in Class 1 and they would like it to be much more so. Curiously, Satisfaction also goes up! Clearly they are quite happy. What we really need to know is what strategies they are having to employ to cope with the 'fighting', 'meanness' and other pupils wanting their own way all the time. Why do they think that you have to compare your work with that of other pupils rather than what you yourself did last time? How can the classroom become a more friendly place?

In Class 3, they seem to have solved this friendship problem. The level here is the highest in the school. However, Friction has gone up and Competition remains high so again it would be good to know what they mean when they say that pupils fight and are mean and how they come to believe that you should compete with other pupils in doing or finishing your work.

Class 4 seems to have the lowest level of friendliness in the school and a high level of Competition and the same level of friction as Class 3. The pupils would prefer much more of the former and much less of the latter. We need to know what changes they think could be made either by themselves, other pupils and/or the teacher (or others) to bring this about.

Class 5 is a more friendly place again but very competitive though without the levels of Friction noted earlier. However, there is still too much, according to the pupils. The level of Difficulty of the work is dropping. Again, where is this Competition coming from? It might be worth asking also about why they think it is such a friendly class.

Class 6 is the friendliest class in the school and the happiest. Friction is down to a low level and Competition is back to the levels noted in the earlier classes though it is still quite high. The pupils would certainly like it to be lower. It would be interesting to know if they feel that it is the competition that is stopping them being even more friendly and/or if lowering it would enable them to get to the very low level of Friction they say they want.

Finally, Class 7. The work is seen as easy but the Competition is high and they don't like it. Friction has gone up again and friendliness down. However, it is still a happy class. What are they competing about? If the work is so easy and you don't have to be smart to do it, does it mean that you feel really bad if you are not top?

Feedback and response

These findings were sent to the school to be discussed by the teachers. Some were found to be surprising but there was a good deal of interest in the picture generated. It was decided to find out from the pupils exactly what they meant by their answers so a second questionnaire was developed in the school and circulated to the pupils.

This second questionnaire was not answered by the younger children, Classes 1-4, as the teachers had problems helping the children to understand the questions. Some of the ideas presented were rather difficult to tackle with young children, e.g. giving the meaning of the word 'work', explaining what they find difficult, the problem of rivalry, etc. The remaining five teachers were interested in the results of their respective classes, and particularly in the comments on verbal abuse, which was mentioned by many of the children, and which suggests that we as adults should look at the problem seriously. This will form the subject of a forthcoming meeting between teachers so that a solution to this problem, which is bothering not only the children but also the teachers, can be found.

Second questionnaire

1. a) What does the word 'work' mean to you?
    b) Do you find the work you do in class difficult?
        Explain why.

2. The atmosphere in the classroom:
    a) Are your classmates rude
        - to you?
        - to each other?
    b) Do you think that children are rude to each other too often in class?
    c) Do you think your classmates get into fights too often?
        Have you ever been involved in a fight?
    d) What do you think could be done to create a more 'friendly' and 'nice' atmosphere in the classroom?

3. Is there rivalry
    a) Amongst pupils in your class?
    b) Between pupils in your class and those in the other classes at the same level?

At home:

c)   Do your parents ask what marks your classmates get?

d)   Do your parents demand that you do better than your classmates?

What the pupils said

Class 5 (age 8-9 years)   To the pupils 'work' means: Knowledge to be acquired (10 pupils), a duty or obligation (4), to get a job (4), being assessed (3), 'I don't like it!' (2) and exercises (2). Only two pupils maintain that their classmates are nasty towards them (both belong to the group of eight which were mentioned above). No pupil states that there is too much verbal abuse in the class. Two pupils maintain that their classmates fight too much.

The main point that interested the teacher was, 'Class 5 is on the whole a friendly class, but there is a lot of rivalry without there being much friction between the pupils. The work is not difficult. What are the origins of this rivalry and why do the children believe it to be such a friendly class?'

The class does a lot of tests which are nearly all formally marked. The teacher uses these marks to inform future work. The second questionnaire showed that the pupils, not the teacher, work out their position in the class. It is the symbolic value attributed to the marks, a value that gives the mark itself far more subjective importance than was originally intended, which explains the results. Eight class members maintain that there is rivalry between pupils. Eleven class members state that their parents ask them what marks their classmates get, and of these, eight maintain that their parents demand that they be better than their classmates. This was particularly the case in Maths. The teacher is now trying to remedy this.

Class 6 (aged 9-10 years)   For most of the class, work means 'a learning process' or 'exercises and lessons'. It may also be a 'duty or obligation', 'learning things about life', or 'a nuisance!' It is difficult if you have missed a lesson. It is not difficult if there 'are clear explanations', 'you listen and work well', 'it's all revision', or 'it's at the right level'. The pupils said that classmates were not nasty to each other or gave abuse. However, whilst most denied that they often fought, nearly all had been involved in a fight at some time. When asked how things might be improved, they felt that it would be better if they all played together, were more kind and entertaining and helped each other. However more than a third of them either couldn't think of anything to say or didn't seem to understand the question. They felt that rivalry was mostly within their own class and was caused, as in Class 5, by either they or their parents comparing marks or demanding that they be 'the best'.

Class 7 (age 10-11 years) The majority of the children consider 'work' to be a synonym for the learning process: lessons, exercises, tests, homework, etc. It is not difficult if you get good explanations, learn your work, listen and are patient. Interestingly, those who felt it was difficult said that it *should* be in Class 7! The pupils felt that there was no nastiness in the class. But half of the pupils felt that they insulted each other too much (this was also true for Class 4). The children rarely fight - but when asked whether they have been involved in a fight, there is a very different response, with more answering 'Yes' than 'No'. Perhaps this can be explained by the fact that the question did not specify whether it was referring to fighting in school or out of school, or perhaps for them 'a fight' signifies not only a conflict between classmates but also between brothers, sisters, cousins, etc. Again, the pupils had no real idea as to how matters might be improved.

There is some rivalry amongst the pupils in the class. Again, it relates to marks. In spite of the teacher's efforts to keep grades and marks 'secret', the children like to know their classmates' results. However, in this class they claim that their parents do not seem to be interested in their friends' results. Nevertheless, their responses indicate that over half the parents demand that their child's be the best - the idea of competition seems to be more important on a family level.

The survey enabled the French teachers to highlight certain concepts that they did not usually think about in their work. For example, the concept of rivalry between children, which seems to be so important for pupils as well as for parents. Some deplore this aspect of school work; however, but the abiding impression is that, even in classes where the teacher does not make comparisons between the children, the home background has a considerable influence in starting up this sort of rivalry as the children grow older. It was also noted that they must monitor the problem of verbal abuse more closely. This is a problem that comes up time and time again, but the questionnaire highlighted the fact that the children consider this a real problem, and therefore the teachers felt they needed to find a solution to this.

Lithuania: a whole school picture

The school we have been working with is a large (2,000 pupils) 12 year comprehensive school in the small, industrial town of Siauliai. This was a 'closed' town during the Soviet occupation as it was next to the largest military airfield outside the Soviet Union. It is now restructuring its economy round light industries and the airfield is to be the main freight airport for Lithuania. The questionnaires were completed by pupils and teachers in Years 1-4 present at the school during a week in January, 1994. Eight hundred and ninety five usable inventories were returned from pupils. One class failed to complete the 'preferred' side of the sheets. Thirty-one teachers returned usable inventories, again one did not complete side 2.

Table 3
Sventupis Mokykla mean scores by classes teachers and children

Year/Group No.		Satisfaction Act.	Pref.	Friction Act.	Pref.	Competition Act.	Pref.	Difficulty Act.	Pref.	Cohesion Act.	Pref.
1	Pupils 177	13.5	14.1	8.9	6.4	11.4	8.4	9.4	7.4	12.1	13.4
	Teach. 5	12.4	14.6	7.8	7.0	11.2	8.2	7.4	6.6	13.8	14.6
2	Pupils 274	12.8	13.9	10.1	6.9	12.8	9.5	8.6	7.4	11.2	13.5
	Teach. 10	12.2	14.5	10.7	5.9	13.6	9.0	7.3	6.0	12.6	13.8
3	Pupils 240	12.8	14.2	9.7	6.6	12.2	8.4	8.5	7.3	11.0	14.2
	Teach. 9	13.0	15.0	7.9	5.0	12.1	8.6	6.3	5.8	12.0	14.8
4	Pupils 203	12.1	14.0	9.9	5.9	10.9	7.0	8.0	6.0	11.5	14.1
	Teach. 7	12.0	14.4	10.4	6.7	13.0	8.3	8.1	5.3	11.9	14.1

The first finding from Table 3, is that the inventory produces meaningful results in a Lithuanian setting. All such devices are subject to the effects of 'faking good': giving the answer that the respondent believes will show them in the best light. The range and pattern of scores suggest that this is not so here. The teachers and pupils agree on the existing characteristics of the lower school and on the direction that any changes should take. It is only on Difficulty that the main difference in perception occurs. The pupils believe that the work they are given is more difficult than do the teachers. The teachers agree that it should be easier and both would want to lower it by approximately the same amount.

This, of course means that the absolute level claimed to be preferred by the teachers is less than that of the pupils. It would be interesting to follow this up by seeking teachers' and pupils' perceptions of the sources of difficulty. On the face of it, one would expect the teachers to be in control of the difficulty of the material presented to their pupils. It is also interesting that, if anything, the pupils' views of Preferred Difficulty are more realistic than those of the teachers. A very low scale score could mean unstimulating boring work unless the sources of difficulty lie in the methods of curriculum presentation rather than content.

The next stage is to examine the structure of the score patterns throughout the four years of classes studied. Here there are some interesting differences and trends. On satisfaction, the teachers feel that classes could be happier places than they are, and the difference between the Actual and Preferred levels remains constant over the 4 years. The pupils begin by feeling that levels in the first year classes are all right but the difference between their Actual and Preferred levels increases steadily from Year 1 to Year 4 when it reaches that level experienced by the teachers. However, examination of the scale scores rather than the differences shows that all levels are reasonably high and stable and that the Preferred levels may be thought to be somewhat unrealistic.

The situation with Friction and Competition is more interesting. Here the scale scores are moderate to low moderate. Both teachers and pupils in all years agree that levels are higher than they should be. The most likely reason for high levels of perceived Competition are teachers' techniques of control and motivation of the learning process. Effects can come from quite subtle indications of a teacher's expectations and what she values in her pupils. Overemphasis on the 'best' work in the class, paying attention to who finishes first rather than which pupils are working hard, singling out individual pupils rather than groups, encouraging pupils always to 'do their own work' rather than setting co-operative tasks, even having a single standard for a piece of work rather than finding something to value in what each child does are all practices teachers can easily fall into. They are also practices which tell the pupils they are only valued in comparison to others and it follows, therefore, that only those few at the 'top of the class' get any real praise. Any praise the others get feels rather like sympathy! This is very similar to the result we noticed in the French data.

With Friction, the situation is even more interesting. The levels fluctuate somewhat but this may be a function of scale composition in relation to the age of the child. What does give us possible indication of the dynamics of it, is the relationship between teacher-pupil differences in actual and preferred scores.

There is a major cross-over effect in Years 1 and 2. Teachers in Year 1 are satisfied that the level of Friction they perceive in their classes is acceptable. The pupils clearly do not. Year 2 teachers firmly reject the levels of Friction they find whilst the Year 2 pupils report the difference between Actual and Perceived Friction as basically unchanged. Our hypothesis is that Year 1 teachers see the perceived friction as a function of beginning school. Young children are thought to be coming to terms with being in close contact with others for protracted periods. The expectation is, 'they will grow out of it'. Clearly, they do not. The Year 2 teachers may believe that Year 1 teachers should ensure that pupils are socialised into the school situation and find the levels of bickering, mutual teasing and impatience with others unacceptable. The differences then level off, whilst the Actual scores fluctuate suggesting that both parties come to accept the situation as unfortunate but unavoidable.

Finally we examined the data for sex differences and for the range of individual responses within classes. We pick out just two features of the sex differences for brief mention. In Years 1 and 2, girls think there is more Friction than boys do and in all years they would prefer less Competition than the boys. It might be interesting how far they see the boys as a source of that competition, as is the case in the UK. Does this Competition come from marks, class position or just plain interpersonal status? The range of responses in each class was indicated by the standard deviation for the scale scores. The larger the standard duration the greater degree of disagreement within the class about the Actual or Preferred level of the characteristic. Eleven classes show large disagreements on Actual Coherence, five of them in Year 3. Eight show disagreement on Preferred Competition, 7 in Year 3. Clearly, Year 3 pupils see the situation in their classes quite differently from each other where these two factors are concerned. Does the 'actual coherence' data mean that there are exclusive groups forming who experience good coherence amongst themselves but reject other pupils? Are there some who thrive on Competition because they have learned how to succeed? There are these and many other hypotheses which we hope the school will consider and let us know the result.

International profile

It is interesting to note in Table 4, how with very different school systems in very different cultures, the overall patterns of results at school level are quite similar. Three scale points cover the range on each variable. Again it is interesting how the Preferred scores tend to be related to the Actual scores. What the pupils can imagine as being better is a relative, not an absolute concept. There is no ideal classroom. This is very heartening. It means that the between-class variations are likely to be real and to be a fruitful starting point for discussion with the pupils of how things can be made more 'pupil friendly'. It also suggests that 'teachers can make a difference'.

Table 4
Mean scores of schools in UK, France & Lithuania

Variable	Satisfaction		Friction		Competition		Difficulty		Cohesion	
Country	Actual	Prefer	Actual	Prefer	Actual	Prefer	Actual	Prefer	Actual	Prefer
UK Sch.1	10.8	12.9	12.1	8.4	12.8	9.0	7.7	7.4	8.4	9.3
UK Sch.2	13.7	13.7	7.0	7.2	8.8	7.9	7.4	7.0	11.6	12.3
UK Sch.3	12.7	13.5	9.5	7.0	11.1	9.2	6.7	6.7	11.0	13.5
France	13.1	13.5	8.4	6.9	12.2	10.7	7.9	7.8	10.7	12.5
Lithuania	12.7	14.0	9.6	6.5	12.1	8.5	8.5	7.0	11.5	13.7

We believe that the instrument has shown itself to be a useful and efficient way of both attaining a view of the interpersonal classroom processes that can be stated in terms readily understood by both teachers and pupils. It can form a starting point for meaningful discussions between teachers, teachers and pupils, or within the 'whole-school'. As the French data clearly indicate, this discussion can be very profitable in enhancing the accuracy of the staffs' perceptions of their school. In all the schools, the importance of the 'affective curriculum' was demonstrated. In Lithuania, this led to adoption of class rules and 'Circle Time' (Mosley, 1993). The work has evolved out of an involvement in 'Europeanisation'. The results give us confidence that communication between schools throughout not only western but also eastern and central Europe can stand on a common basis.

References

Albany E.A. (1986) *Challengers: A Teacher's Handbook.* (Harlow, Longman).

DES (1975) *A Language for Life: Report of the Committee of Enquiry chaired by Sir Alan Bullock, 'The Bullock Report'.* (London, HMSO).

DES (1982) *Mathematics Counts: Report of the Committee of Enquiry under the chairmanship of W.H.Cockroft, 'The Cockroft Report'.* (London, HMSO).

DES (1989) *Discipline in Schools: Report of the Committee of Enquiry chaired by Lord Elton, 'The Elton Report'.* (London, HMSO).

Fraser B.J. (Ed.) (1986) *The Study of Learning Environments, Vol. 1.* (Western Australia, Curtin University of Technology, Science and Maths Education Centre).

Fraser B.J. (1989) *Assessing and Improving Classroom Environment Monograph No.2.* (Perth, Western Australia, Key Centre for School Science and Mathematics).

Fraser B.J. and Fisher D.L. (1983) *Assessment of the Classroom Psychosocial Environment*. (Western Australian Institute of Technology).

Johnson M. (1975) *A Longitudinal Study of Student Performance at a College of Education*. Unpublished M.Ed. Thesis, University of Manchester.

Johnson M. (1995) *Report on Drama Research Project*, Manchester Metropolitan University. (In preparation).

Johnson M. and Martineniene R. (1994) 'This is our class and we like it' in *Mokykla* 1994 No. 9, pp 5 to 10.

Kelly G. (1963) *A Theory of Personality*. (New York, Norton).

Lewin K. (1951) 'Field Theory' in D.Cartwright (Ed) *Social Science; selected theoretical papers*. (New York, Harper & Row).

Mosley J. (1993) *Turn Your School Around*. Wisbech, L.D.A.

Warham S.M. (1993) *Primary Teaching and the Negotiation of Power*. (London, Paul Chapman Publishing).

19 Conflict between social groups: cognitive psychology and the reduction of conflict between groups

Geneviève Vinsonneau

Introduction: the notion of social groups

When social participants are brought together in structures either formal (schools, professional) or informal (religious, ideological, political ...), or when they are endowed with certain common attributes (such as sex or ethnic characteristics), bound together by their links to a common source (nation, family), or their involvement in a collective activity (leisure, professional or non-professional involvements, social engagement activities that transform their world environment), or that they share a common fate, they form what cognitive psychology calls a social group.

In psychology there are many studies of groups, which whilst they all are of great interest do not all deal with the same phenomena. Three areas of study can be distinguished: the analysis of the one-way influence exercised by a collection of individuals on a single person, corresponding to the phenomenon of social conformity; the observation of mutual functional interactions within a group that must complete a common task; and finally, the consequences on individual psychology of the fact that the group has, for its members, a reality, a function and a value. In this perspective the motivation of the participants in the life of the group is essential.

After the Second World War, an important field of study was developed, characterised by what Doise (1985) has called, 'essentially (...) a humanist and universalist vision, inherited from the Siècle des Lumières, whose aim was to combat prejudice and inter group discrimination'. This approach, illustrated in particular in the work of Adorno et al. (1950), Rokeach (1960), and Sherif

(1966), studies the relations that develop between alien groups, and the project that implicitly animates it aims to re-establish in the broader society a balanced cognitive and effective functioning. Such studies, which were intended to provide tools for the appeasement of social conflict, are today relegated to the background. New research has recently brought to light methods which bear no comparison with what had been claimed beforehand; the structures that were once thought to be occasional perversions of social reality, now appear to be techniques inherent in the normal psychic life of human beings and not the unhappy consequence of conflict - provoking social reality.

From individual psychology to the processes of belonging to a social group

In the 19th century western thought gave birth to two theoretical schools that underlie the various scientific analyses of the elaboration of human relationships in societies divided by inequalities. The first comes from Marx's analysis of capitalist society, the second is rooted in Freudian theory. Conventional Marxism suggests certain tools that supposedly explain the mechanisms of social discrimination. Borrowed from sociology and economics, this model envisages conflict between groups and individuals solely from the angle of economic differences and conflicting objectives. Social conflict is the result of the capitalist organisation of societies; social revolution, in which the egalitarian aspirations of the oppressed will confront the ideology of the oppressors - who are supposed actively to defend their privileges - will put an end to social conflict.

Looking at German society between the wars these predictions proved unreliable: the observations of Theodor Adorno, Max Horkheimer and Erich Fromm showed that even when capitalism's troubles occurred - economic crisis, rising unemployment - as predicted, individuals caught in this social machinery did not, as had been presumed, adopt the doctrine of revolution. Instead one had to face the rise of mass irrationality and of thinking littered with prejudice made legitimate by the official Nazi doctrine. By invoking natural variables, Nazism divided the world into a 'dominant race' and 'inferior' races. For the thinkers of the German Institute of Social Research, the classical Marxist interpretation had to be challenged. For them, it became possible that individual economic motives were not as determinant as had been imagined; in particular the origin of the discriminatory processes were perhaps not linked to socio- economic historicity, but to the personal history of the individual: the Freudian concepts coming together with the necessary tools for exploring the historicity.

The researchers' efforts (Adorno et al., 1950) centred on the attitudes expressed regarding ethnic minorities. Two thousand questionnaires were distributed in California, where the members of the German Institute of Social Research had sought refuge when Hitler came to power. The populations on which the research was conducted were diversified although exclusively White and non-Jewish, owing to the aim of the study: to investigate attitudes towards the Black and Jewish minorities. The mental structure observed was meant to be expressed by four measurements identifiable through a series of scales of attitude:- anti-Semitism, socio-political conservatism, antidemocratic tendencies, and ethnocentrism. Each subject had to express his/her degree of agreement/disagreement on a six point scale (strong, moderate or weak agreement, strong, moderate or weak disagreement) with a statement such as, 'most Negroes would become arrogant and unpleasant if they were not kept at a distance' or 'whoever employs large numbers of people should make sure they do not employ a high percentage of Jews'. Results showed a high degree of correlation between the different prejudices, suggesting that prejudice should be considered as a general frame of mind and not as a specific disposition towards a particular minority. Finally, the study showed clearly that prejudice is typical of certain types of personality, to whichever group they belong.

This being established, the authors met, and interviewed, the subjects of the two most extreme sub-samples, in order to identify the personality profile which according to them was typically 'fascist'. Such a profile should explain the 'fascist' personality's vision of the world, what today would be referred to as its cognitive style, and its unconscious motivations, in other words, its type of affective functioning. The data from the interviews allowed the pinpointing, in this 'authoritarian' personality, of the frequent rigid use of clichés in evaluative judgment and, as a consequence, of a difficulty in thinking of objects and people in terms of their own characteristics. This authoritarian personality was further characterised by a strong tendency to structure the world according to a hierarchy, assigning a specific place to each individual and to each group within an ordered universe. From a cognitive point of view, having thus, so to speak, identified the syndrome, the authors postulated that the origins of such a personality structure were to be found in excessive parental authority, that caused certain blockages during the 'normal' management of reactions. These include ambivalence, through which the subject feels both love and hatred for his parents, and the capacity to transfer this ambivalence beyond the parental system. If the parental authority is excessive, it is impossible to structure this ambivalent functioning and repression rules together with the ensuing guilty feelings. Fighting these guilty feelings, subjects transfer their negative reactions on to 'scapegoats'. In this way, the positive feelings can be uniformly fixed to the parents under the form of idealised images. This mechanism creates in the adult a deep attachment to any idealised parent substitute: heroes, religious leaders, political leaders, ... and to the law, as well as to a simultaneous idealisation of the past and of the future at the expense of the present. Anything that appears to violate the law is disliked, any transgression of custom and of the established order is condemned. Through displacement, such a mode of functioning renders possible the satisfaction of taboo desires. In order to define generically this fascist syndrome, the authors introduced the concept of 'ethnocentrism'. They built a scale for the measurement of virtual fascism, the F scale, which was then used in numerous psychological studies as a scale for the diagnosis of antidemocratic attitudes.

This analysis that gives prominence to the psychological point of view and ignores environmental factors has often been criticised. For example, Pettigrew (1959) noted that the variation in the scale of prejudice against Blacks between the north and the south of the USA did not reflect the distribution of 'authoritarian personalities' in these two areas, but that it was a consequence of a socio-historical causality independent of the subject. In Great Britain, The Netherlands and Germany, recent planned studies have been developed in order to observe the strong influence of socio-cultural factors on the mechanisms of attribution of ethnic stereotypes. Schönbach (1981) showed that the prejudice of young West Germans towards the Turkish and Italian immigrant workers varied with the education received and not with 'cognitive style' of the subject; whereas, according to the theoreticians of the 'authoritarian personality', cognitive style is either rigid or flexible and should push the inter-group behaviour of subjects in different directions. If education affects the manner of stereotyping foreign ethnic groups, it does not imply that prejudice diminishes as the level of instruction rises. Stereotype derivation depends in the first instance on the wider social frame and the dominant ideology in which it is produced, so that the content can change without there being a diminishing of the phenomenon of discrimination at work in the attribution of stereotypes. We will return to this point at the end of the chapter. The development of the strategies of stereotype attribution must be apprehended as a whole, and placed in its socio-historical context. Billig (1984) observed that in contemporary western democracies, where tolerance is the norm, attitudes of racial segregation do not have the same function and are not accompanied by the same evaluations as their counterparts in officially segregationist cultures (Nazism, Apartheid). The will to fall within the dominant norms and to conform as much as possible (whilst still demonstrating the signs of our own specificity, which Codol (1975, 1984) has called the phenomenon of 'higher conformity of the self' or 'PIP effect') encourages social actors to manage their representations and behaviour according to varying strategies. If the wider societies in which it occurs are subjected to opposed ideological pressures, this can easily lead to the expression of different behaviour from one society to another, notwithstanding the apparent similarity of the respective systems of inter-ethnic relations in which this behaviour is organised.

Returning to the previous studies, Rokeach (1960) thought of analysing the possible ways of adhering to one or other ideological system, beyond the actual layout of a series of ideological attitudes, and beyond the ideological content presented: 'In order to understand the functioning of a system of beliefs or ideological representations, as well as the institutions that regulate them, it is much less important to approach them at the level of the specificity of their discourse than to highlight a certain number or recurring systematic structures that underlie the most varied beliefs and ideological representations' (Deconchy 1984). It is the pinpointing of that which is constant which allows for the development of a scientific understanding of ideological systems and the way they work. According to Deconchy: 'In describing the structures of the 'dogmatic' processing of information and reading the social surrounding, Rokeach attempts to establish a pre-existing form of the manipulation of ideological objects'; man filters and organises his reading of his surroundings and specifically of his social surroundings with the help of a 'Belief disbelief system'. This can become a set of beliefs that the subject adopts, articulated to another set of beliefs that he refuses to adopt. This belief/disbelief system, be it that of a group or an individual, is situated on a continuum ranging from an open, flexible model, to a rigid one. The degree of dogmatism depends on the relationship between the set of beliefs and of disbeliefs; the greater the separation of these two series, the higher the dogmatism. The contrast between beliefs and disbeliefs, on a given subject, as well as the tendency to lump together and reject totally the disbeliefs, gives the measure of dogmatism of the 'cognitive structure' of the subject. The degree of dogmatism of a cognitive structure is also revealed through the greater or lesser dependence of peripheral beliefs on central beliefs: the higher the dependence, the stronger the dogmatism. Another dimension which can give an indication of the degree of dogmatism of a cognitive structure is the approach to time. Dogmatism goes hand in hand with the depreciation of the present and over-valuation of the past and the future simultaneously. Rokeach recognised dogmatism at work in certain specific types of institution, but his observations were made upon individuals. He used the usual attitude scales to analyse, in a monographic mode, an invoked phenomenon. We will now look at what social psychology can teach us when individuals act as members of social groups, and not as individuals.

Group projects and changing relations between social actors

Amongst the first attempts at experimentation on groups in a natural setting, Sherif's studies between 1949 and 1954 in the USA should be highlighted. This was a research programme in competitive interaction situations within the framework of the theory of 'conflict of interest'. Boys of 11 to 12 years of age, whose sociological and personal characteristics were rigorously controlled, were brought together in a real holiday camp for around three weeks; the subjects were unaware of the experimental aspect of the research. In the first instance, mock instructors observed the consequences of splitting up the children into different groups. After eight days of communal living, a majority of children chose their new friends from within the group to which they had arbitrarily been assigned, at the expense of the spontaneous friendships which predated the division into groups. A structure appeared within each unit with a specific distribution of status and roles; norms of functioning appeared that were different from one group to the next. The discourse in these various formations established a social distance between them, separating the team mates referred to as 'us' from the adversaries who became 'them'. The authors then studied the conflicts that appeared between these initially peaceful groups; they introduced a series of incompatible goals, with the success of one group only possible through the failure of the other. In other words they created a competitive situation. Facts showed that competition gradually transformed itself into hostile rivalry between the groups and the members of the protagonist groups. Contemptuous attitudes towards the foreign group and stereotypic images, also unfavourable, spread and became familiar. These established a precise social distance within the home group and between the different groups. In all the formations solidarity and self valorisation increased, so that team mates tended systematically to overestimate their possibilities and, quite oppositely, underestimate those of the opposing group. The organisation and the habits established within each group were transformed at the same time. The third set of observations consisted of attempts to reduce the conflict created by incompatible goals. Keen to re-establish good relations between the young boys, transformed into ferocious adversaries, the authors of the experiment failed in their attempts at pacification, whether they attempted it through moralising speeches or through pleasant contact between individuals of different groups. Conflict appeasement only became possible after the realisation of a series of 'super ordinate' goals, vital not only for the groups but also requiring interdependent co-operation of all members of the groups.

These experiments, in the end, show that inter-group conflict is independent of personal neurotic tendencies. At the peak of inter-group conflict, solidarity and co-operation were reinforced within each party and the structures and respective distributions of role and status were transformed. Moralising discourse and the multiplication of pleasant contact did not reduce conflict unless they accompanied a series of interdependent activities between the groups aiming towards a supreme goal. Only in this case did the previously ineffective solutions become effective and contribute to the reduction of hostilities. Since actual conflicts of interest and/or competitive goals create hostility between social groups, it is possible that the analysis of the objective conditions facing groups can, by itself, explain the psycho-social mechanisms at play when groups meet. The theoreticians of social identity do not, however, see matters in this light. These authors show that the simple fact of being informed of the presence of another group induces in members of a given social group differentiating mechanisms. There is a separation of that which is of home group from that which is of the foreign group.

Groups and social cognition

Following up Sherif's work, Tajfel and his collaborators (1971) observed that the simple fact of dividing people into categories provoked the differentiation of attitudes from one category to another. They looked for the minimal conditions likely to provoke the phenomena of inter-group discrimination. In order to do so, they asked the pupils of one school to participate in a task, supposedly of visual perception, and told them that they would be divided into two groups according to their answers. Individuals were in fact randomly assigned to a group and told in private what their categorical affiliation was, whilst the position of the others was kept secret. A decision-taking task was then submitted to them: on the basis of different matrices of numbers, children had to divide amounts that corresponded to the remuneration for the experiment. This they did, knowing only the group affiliation of the receiver, with the amount going to each group being equally distributed amongst its members. Under this condition the members of the group were uniformly ready to favour the members of their own group; when it was possible they did it at the expense of the members of the other group, and in the opposite case, they reduced the gain to their group, and therefore to themselves, in order to maintain a positive discrimination between them and the other group.

To explain these results Tajfel proposed the model of 'social identity' linked to Festinger's (1957) 'theory of social comparison'. The individual judges his opinions and capacities by comparing them to those of others, and self evaluation varies with the social identity bestowed upon each individual through his belonging to various social groups, so that identity is all the more gratifying as the comparison is to the advantage of the home group. The study of the mechanisms of social categorisation explains certain of the processes of identity. First of all, what is a 'categorisation'? It is an activity at the origin of perception that consists in placing a stimulus into a certain class of stimuli. Since Bruner's (1957) studies, perception is envisaged as an activity subordinated to the building of various category systems through which stimuli are classified, identified, interpreted, in order to adapt to reality. Individuals perceiving elements of the outside world or of themselves are equipped with hypotheses as to what they are supposed to perceive. All perception is therefore put in the same category as decision-taking; it is composed of an inductive operation - the attribution of a stimulus to the class of perceptions with which it is grouped - and a deductive operation through which are assigned to the stimulus the characteristics of the class of stimuli, as a whole, to which it has been associated. To perceive is, therefore, to decide on what must be perceived, on the basis of discriminating hints, derived from the motivation of the subject and the conditions of the situation.

Tajfel explains how the processes of the categorisation allow us to simplify and order our environment: categorisation works through the grouping of objects that are (or appear) similar on certain dimensions (whereas they differ on other aspects) and distinct from other objects on those dimensions. If such an activity of structuring simplifies reality and makes it more understandable and controllable, it does also present a few problems. With the systematisation of information appear the transforming mechanisms of assimilation and contrast: the former enhances similarities of objects belonging to the same category, the latter the differences between objects of different categories. In other words, the main consequences of categorisation are increases in the perceived differences between categories and in the perceived similarities within categories.

The need to give oneself a favourable identity in the comparison between the home group and foreign groups has inescapable consequences:

1. Given the heterogeneity of society, composed of superior and inferior groups, of dominating and dominated groups, the individual will always attempt to belong to the groups capable of giving him the conditions of a satisfactory social identity.

2 When, for various reasons, the home group does not satisfy such a need, the individual will be tempted to abandon it to join groups better valued socially.

3.   If it proves impossible to abandon a group, either objectively - it is not possible for example to change one's ethnic characteristics - or subjectively - as when the values involved in the building of identity are highly conflictual - the individual can attempt to change the situation that poses the problem, either by fighting to change the system generating the negative values which affect him, or by developing strategies of social creativity which bring about new dimensions of comparison that, for once, favour the home group.

(The groups of lower social status are those which operate such strategies. They can consist in developing new dimensions through which the home group, previously devalued, becomes incomparable and therefore necessarily the best on this dimension. Lemaine (1966), for example, set up an experiment in which groups of children would be compared to one another in the building of a hut. In the performance of this task one of the groups was handicapped by being deprived of string which the other group had. Without this resource, the children lost interest in the hut and started making gardens, and tried to have beauty recognised as an important dimension in the feared comparison. Another strategy that creates the tools of a positive social identity involves redefining in positive terms that which had previously been judged as negative. This is what occurred with Black Americans who by proclaiming "Black is beautiful" were reversing the usual negative evaluations given their group. A third strategy appears when individuals turn to a new group to be able to make comparisons that will be in their favour. It happens in the USA where poor Whites develop a form of racism to distinguish themselves from Blacks in similar circumstances.)

4.   The confrontation of social groups is automatically accompanied by the phenomena previously described, and actors from different backgrounds build their respective identities by comparing their group of origin with other similar social groups. Comparison with radically different groups from an economic, social and cultural standpoint can be important if the differences in status are perceived as unjust and likely to be reduced.

Can the knowledge of social psychology help reduce inter-group conflict?

In other words, has social psychology brought to light variables which are in fact levers capable of transforming reality for the better? In situations where groups meet, individuals' behaviour is largely determined by their respective group membership. The relations which are then established are not interpersonal but inter group ones, marked by social status, power and material inter-dependence. Sherif's (1966) theory of conflict of interest, and Tajfel's (1978) theory of social identity let us re-conceptualise the variables relating to social relations between individuals in terms of group membership and away from psycho-individual considerations. All meetings between groups are potentially conflictual situations, and no intervention upon them is insignificant: the manipulation of the contact can have negative as well as favourable effects on communication. Furthermore, one must not believe that a successful experiment in collective contact carries its effects to all other situations uniformly; the change of attitude is selective, it occurs in specific situations and does not generalise itself eitherto the various situations of life in society, or to the various groups. Cook (1978), for example, showed that a change of attitude caused by co-operative inter-racial contact occurred only if the specific interventions reinforced the generalisation, and that only when the initial attitude towards the foreign group was favourable did this contact develop the generalisation of positive attitudes towards the group.

In a heterogeneous and stratified society, in order to understand the contact situations between different socio-ethnic groups one must analyse the objective constraints and the political system in place. Policies in general must be considered and the policy on immigration in particular, for it has a determining effect on the modes of perception of the minority groups. When a society claims to incorporate all the differences among groups by having them all adopt the dominant values and norms, it practises a policy of assimilation. When, on the other hand, it attempts to maintain for each group its own specificity whilst at the same time attempting to integrate the subcultures into the wider social tissue, it is attempting to establish 'multiculturalism', or a 'culturally plural' society, encouraging the development of distinct cultures and varied ethnic identities. 'In such a perspective, harmony among the groups can be established by the creation of common and regular evidence of identity' (Turner 1979). The maintaining of inter-cultural categorisation contains within itself the risk of latent inter-group conflict inherent to social categorisation, whilst presenting the advantage of preserving within the groups the advantages of this conflict. These are: the reinforcement of moral values, the narcissistic satisfaction due to the favouritism showed to the home group, the improvement of the conditions for the elaboration of personality (given the solid role models), the increase in inter-group solidarity. In such circumstances, the communication between individuals of different groups can be good so long as the contact between these groups is socially recognised as a pleasant situation. Only then, can we attempt to increase the beneficial effects of a successful meeting or exchange. The knowledge of the cognitive phenomena previously described means we can lay down certain ground rules for interventions of this nature.

Providing superordinate goals is an efficient way, in the first instance, of getting the foreign groups to build mutually favourable images of each other, and of transforming their attitudes: each group is useful to the other in achieving the common goal. The goals to be achieved need to be attractive to, and wanted by, all groups involved: they must not be imposed; they must be important but also unattainable by any group on its own. Worchel (1979) showed that for a co-operative venture to be effective it must also be a success: if it ends in failure the blame is laid on the group to which we do not belong, that group becoming the scapegoat towards which hostility is directed and about which negative representations are formed (unless individuals have at their disposal a satisfactory explanation that is not built at the expense of the foreign group).

Today the concept of interdependence is preferred to that of the super-ordinate goal. Interdependence can be negative and lead to conflict, as when two countries rely on the same resource (such as fish) that both want to own; it can also be positive and lead to co-operation with each group needing the other to reach the goals it has set itself. Offering common goals which place individuals in a situation of positive interdependence, and which push them into successful co-operation, is therefore an efficient means of reducing the negative aspects of conflict.

Cross group membership is another way of reducing the consequences of inter group conflict. Classical research on social categorisation considered individuals in dichotomous situations: two categories were opposed and subjects belonged either to one or to the other. Social reality is much more complex, consisting of categories overlapping each other and not necessarily juxtaposed. A male individual can, at the same time, be young, American, of a certain profession, etc.. His social identity is the result of the crossing of his various category memberships: sexual, national, professional, etc.. Studies by Doise and Deschamps (1978) showed that under those conditions, the process of category differentiation tended to diminish, even disappear. This can be explained by the simultaneous action of the processes aiming to increase the differentiation (which is a consequence of individuals being members of two distinct categories) and those aiming to reduce it (as a consequence of another, shared membership). For Tajfel and Turner, the reduction of category differentiation is due to the great increase of information in situations of crossed membership which renders too complex the task of social comparison needed in identity processes. For Wilder (1978), the reduced perceived homogeneity inside the foreign group in cases of crossed memberships causes the drop in differentiation. Whichever might be the case, one reduces the risks of inter-group conflict by multiplying the memberships of the social actors. Ethnologists had already noticed that by resorting to category crossing (through marriage, for example) conflict control and management was facilitated. Certain experimentalists offer more artificial interventions to attempt to reduce actual conflicts: by introducing alternative categories in a laboratory setting, they hope to set in motion effects that would persist beyond that original setting. Questions can, however, be asked about the effectiveness and validity of these interventions.

From another point of view, the reintroduction of individualising perceptions between members of foreign groups is also very important in conflict reduction. With social differentiation, there occurs a phenomenon of homogenisation within the groups, that is de-individualisation. If the foreign group is not perceived as homogeneous, if the individuals that comprise it are considered in their personal uniqueness, the meeting will take place at the level of inter personal relations, and the bi-categorisation which is at the heart of the conflict will lose its importance. The individualisation of the members of the foreign group could, furthermore, make evident certain personal similarities likely to increase the attraction between individuals, thus reducing the risk of conflict. The effect of interpersonal attraction, under these conditions, is much discussed: opinions and experimental results are divided. On the one hand, Stephan and Stephan (1985) predict the accentuation of similarities (insisting on bringing together Blacks and Whites, in the USA, who share the same moral values); on the other, Salomon and Swanson claim that inter-group contact is the cause of the need to reaffirm oneself among certain groups. Highlighting similarities could in effect present the danger of stimulating the tendency to favour the home group. Amir (1976) showed that two groups of very similar status felt threatened by this similarity and reacted by increasing discrimination, using it to re-establish the wanted distance for a greater comfort in identity. Brown (1984) observed that under certain conditions of positive co-operation between groups, the perceived similarities among groups could go hand in hand with an increased attraction between them.

Not only does the beneficial effect of inter-individual similarity across groups remain hypothetical, but, as we previously noticed, the generalisation of these effects to other individuals and other situations is also hypothetical. We should therefore refrain from any great enthusiasm when we act at this level.

After having considered the conditions under which potentially conflicting groups meet, let us now see the possibilities of intervention on mutually unfavourable representations.

Social psychology and stereotype change

Well before the arrival of the cognitive approach, phenomena linked to social stereotypes were of interest to researchers in Human Sciences. Studies made at the time tended to remain descriptive; they did not help in the comprehension of the underlying mechanisms of stereotype formation, stability or possible variation. With the development of a field of study on social cognition, since the seventies, has come the attempt to identify factors involved in cognitive stereotyping. In an attempt to control the negative effects associated with this phenomenon in social reality, the emphasis was laid on the mechanisms involved in stereotype change.

What is to be understood by stereotype in this perspective? Whether it is considered a priori as bad (the point of view held by Allport and Adorno, most interested in social factors), or not necessarily so (as the cognitists claim), a stereotype is always a mode of information processing (by consensus or otherwise) which generalises (in, what lots of authors think, an abusive and erroneous manner) information (true or false) and applies it as a set in a rigid manner to a social group. The authors involved in the field disagree on many points but one can say that stereotypes represent a certain type of social categorisation, and that what needs to be explored in them is not so much the content, subject to the changing circumstances of social life, as the mechanisms at the root of their production. The cognitive functioning in itself is what is to be understood. How does the stereotype, as a cognitive structure, become a tool for the organising and processing of information? Basing himself on an experiment pertaining to the perception of physical objects, Tajfel (Tajfel and Wilkes, 1963) checked the existence of mechanisms of assimilation and contrast in the perception of social objects. Confronted by two sets of stimuli to be perceived, subjects will tend simultaneously to accentuate the differences that separate the two sets (contrast), and the similarities of the elements within one set (assimilation). In 1971, with his collaborators, the same author showed that when subjects are deprived of any relevant information to make the social comparisons necessary for their identity building, they seize any available factor to establish a positive social differentiation.

The principles of assimilation and contrast, and more generally, of category differentiation, seem to operate whatever happens. The taking into account of motivational factors in Social Identity Theory (Tajfel, 1978; Turner, 1979) explains how the recourse to stereotypes is a necessary operation in situations of social comparison that allow social actors to build for themselves a social identity that is to their advantage. The purely cognitive approach envisages the stereotype as the foremost tool for investigating reality as it processes social reality in its complexity. Certain recent studies have therefore been concerned with the conditions in which stereotypes are used (the accessibility of the memorised social categories, complexity of the task to be performed, effects of a category expectation on perceptive judgment, conditions under which the information kept in memory was acquired, etc.) and show, amongst other things, that the activation of this mechanism is not systematic and that certain factors can affect their creation.

It is clearly important to know to what extent we can expect to change stereotypes. We have seen previously that in conflict situations, hostility appears between members of rival groups, mutual images deteriorate and are transformed into clichés, applied in an automatic and rigid manner to bring about the development of other even more negative attitudes that reinforce the conflict. By a coming together of emotional, socio-cultural, and cognitive factors, stereotypes are crystallised and resist very strongly any attempt at change. Memory is selective: it stocks preferentially that which confirms stereotypes, and the comprehension of observed human behaviours follows stereotyped models provided by the environment about them and by the social actors that perform them. Hewstone and Jaspars (1982; 1984) explain how, through differential attribution of the division between internal and external, attribution permits the preservation of stereotypes in inter-group situations is achieved. Behaviour that confirms the stereotype is justified through internal causality, and counter stereotypic behaviour is explained by the setting, and is not, therefore, a consequence of the personal characteristic of the social actor.   Since the 1980s cognitivists have proposed different models for stereotype change. These models focus on information likely to contradict the stereotype. The first refers to the concept of accumulation, which considers that information going against the stereotype has no chance of modifying it unless it is repeated beyond a critical level after which it would start to be effective (Rothbart, 1981). According to another point of view the change can occur suddenly from one piece of information, provided it is relevant and strong: the conversion model (Rothbart, 1981). A third model, called 'subdivision' or 'sub-categorisation', envisages stereotypes as hierarchical structures established from personal experience. In this case, when counter-stereotype information appears there are two possibilities. In the first possibility, the information concerns certain members of the group to which the stereotype is applied, following which the subject then divides the group into various subgroups for some of which the stereotype still applies and the others for which it is transformed because of the information. In the second scenario, the information is more broadly based on the group and the change is therefore more generalised causing the stereotype to change (Taylor, 1981; Ashmore, 1981; Brewer et al., 1981). The experimental studies by Weber and Crocker (1983) show that the manner of distribution of the information and its amount are both important factors in the changing of the stereotypes.

Since 1992, Hewstone and various colleagues have undertaken a series of empirical studies whose aim was to test the different models of stereotype change. The first thing they showed was the effect of the typicality of the members of the stereotyped group with whom the contacts, potentially leading to change, are made. This influences the effect of the information: the generalisation leads to the evolution of the stereotype, only if the contact is made with an individual perceived to be typical of the stereotyped group, and not if he is perceived as atypical (Hewstone and Brown, 1986). On the other hand, in homogeneous groups, centred information has more impact on stereotype change than information dispersed among the group. In heterogeneous groups, the mode of distribution of the information can have an effect on the probability of subdivision, with the concentration of information, the risks of subdivision are increased (Johnson, Hewstone and Aird, 1992). Finally, Johnson and Hewstone (1992) showed that to every stereotype corresponds a prototypical individual who optimises the group characteristics in question: the more the group members differ from that prototype the more they are likely to be the cause of stereotype change.

In addition to the information presented to change stereotypes, various other factors intervene:

- the quality of the information already absorbed and which is at the source of the stereotype;
- certain emotional aspects;
- personal implications, 'the outcome dependency' (Fiske, 1984);
- the 'inter-group anxiety factor' (Stephan & Stephan, 1985).

To sum up, together with Hewstone (1986), we can say that a stereotype is likely to change if:

- the new information is about individuals very typical of the group and this allows for the generalisation to the group;
- the subjects are particularly keen to change their established stereotype;

- the conditions of reception of the new information are not going to bring out anxiety among the groups.

References

Adorno T.W., Frenkel-Brunswik E., Levinson D.J. and Sanford R.N. (1950) *The authoritarian personality* (New York, Harper).

Amir Y.(1976) 'The role of intergroup contact in change of prejudice and ethnic relations', in Katz P.A.(ed.) *Towards the elimination of Racism*, (New York, Pergamon).

Ashmore R.D., (1981) 'Sex stereotypes and implicit personality theory' in Hamilton D.L. (ed.) *Cognitive processes in stereotyping and intergroup behaviour* (Hillsdale N.J., Erlbaum) pp37-81.

Billig M. (1984) 'Racisme, préjugés et discriminations' in Moscovi S. (ed.) *Psychologie sociale* (Paris, P.U.F) pp449-472.

Brewer M.B., Dull V.,and Lui L. (1981) 'Perceptions of the Elderly: stereotypes as prototypes'. *Journal of Personality and Social Psychology* vol.41 pp656-670.

Brown R.J. (1984) 'The effects of intergroup similarity and cooperative vs. competitive orientation on intergroup discrimination'. *British Journal of Social Psychology* vol. 23 pp21-33.

Bruner J.S. (1957) 'On perceptual readiness', *Psychological Review*, vol.64 pp123-152.

Codol J.P. (1975) 'On the so-called "superior conformity of the self" behaviour: twenty experimental investigations', *European Journal of Social Psychology*, vol.4 pp457-501.

Codol J.P. (1984) 'La perception de la similitude interpersonelle: influence de l'appartenance categoriélle et du point de référence de la comparaison', *L'Année Psychologique, a,* vol.84 pp43-56.

Codol J.P. (1984) 'Social differentiation and non-difference', in Tajfel H. (ed.) *The Social Dimension* (London and Paris: Cambridge University Press and Maison des Sciences de l'Homme).

Cook S.W. (1978) 'Interpersonal and attitudinal outcomes co-operating in inter-racial groups', *Journal of Research and Development in Education,* vol.12 pp97-113.

Deconchy J.P. (1984) (a) 'La Résistance à la validation expérimentale d'une connaissance portant sur les comportements "idéologigues"', *Archives de Sciences Sociales des Religions,* vol.58 pp7-138.

Deconchy J.P. (1984) (b) 'Rationality and social control in orthodox system' in Tajfel H. (ed.) *The Social Dimension. European Developments in Social Psychology,* (London, Cambridge University Press).

Deconchy J.P. (1984) 'Systèmes de croyances et représentations idéologiques' in Moscovi S. *Psychologie sociale* (Paris, P.U.F) pp331-255.

Doise W., Deschamps J.C. and Mugny G. (1978) *Psychologie sociale expérimentale* (Paris, A. Colin).

Doise W. (1985) 'Nouvelles recherches sur les relations intergroupes' *Psychologie française* no. 30-2 pp141.

Festinger L. (1957) *A Theory of Cognitive Dissonance,* (Stamford, Ca., Stamford Univ. Press).

Fiske S.T. (1984) *Social Cognition,* (Reading Ma., Addison Wesley).

Hewstone M. and Jaspars J. (1982) 'Intergroup relations and attribution processes' in Tajfel H. (ed.) *Social identity and intergroup relations* (London and Paris: Cambridge University Press and Maison des Sciences de l'Homme).

Hewstone M. and Jaspars J. (1982) 'Explanations for racial discrimination: the effect of group discussion on intergroup attributions', *European Journal of Social Psychology* vol.12 pp1-16.

Hewstone M. and Jaspars M.F. (1984) 'Social dimensions of attribution' in Tajfel H. (ed.) *The social dimension* Vol 2, (London, Cambridge University Press) pp379-404.

Hewstone M. and Brown R. (1986) 'Contact is not enough: an intergroup perspective on the "contact hypothesis"' in Hewstone M. and Brown R. (eds.) *Contact and conflict in intergroup encounters* (Oxford, Blackwell).

Hewstone M., Johnston L. and Aird P. (1992) "Cognitive models of change: (2) Perceptions of homogeneous and heterogeneous groups", *European Journal of Social Psychology* vol.22 pp235-249.

Johnston L. and Hewstone M. (1992) 'Cognitive models of stereotype change: (3) Subtyping and the perceived typicality of disconfirming group members', *Journal of Experimental Social Psychology*, vol.28 pp360-386.

Lemaine G., (1966) 'Inégalité, comparaison et incomparabilité: esquisse d'une théorie de l'originalité sociale', *Bulletin de Psychologie* vol.20 pp24-32.

Pettigrew T.F. (1959) 'Regional differences in anti-Negro prejudices', *Journal of Abnormal and Social Psychology* vol.59 pp28-36.

Rokeach M. (1948) 'Generalised mental rigidity as a factor in ethnocentrism', *Journal of Abnormal and Social Psychology* vol.43, 3 259-278.

Rokeach M. (1960) *The open and closed mind: a study of belief and disbelief systems* (New York, Basic Books).

Rothbart M. (1981) 'Memory processes and social beliefs' in Hamilton D.L. (ed.) *Cognitive processes in stereotyping and intergroup behaviour* (Hillsdale, N.J, Erlbaum) pp145-181.

Schönbach P.(1981) *Education and intergroup attributes* (London, Academic Press).

Sherif M. (1966) *Des tensions intergroupes aux conflits internationaux* (Paris E.S.F.).

Sherif M. (1966) *Group conflict and cooperation: their social psychology* (London, Routledge and Kegan Paul).

Stephan W.G. and Stephan C.W. (1985) 'Intergroup anxiety', *Journal of Social Issues* vol.41, pp157-175.

Tajfel H. and Wilkes A.L. (1963) 'Classification and quantitative judgment,' *British Journal of Psychology* vol.54 no.2 pp101-114.

Tajfel H., Billig M., Bundy R.P. and Flament C. (1971) 'Social categorisation and intergroup behaviour', *European Journal of Social Psychology* vol.1, pp149-178.

Tajfel H. (1978) *The social psychology of minorities* (London, Minority Rights Group).

Tajfel H. (1978) *Differentiation between Social Groups, Studies in the Social Psychology of Intergroup Relations* (London, Academic Press).

Taylor S.E. et al. (1978) 'Categorical and contextual bases of person memory and stereotyping', *Journal of Personality and Social Psychology* vol.3, pp778-793.

Taylor H. (1981) 'A categorisation approach to stereotyping' in Hamilton D.L. (ed.) *Cognitive processes in stereotyping and intergroup behavior* pp83-114.

Turner J.C. (1979) 'Comparaison sociale et identité sociale: quelques perspectives pour l'étude du comportement intergroupes' in Doise W. (ed.) *Expériences entre groupes* (Paris, Mouton) pp151-184.

Weber R. and Crocker J. (1983) 'Cognitive processes in the revision of stereotypic beliefs', *Journal of Personality and Social Psychology* vol.45 pp961-977.

Wilder D.A. (1978) 'Reduction of intergroup discrimination through individuation of the outgroup'. *Journal of Personality and Social Psychology*, vol.36 pp1361-74.

Worchel S. (1979) 'Intergroup Cooperation' in Austin W. and Worchel S. (eds) *The Social Psychology of Intergroup Relations* (Monterey, Brooks/Cole).

20 Multi-ethnic marriage and interculturalism in Britain and the Netherlands

Christopher Bagley, Angela van Huizen and Loretta Young

Introduction

One defining factor of an ethnic group is the degree to which it is endogamous from generation to generation. Minority ethnic groups which are highly exogamous (choosing marriage partners from outside their traditional ethnic group) are likely to be absorbed into mainstream ethnic groups in the course of one or two generations, according to the rate of intermarriage, the degree to which new and relatively unacculturated migrants arrive in the host country and present themselves as potential marriage partners.

Research in Britain (Bagley, 1972a and 1979) has indicated surprisingly high rates of intermarriage between different ethnic groups (e.g. indigenous whites, and black people of Afro-Caribbean descent, with about 25 percent of the latter group marrying outside their traditional ethnic groups). Follow-up studies of mixed marriages (and 'mixed race' children of these marriages) in Britain and Canada have indicated quite good social and psychological outcomes for both the partners of these marriages, and their mixed race children in comparison with control families and comparison children (Bagley and Young, 1984; Bagley, 1993) These findings are welcome, given the embedded patterns of racism in some sectors of British society (Bagley and Verma, 1979). Frequently, however, mixed-marriage couples are professional or upper blue-collar people who can often escape the day-to-day racism which ethnic minority residents in working class or council housing have to endure.

Contrasts between Britain and The Netherlands

In contrast to British colonial policy which held racial and ethnic minorities at a distance, Dutch colonial policy in the East Indies was one of absorption, granting Dutch citizenship to those who converted to Christianity and absorbed various aspects of Dutch culture (Bagley, 1972b). When the Dutch were forced to leave Indonesia, they were accompanied or followed by many thousands of 'repatriates', mostly descendants of mixed marriages between Dutch settlers and native peoples. Although absorbing this large group of repatriants into a country still recovering from the ravages of war caused many economic difficulties, a surprising reservoir of goodwill by politicians and populace alike assisted the absorption of an ethnic group which was visibly different (in terms of skin colour) but not culturally different (in terms of religion and language). Comparative evidence from the 1970s indicated that the Dutch general population held more tolerant attitudes (including acceptance of ethnic intermarriage) than did the British (Bagley et al., 1979), provided that the ethnic minority partner was similar in terms of religious affiliation (Catholic, Protestant or secular). Thus the Dutch were more accepting of a 'black Dutchman' than they were of a light-skinned 'guest-worker' (Hagendoorn and Hraba, 1987). In contrast, British racism seems to be deeply embedded in negative perceptions of skin colour (Bagley et al., 1979). There seems to be general evidence of greater acceptance of individuals with different skin colour in Dutch society provided that the individuals conform to Dutch mores. In the past the system of 'pillarisation' has aided this process: immigrants were absorbed into vertical segments of a plural society which supported a framework of consensus about the structure of government and the allocation of resources (see Bagley, 1972a and 1983 for accounts of the Dutch plural society, and of changing Dutch social structure). While in Britain, racism is often blunt and direct, in the Netherlands it is more subtle, indirect and pseudo-moralistic (Pettigrew and Meertens, 1995). While the black immigrant from Surinam may be judged on moral grounds for unseemly conduct, it is for migrant workers such as Turks and Moroccans that more direct racism is reserved (Hagendoorn and Hraba, 1987).

The 1970s saw rapid social change in The Netherlands as the Dutch became absorbed in the social and political realities of the European Common Market, and the influence of the traditional churches declined, resulting in the crumbling of the traditional pillars of Dutch plural society described by Bagley (1972b). Coincident with (or because of) these social changes, Dutch attitudes to a new group of colonial immigrants, descendants of slaves from Africa and of plantation workers for India and Java, now resident in the former Dutch East Indies (including Surinam) became much less tolerant (Bagley, 1983; Cross and

Entzinger, 1988). Here is a paradox, which forms the basis of the present research: ethnic or racial intermarriage, which has traditionally aroused the deepest ire of the racist lobby (Pettigrew and Meertens, 1995), has increased in Britain (despite its colonial policies of intolerance, and traditions of blue collar racism) while some kinds of ethnic intermarriage in The Netherlands, once accepted, may be more problematic with the trends towards secularisation in Dutch society.

Previous studies of mixed marriages in Britain, the United States and Canada indicate that despite observable racial differences, the couples usually have some important psychosocial similarities (Bagley, 1979 and 1993). There is often a shared religion, profession and mutual friends. Where religious backgrounds are different, one of the partners will often convert; this happens most often when the partner is Islamic. Sometimes mixed marriages are unnoticed by the wider community, but do represent profound acculturations, such as the Ibo-Jamaican marriages in South London, reflecting the fact that the two groups settled in the same areas.

In addition, in England there are unnumbered mixed marriages of Europeans: Irish and English, Poles and English, French and English, and so forth. Often these marriages reflect the acculturation of refugee groups (in the case of the Poles) or religious similarity (in the case of the Irish). A whole variety of marriages 'mixed' by culture, religion and language exist in Europe, too numerous to be counted by statisticians, and too uninteresting to be studied by sociologists. Yet these mixed marriages are very important in the future of Europe; in the very long run, the peoples of the European Common Market (and their former colonies) may become a single ethnic group, divided only by compromises between different religious groups (Christianity, Islam, Judaism, Hinduism and other world religions) who share common values with regard to political compromise and co-operation, within a shared framework of values.

This is a highly optimistic and idealistic hope, nevertheless, based on previous research studies of racially mixed marriage couples and their children (Bagley and Young, 1984; Bagley, 1993). Our working hypothesis is one of few differences in adjustment and social experiences compared with non mixed couples.

A comparative study of ethnically mixed marriages

The study reported here is based upon a comparison of the most salient type of mixed marriage, that between a white person of wholly European (or Caucasian) ancestry and individuals who are visibly different in terms of skin colour or facial features (individuals with origin in or descent from Africa, the Caribbean, the Indian sub-continent, Indonesia, Malaya, Philippines, Singapore, and Hong Kong). The final sample of 59 couples (25 in Britain and 34 in The Netherlands) was obtained in Britain and The Netherlands through opportunity or 'snowball' sampling, asking the initial mixed couples if they knew of any other racially mixed couples. Participation rates were high (93 percent in Britain, 25 of 27 couples approached; and 87 percent in The Netherlands, 34 of 39 couples approached). We asked couples for personal interviews, and completion of questionnaires, only if they had one or more child of school age, since one focus of this study was on the adjustment and social experiences of 'mixed-race' children.

All couples interviewed were able to nominate at least one other mixed couple. The same 'snowball' technique was used in obtaining control couples in mono-ethnic marriages: enough potential control families were found until we had obtained matches for the multi-ethnic marriages in terms of age, educational achievement, current employment status (for wife and/or husband), and number and ages of children. The mixed couples and control samples obtained were in stable blue collar employment sectors (48 percent in Britain and 38 percent in The Netherlands) or in white collar professional or semi professional jobs (52 percent in Britain and 62 percent in The Netherlands).

Measures employed

The instruments used were similar to those in a Canadian study of ethnically mixed marriages (Bagley, 1993). These included the Middlesex Hospital Questionnaire (MHQ) measuring psychoneurosis (Bagley, 1980); a measure of depression - the CESD scale (Radloff, 1978); the Coopersmith self-esteem inventory for adults (Bagley, 1989); an assessment of the quality of marriage; and information on religious participation. These measures were chosen because of their previous utility in British and Canadian studies of community mental health (Bagley and Ramsay, 1985). For the Dutch portion of the study, instruments were translated into Dutch and administered by a Dutch interviewer (A.V.H.)

Questions were also asked about the degree of acceptance of the fact of the mixed marriage by close relatives, and the wider community (in terms of expressions of approval, and discrimination). We asked too about slights or difficulties experienced by mixed-race children which appeared to parents to be based on physical and/or cultural differences.

Results

The types of mixed marriages in each culture are detailed in Table 1 (at the end of the chapter). While there was not a complete correspondence between the two cultures in types of mixed marriage, the actual ethnic combinations in both cultures were independent of mental health profiles, and experience of discrimination. Educational levels were similar across the samples, and number and ages of children were unrelated to adjustment outcomes. No demographic factor (social class, educational level and numbers of children) has any significant link to measures of adjustment and community experience in either culture.

Table 2 (at the end of the chapter) indicates that mental health profiles for the mixed and non-mixed couples in both cultures are quite similar, without any excess of either very good or very poor mental health in any of the groups (the proportions falling into clinical groups are based on the partner in the marriage who had the least favourable score). The incidence of depression and psychoneurosis implied by these figures is very similar to that obtained in normative samples using these instruments.

Families in both Britain and The Netherlands were equally accepting of the mixed marriage, although 24 percent of close relatives in each culture were at least 'somewhat' disapproving.

Correlational analysis (table not shown) indicated no significant links between family acceptance of marriage, and mental health or marital adjustment.

Mixed couples experienced similar levels of discrimination as adults in each culture, but the British mixed couples reported significantly more discrimination experienced by their children. This most often took the form of insults and name-calling at school, and sometimes, bullying. These negative factors are likely to be experienced by many ethnic minority children in British schools, regardless of whether or not they are from mixed parentage: the British parents confirmed this view, suggesting that school peer groups tended to classify the child by minority, rather than majority racial or cultural group. No incidents of discrimination against the mixed-race child by a child from a minority group were recorded. In contrast to the British children, white Dutch children were much more accepting of the mixed-race children.

Interesting differences emerged with regard to church attendance: mixed couples in both cultures attended church significantly more often than control couples - a confirmation of Canadian results on mixed marriage couples (Bagley, 1993).

Discussion and conclusions

The amount of mixed marriages (between individuals of different race or ethnicity, and different cultural backgrounds) is an important indicator of a movement towards interculturalism both within E.E.C. countries and between countries of the European Union. Figures for Britain suggest that around 25 percent of those with ethnic origins in India, Africa and the Caribbean who have settled in Britain are in a racially mixed marriage with a white, European partner. We have no comparable data for The Netherlands, although simple observation indicates the presence of many mixed marriage couples in a cosmopolitan city like Amsterdam. Previous findings of greater ethnic tolerance in The Netherlands were only partially replicated, in that adults in each culture were equally likely to experience prejudice or discrimination. Only in the case of racism experienced by children of mixed marriages was there less apparent prejudice in Dutch society. This finding is, however, supported by the comparative study of Pettigrew and Meertens (1995) which found that in Britain it is the young who express the most blatant prejudices, whereas in The Netherlands (as in France) it is older people who express the most attitudinal racism.

It is likely that rates of intermarriage between 'racially' similar peoples from France, Britain and Germany are high. In a hopeful sense, the 'common market' may also become a 'common family'. Our hypothesis for future research is that in these countries too, mixed-race couples will have good adjustment, despite the existence of reactionary groups in all of these countries. As Hagendoorn and Hraba (1987) have shown in The Netherlands, despite the emergence of extreme right wing groups (parallelled by the rise of such groups in Germany, Britain, France and Italy) verbal acceptance of mixed marriages (as measured by the Bogardus social distance measure) is high, and the proportion accepting ethnic minority individuals as potential members of their family by marriage is much greater than the proportion rejecting the idea.

Results of the present study should be regarded as tentative. First of all, the samples are small. Secondly, the manner of obtaining the sample may have involved certain biases. Unlike the Canadian study (Bagley, 1993) which was based on random sampling of 2,000 adults, the present study used a network or snowball sample. Asking each interviewed pair to nominate other mixed couples may oversample couples who are likely to have a supportive peer group of other mixed-race couples. This might also account for the relatively high proportion in both Britain and The Netherlands who participate regularly in church life, couples nominate mixed couples who they know best in the context of church life. An alternative is that shared religious values overcome what seem to the couple (although not perhaps to outsiders) to be trivial physical differences. Indeed, marriage across religious lines may be more difficult for each party than marriage across racial lines where both parties have similar religious, educational and professional backgrounds.

We conclude that mixed marriages are an important index of interculturalism and of a movement towards tolerance and racial harmony in important sectors of Dutch and British society. While the adjustment and marital happiness of the mixed couples are similar across both cultures, children in The Netherlands are less likely to experience prejudice and discrimination. This could mean that there is less institutional racism in The Netherlands, a possibility which should be investigated by further comparative research. Finally, we advocate more research on the values and norms which European societies have regarding mixed marriages of various kinds. In the past, opposition to 'miscegenation' has been the marker of extreme racism. Does there remain in European societies a polarisation of forces on the far right (in Britain, France, Italy and Germany) whose opposition to interculturalism in general, and mixed marriages and mixed-race children in particular, is of such salience that it may influence how mixed marriages couples relate to their wider community? This is an interesting and important area for future research.

References

Bagley C. (1972a) 'Patterns of inter-ethnic marriage in Great Britain', *Phylon*, vol.33 pp 373-379.

Bagley C. (1972b) *The Dutch Plural Society: A Comparative Study in Race Relations*, (London, Oxford University Press).

Bagley C. (1979) 'Inter-ethnic marriage in Britain and the United States from 1970-77', *Sage Race Relations Abstracts* vol. 4 pp 1-22.

Bagley C. (1980) 'The factorial reliability of the Middlesex Hospital Questionnaire'. *British Journal of Medical Psychology*, vol. 53 pp 55-58.

Bagley C. (1983) 'Dutch social structure and the alienation of black youth', in C. Bagley and G.Verma (Eds.) *Multicultural Childhood: Education, Ethnicity and Cognitive Styles* (Aldershot, U.K., Gower Press).

Bagley C. (1989) 'Development of a short self-esteem measure for use with adults in community mental health surveys'. *Psychological Reports*, vol. 65, pp 13-14.

Bagley C. (1993) 'Psychological and social adjustment in racially-mixed marriages', *International Journal of Marriage and the family*, vol.1, pp 53-59.

Bagley C. and Ramsay R. (1985) 'The prevalence and correlates of suicidal behaviours, attitudes and associated social experiences in an urban population' *Suicide and Life Threatening Behavior* vol.15, pp 151-160.

Bagley C.,Verma G., Mallick K., and Young L. (1979) *Personality, self-esteem and prejudice* (Aldershot, U.K., Saxon House).

Bagley C. and Verma G. (1979) *Racial Prejudice, the Individual and Society*, (Aldershot, U.K., Saxon House).

Bagley C. and Young L. (1984) 'The welfare, adaptation and identity of children from intercultural marriage', in Verma G. and Bagley C. (Eds.) *Racial relations and Cultural Differences* (pp 247-258), (New York, St.Martins Press).

Cross M. and Entzinger H. (1988) *Lost Illusions: Caribbean Minorities in Britain and The Netherlands* (London, Routledge).

Hagendoorn L. and Hraba J. (1987) 'Social distance towards Holland's minorities: discrimination against ethnic outgroups', *Ethnic and Racial Studies* vol. 10 pp 120-133.

Pettigrew T. and Meertens R. (1995) 'Subtle and blatant prejudice in western Europe'. *European Journal of Social Psychology* vol. 25, pp 25-75.

Radloff L. (1977) 'The CES-D scale: a self-report depression scale for research in the general population', *Applied Psychological Measurement* vol. 1 pp 350-401.

Table 1
Types of mixed marriage in the British and Dutch samples

	Britain	The Netherlands
Afro-Caribbean male & European female	27%	18%
Asian male & European female	20%	21%
Oriental male and European female	12%	18%
European male and Afro-Caribbean female	12%	15%
European male and Asian female	13%	15%
European male and Oriental female	16%	13%
Number of Mixed Marriages	25	34

Note: 'Asian' includes those with ethnic and racial origins in India, Pakistan, Indonesia and The Philippines 'Oriental' includes those with ethnic and racial origins in Hong Kong, Singapore and China. 'Afro-Caribbean' includes those with ethnic and racial origins in Africa, the Caribbean, Guyana and Surinam (an Indian person of Guyanese origin would be classified as 'Asian').

Table 2
Comparison of social participation and personal adjustment in mixed marriage couples in Britain and The Netherlands

	Britain		Netherlands		
	Mixed	Controls	Mixed	Controls	
	N=25	N=254	N=34	N=34	
Marriage 'very happy' or 'happy' (wife's judgement)	84%	80%	82%	84%	A
Depression score 31+ on Radloff measure (clinical cut-off)	8%	12%	9%	9%	A
Psychoneurosis score in clinical range	12%	12%	15%	12%	A
Self-esteem in highest quartile range of normative group	28%	24%	23%	26%	A
Experienced events of discrimination as a partner in mixed marriage	20%	-	15%		
Family (very) accepting of the mixed marriage	76%		76%		
Child of marriage has experienced discrimination	52%		15%		B
Couple attended church in past month	52%	20%	59%	23%	C

Note :
A   indicates no significant difference between mixed couples and controls in either culture; and no significant difference between respondents in Britain and The Netherlands

B   indicates a significant difference (Chi-squared 9.4, 1.d.f. p<0.01) between British and Dutch mixed couples.

C   indicates significant differences between British mixed couples and controls (Chi-squared 8.1, 1 d.f., p<0.01); and between Dutch mixed couples and controls (Chi-squared 8.7, 1 d.f. p<0.01).

Part VI

Conclusions

21   Pluralism and the future of multicultural education

Gajendra K. Verma

The past two decades have seen enormous changes in European society. Although the old colonial powers have now put their imperial past firmly behind them, the legacy of those colonial enterprises still has impact, since an important sector of the population in France, Britain, the Netherlands, Portugal and Belgium have cultural origins in former colonies in Asia, Africa and Central and Southern America. Many countries too have considerable populations of 'guest workers' who with their families and children are now permanent settlers in many European countries. Parallel to the increasing integration of the European states, voices of nationalism and ethnic identity have become increasingly strident, and at times violent. Often, as is the case with Britain's occupation of Northern Ireland, this violence is deeply rooted in historical dramas enacted centuries earlier. One political solution which has emerged for grappling with these ancient wrongs (the suppression of religion, and the practices of subjugation and slavery) has been that of cultural pluralism within a political framework of equality between contrasted groups. Parallel to this is the right of any individual not to belong to any particularly 'cultural or ethnic minority'. The increasing rates of ethnic intermarriage in Europe (described in the chapter by Bagley and colleagues in this volume) are important markers of movement not towards assimilation as such, but to the creation of a new cultural bloc within a plural society based on *interculturalism*. What implications does interculturalism have for educational practice and policy in the twenty-first century?

Pluralism in political cultures implied by recent social change in Europe is an elusive and complex concept. In the broadest sense, pluralism refers to heterogeneity of cultural groups within a national or societal boundary in terms of ethnicity, culture, language, religion, social class, and so on. Every society is plural to some degree, whether or not it has achieved the broad aims of pluralism, in terms of both equity of treatment for different ethnic, linguistic and religious groups, and the recognition that there are different blocs in society contrasted by ethnicity, broadly defined. The process of achieving such a pluralist democracy generates debate and discussion, even conflict, to arrive at a true recognition of differences and equality which are grounded in mutual respect for the groups involved. In this process, education has an important part to play in the development of individuals - intellectually, affectively, physically, socially and morally - in the development of the wider society.

Education in a plural society ought to teach people to feel comfortable with differences of attitudes, values, life styles, beliefs and so on - indeed, to expect them as a fact of life. Differences provide the identifying markers around individuals and render them unique and distinct. Education should help young people to become aware of this reality, and teach them to become more sensitive and more positively receptive to difference.

Much of education has to do with the transmission of knowledge and skills that will equip young people to survive and prosper as they mature. That has often been described as the instrumental approach: what knowledge and skills are needed to become a doctor, or a lawyer or an artist? These are not unimportant considerations: as we know, people tend to be defined, and to define themselves to a significant degree by what they are, by the jobs they do. But I believe there is more to education than that. It is not, or should not be, merely a process through which people go in order to learn how to *do* things; it is also a process which should help them to *become themselves*.

One of its tasks will be to encourage and disseminate a recognition of personal rights and responsibilities since without them, personal freedom is a *meaningless* term and a truly democratic society cannot survive. By accepting this task, education could become a powerful force in helping to bring about a culture of peace and international understanding. It will make it possible for diversity of behaviour and belief to be not only *accepted* but *welcomed*.

At a time when the media show us, every day, examples of intolerance, violence, social discrimination and the abuse of human rights resulting from cultural, political or religious differences, the values of tolerance, respect for others and international understanding must assume paramount importance. Major international organisations such as UNO and UNESCO have tried to address these challenges. It is not to denigrate their efforts and their achievements to say that they have, in a fundamental sense, *failed*. I would argue that *failure* was inevitable given the forces ranged against them - forces that feed from ignorance, intolerance, and discrimination. The theory of intercultural education proposes that these forces can be overcome, with educational strategies as the basis for increasing and supporting *knowledge*, *tolerance, mutual understanding,* and *respect.* But this can only be brought about through a fundamentally positive commitment to education; this achievement must form a major political objective for the next century.

A sine qua non for achieving these idealistic goals is that universal, high quality primary, secondary and college level education ought above all else to be freely available to all, world-wide, regardless of ethnic, gender, religious or socio-economic status. The Golden Rule of intercultural education is that it should be the responsibility of civilized societies to find the means of making the opportunities to acquire education available to all in a *fair and just* way. Education should not just be the province of a privileged élite, even though we will need to continue to promote excellence in achievement, not neglecting the needs of gifted children and adolescents of both sexes.

While promoting the intellectual, social and affective development of the individual to satisfy his or her needs, education must strive to meet the responsibilities implied by the demands of individual freedom and social responsibility. What I would emphasise is the need to provide for tomorrow's young people a sense of balance between, on the one hand, the rights and freedoms and responsibilities of the individual and, on the other, and understanding of and respect for those of other individuals, cultures and other societies. The evidence from social psychology indicates that adolescents with high self-esteem tend to be confident in their abilities and achievements, and are accepting of moral codes of just and equal treatment, including the reduction of intolerance: to esteem oneself leads to acceptance of others. But those with poor self-esteem, who are denigrated and rejected by society have both poor self-esteem and a desperate, unhappy ethnocentrism (Bagley, Verma, Mallick and Young, 1979). Educational policies should not only promote the acquisition of knowledge and skills, they should also support the emotional well-being of students. Without there being a harmony between these goals, there is the real risk of society degenerating into competing groups engaged in internecine warfare and ghettoization, and of humanity being overtaken by inhumanity.

We cannot turn a blind eye to disturbing signs of re-emerging violence, intolerance, ethnic cleansing, anti-semitic, anti-democratic activity. Education must play its part in leading future generations away from the brink of the volcano. The flashpoints around us in the world today should serve as a reminder of the danger of overlooking this important issue.

Human rights have become a dominant theme in the last twenty-five years and more. I will comment on one aspect - intercultural education - which has been part of my personal experience, as an Indian living in Britain for all of my professional life. Intercultural education is concerned with the development of *reciprocal* relationships and interaction between individuals and communities.

Values, ways of life and aspects of cultures may be shared and modified whilst, at the same time accepting the need to understand the differing traditions and structures of communities within a country. *Intercultural* education is also about identity. It is based on the premise that *each* person has a number of *overlapping* identities. Human rights education needs to be firmly based on an intercultural approach which goes beyond perceptions of others based on stereotypes constructed out of ignorance, fear and envy.

Cultural diversity has been a fact of life in the countries of East and West, North and South for *many* centuries. The implication of this has been the presence within most nation states of contrasting cultural, ethnic, or racial groups. Since the processes of settlement and the history of different nations vary considerably, the cultural profile of different regions within any particular country in Europe also varies. However, contemporary recognition of the value of cultural, linguistic and religious diversity and their educational implications are global and more recent.

Over the last four decades the classical concept of a culturally homogeneous society has been challenged more openly. In some countries, the process of 'pluralized integration' - political, social and economic - is well under way (e.g. the European Union; and the North American Free Trade Association ,of Mexico, Canada and the U.S.A.). In all countries, the salience of cultural, religious and linguistic differences between groups have been reconsidered in an era of 'positive nationalism' and the expansion of positive aspects of ethnic and cultural identity.

Definition of the term 'culture' is both complex and problematic. A common ambiguity inherent in any discussion of culture is the interchangeable use of the terms 'race', 'ethnicity', and 'culture'. For example, educational programmes tend to adopt certain strategies variously labelled as 'multicultural', 'multiracial', 'multiethnic', 'anti-racist' and, more recently, 'intercultural'. Such approaches to teaching have been supported by some and criticized by others. Thus, the relationship between cultural diversity and education has become an area of increasing controversy. In a culturally diverse society, such controversies and debates inevitably involve issues such as value systems, language, relationships between different ethnic groups when needs and interests conflict.

One of the factors which has contributed to confused thinking in the area of multicultural education is the notion of defining culture primarily in terms of ethnicity. Such a perspective assumes that there are single Chinese, Malaysian, Indian, or English cultures. Such an oversimplified definition does not allow for two important factors. First, culture is not a *static* entity. Rather, it is *dynamic* and changes over time in interaction with political, economic, ecological and social factors. Second, a 'culture' is not *objective*. Any attempt to describe it must allow for the way in which it is *perceived* by different individuals living in that particular culture.

There are some, quite fundamental considerations about the nature of education at all levels that need to be reaffirmed. Almost for want of a better form of words I refer to them *the moral dimension*. It is important when using the word 'moral' and its derivatives, to try to divorce it from any religious sense: rather, it is one important goal of education, as Durkheim (1926) showed so clearly in his writing on educational sociology. The use of the concept is well exemplified in the work by Power and associates (1992) on "A Raft of Hope: democratic education and the challenge of pluralism", a creative response to the ethnic conflicts in Los Angeles in the previous decade.

The term 'moral education' is used in the sense of the human values and motives which determine education's nature and processes. In the beginnings of education, in Britain at least, there was no doubt about it: all learning led to God and this belief is still enshrined, in *fossilised* form, in, for example, the University of Cambridge where, in formal processions, the Vice Chancellor is followed by the Professor of Theology, with those professing other disciplines arranged behind them. Nowadays the position of authority is not nearly so clear; but that does not mean that motives are not powerfully at work. Take, for example, the introduction of the national curriculum in England. Launched in 1988 as part of a series of reforms designed to improve the quality of education nationally, it represented a new departure. Previously, head teachers and local education authorities exercised power and discretion over *what* was taught and *how*. That power and discretion went largely unchallenged, other than by a broad and rather loose framework provided by the independent public-examination boards and, to a much lesser extent, by parental and public expectations. When it came to drawing up the detailed specification for the national curriculum, why was it that the two subject areas over which there was most controversy were History and English? The answer, I believe, had to do with the way those two subject areas most obviously capable of defining the current sense of *Englishness*.

As soon as selection of materials enters the education process, and selection *always* does, then the motives which influence that selection become important because they are usually, if not always, the product of some moral system. Converging on this process is the rise of information technology. The power of computer technology is already daunting and is currently doubling every two years while at the same time getting cheaper.

Just as in many countries of the world, the government has taken control of what children shall be taught, the last decade has seen the development of multinational media corporations. Their prime concern is growth which they achieve by expansion, by diversification and by aggressive take-overs of their competitors. Their invasion of the computer software industry seems only a matter of time.

There is a danger that the education of our children - centrally directed by government and mediated through a technology controlled by huge corporations having allegiance to nobody but themselves - will be driven by implicit moral agendas of globalization over which neither parents nor teachers will have control. I see this trend as part of the *privatisation* of knowledge - and this process appears to be accelerating. The concept of intellectual property rights traces its origin to the laws governing copyright. Few would argue that authors should retain control over the books or parts of books that they have written whilst welcoming the free use (preferably with *acknowledgement*) of the ideas they contain. What is unwelcome is the concept of knowledge as an intellectual commodity to be used, concealed or disposed of on the basis of the 'owner's' perception of personal or organisational benefit.

One final example of this process: there is an international interest in the biological sciences in techniques to identify and modify genetic structures. As fragments are decoded, some of the researchers are not reaching for their word processors to publish their successes. Their first step is to *patent* their discovery. As one scientist observed, it is as if a group had discovered long ago some or all of the letters of the alphabet and had patented them for their exclusive use, thus ensuring the intellectual poverty of all, except themselves!

Education in both its cognitive and moral forms is about the *exchange* of knowledge. New technology makes that exchange rapid, universal and cheap. It is potentially a great opportunity and educators should, and do, welcome that opportunity. But like all things with great *potential for good*, it holds within itself the *same* potential for *misuse*.

What core issues should be identified as central to a civilised society and which we would want to be carried forward into the next century? I think that we might well wish to transmit the following through the young people for whom we have responsibilities today:

- Tolerance;
- Belief in a world community with a recognition of, and delight in difference;
- The just treatment of all peoples;
- Respect for all; and,
- Intellectual freedom.

These provide some *purposes* for teaching. The transmission of knowledge and skills from us to our students and from them to children is not, of itself, enough. Without a moral dimension to it that is not just *inherent* but *made explicit*, our students will have no sense of what teaching is for - other than the priorities of personal or national advancement.

It is in the area of school education that we will need to achieve the greatest changes and break throughs, if a plural and harmonious society is to survive and flourish. I do not deny that higher education will still have to give the lead but believe that the major educational challenge will face the school system. This will be to elevate the levels of skills and knowledge in the weakest sections of the school population. At present, too many youngsters fall by the wayside, de-motivated and/or rejected by the educational system.

Such a challenge is not one driven by egalitarianism. Rather, it is one driven by the recognition that society is becoming more and complex will continue to create more specialized and demanding occupational and civic roles. If people are to be able to cope with life - at work and at play - in that society, they will need to have acquired higher levels of skill and knowledge than the bare minimum required today. That minimum threshold of achievement will continue to rise. Failure by the schools to get children to achieve those standards will effectively disenfranchise them in their adult lives.

Education in most developed countries has failed because it has not been based on an integrated or ethical approach. All attempts at reforming or enriching curricula are evidence of this because reforms were designed to overcome these shortcomings and yet have so far failed to deliver. As we are nearing the end of this century there is a new belief in education and knowledge. It is a basis for the personal development and for the development of the welfare of society as a whole. It is being widely accepted that education and knowledge are the main instruments for change, innovation and growth in society.

Despite some optimism, we cannot a blind eye to disturbing signs of re-emerging violence, intolerance, ethnic cleansing, and anti-semitic and anti-democratic activity. It is the responsibility of educators to lead future generations away from the brink of the volcano. Such flashpoints should serve as a reminder of the dangers of getting them wrong.

Education is about the exchange of knowledge. Technology provides great opportunities and educators should, and do, welcome those opportunities. But like all things with great potential for good, it holds within itself the same potential for misuse. The frontiers that exist to divide nations and peoples will not disappear in the short term. However education *can at least* begin to dismantle the barriers which exist in our minds. It is vital that education should have a more humanist dimension, and this would help to strengthen ethical and moral dimensions.

Education in the twenty-first century must seek a balance between its role as an instrument of human integration and as the agent of a global vision. In this way, education should strengthen the cultural identity of a particular society and also create the ability to see the world in its unity within its plurality.

The quality of education is currently an important issue in countries all over the world. There is a steady increase in participation in formal schooling, reflecting trust and belief in the value of education. Schools are seen as instruments contributing to social and economic progress. They are expected to 'produce' more and more better-educated individuals the result of which will be to lead to higher incomes, not only for the benefit of the individuals concerned, but also for the community of which they are part.

Educators talk about the importance of culture and about the need for children and young people to build up a sense of cultural identity and sensitivity to other cultures, and yet, a careful analysis of what teachers are required to do in the classroom does not provide adequate assurances that enough is being done to teach children these values. The development of a cultural identity and a sensitivity to others are not built up automatically: they can only be outcomes of a curriculum designed to achieve them.

Our expectations of schools have risen - and rightly so. Our expectations of excellence should continue for *all* children and young people regardless of their circumstances. Yet that process, which is described by that rather ugly term *levelling up*, has not been driven by altruism alone. It has also been born of necessity. With the material progress that has been made in the last fifty years, the complexity and amount of change in the basic social order in societies, daily living and occupational roles have become more complex and demanding. This has placed increasing demands for skills and knowledge even upon those in the least advantaged groups of society. This increase in levels of knowledge and skills must be maintained if our society is to grow and develop in positive and tolerant ways, which do not demean the least motivated students. Parallel to this, economists and politicians must devise policies which do not marginalize the least able through perpetual unemployment. "The devil makes work for idle hands" the old saying goes: translated sociologically, this implies that aggressive, destructive racism will become the province of the chronically unemployed.

Will the momentum of educational change, designed to address the moral goals I have outlined, continue? With a centrally directed curriculum, the *power* of what is *knowledge* is not in the hands of the local community but in the hands of those in central government.

I wonder when we reflect on our own educational experience whether what we *value* was the *contact with other people* rather than simply *the qualifications we gained* in the process. When we look back on the formal education we received, do we remember more the *persons* (favourite teachers, best friends) than the actual *content* of the curriculum?

If we are concerned about the promotion of values and attitudes that will help to make the world a better place to live in, then the quality of the *interaction* is more important than the *knowledge and skills* imparted. With technological advances, machines may provide us with more efficient ways of acquiring skills and knowledge. However, I am highly sceptical as to whether those machines, even those of tomorrow, will be able to provide the sort of interactional skills needed to play a full and responsible role in society.

Conclusions

The changes that are with us now are likely to continue in some form or another into the future. Their exact natures are, ultimately, unpredictable. Fields of knowledge will change as will their content. Methods of teaching will be affected by constraints that can only be guessed at, and by opportunities brought about by technological progress that we cannot foresee. As educators, it will remain our moral responsibility to ensure that students are provided with the best that we can deliver. That, at least, will remain a constant.

There are, however, other considerations that will remain. I have dwelt at length on the way technological advance and the external control of the curriculum are converging. This convergence makes it all the more important that we remain vigilant about the motives (referred to above as the *moral dimension*) underlying the knowledge we transmit.

The chapters in this book illustrate the interesting and challenging complexities which face the movement for intercultural education. Education in the twenty-first century can become an essential contributor to integration, to a culture of peace, and to international understanding. Through this, we can assure respect for diversity, whether diversity of behaviour, or diversity of philosophical or religious belief.

Perhaps we might then all be able to live comfortably in a world of which Gandhi had a vision:

'I do not want my house to be walled in on all sides and my windows to be stuffed. I want the cultures of all lands to be blown about my house as freely as possible. But I refuse to be blown off my feet.'

References

Bagley, C., Verma, G., Mallick, K. and Young, L. (1979). *Personality, self-esteem and prejudice*. Aldershot: Ashgate-Gower.

Durkheim, E. (1926). *Moral education*. New York: Free Press.

Power, F.C. and Power, M. (1992). 'A raft of hope: democratic education for the challenge of pluralism'. *Journal of Moral Education*, 21, 193-205.